The Making of
MARK
TWAIN

Mark Twain, 1870.
MARK TWAIN MEMORIAL, HARTFORD, CONNECTICUT

The Making of
MARK TWAIN

A BIOGRAPHY

John Lauber

American Century Series

The Noonday Press
Farrar, Straus and Giroux
New York

Library of Congress Cataloging-in-Publication Data
Lauber, John.
The making of Mark Twain.
Bibliography: p. 280
Includes index.
1. Twain, Mark, 1835–1910—Biography. 2. Authors, American—19th
century—Biography. I. Title.
PS1331.L38 1985 818'.409[B] 85-6169

CONTENTS

The Making of
MARK
TWAIN

LITTLE SAM

In a two-room frame house with a lean-to kitchen, in the "almost invisible village" of Florida, Missouri, a seven-months child was born to Jane and John Marshall Clemens on November 30, 1835—increasing the town's population by one whole percent, as that child would later write. His parents had him christened "Samuel Langhorne," but he promptly became "Little Sam." Weak and sickly, he may have seemed an addition of very doubtful value to the family. For Jane and John Marshall Clemens had four children already, and they were poor—proud, but poor.[1]

John Clemens was only thirty-five, but his greatness, such as it was, already lay behind him. In the early days of his marriage he had been the leading citizen of the tiny settlement of Jamestown in the "Tennessee Knobs," the hill country of eastern Tennessee. There he had practiced law, served as county commissioner and clerk of the circuit court, and "kept store," selling the ribbons and calicoes, the salt fish and coffee and sugar and molasses, the powder and shot, that country people could not produce for themselves. He had been trained to the law, but in the backwoods a man turned his hand to whatever offered itself. In Jamestown he had prospered modestly; by the standards of east Tennessee, the Clemenses were "gentry." He had a profession, he owned slaves, he had ancestors, he was "Squire" to the villagers.

The family lived according to its status; their house had two windows to a room and plastered walls—luxuries then still largely unknown in that region. And John Clemens bought land on a gigantic scale, eventually acquiring about 75,000 acres, supposed to be rich in copper, iron, coal, timber, and waterpower, at a cost of less than a cent an acre. It was an investment in the future; the "Tennessee Land" was to be the Clemens estate, ensuring his children's fortune, if not his own. Then hard times came. Short bursts of prosperity, followed by long declines, were to form the pattern of John Clemens's life. One by one the slaves were sold, the family moved to even smaller and remoter settlements, the father no longer able to practice law but still keeping store, more or less unsuccessfully, until they were reduced to a two-room cabin. In the America of the 1830s the answer to failure must have seemed obvious—to move West. Opportunity came with an invitation from John Quarles, Jane's brother-in-law, to join him in Missouri. In the spring of 1835, John Clemens sold everything but the Tennessee Land—that was inviolable, the future greatness of the Clemenses depended on it—loaded his family and their one remaining slave into a two-horse carriage and set out on the long, slow journey to Missouri. Jane Clemens was already pregnant.

Small and poor as it was, with a scattering of cabins and houses along the two streets "paved with . . . tough black mud in wet times, deep dust in dry," as Mark Twain was

to describe it, Florida might have seemed a hopeful place
to John Clemens, a dreamer, a man who preferred to live
in the future. It had its sawmill and its flour mills and its
distilleries, its location on the Salt River. There was talk of
improving the river to make it navigable for steamboats,
even of building a railroad. And there was rich land
around, sure to be overflowed by the tide of emigration.
To its boosters, there could be no doubt that all those ad-
vantages made this a "favorable point for the founding of
a great commercial town."

More important, there was John Quarles, a substantial
farmer, genial, popular, and respected, to help the family
to a new start. Again John Clemens seemed to prosper,
keeping store in partnership with Quarles, buying land, becoming a judge of the county court, and so making himself
"Judge Clemens" for life—the South loved titles. He took
the lead in civic improvements; he could always mind the
public's business better than his own. He became a trustee
for the newly incorporated Florida Academy; when the legislature appointed commissioners to raise capital for the
Salt River Navigation Company and the Florida and Paris
Railroad Company, to connect Florida with the county
seat, his name headed both lists. But the country was entering a depression; the river was never dredged, the railroad was never built, and the Clemens store was doing
badly.

He had withdrawn from his partnership with Quarles,
and his oldest boy, Orion, now served as clerk. Hopelessly
absent-minded, fatally unbusinesslike, Orion would always doom any enterprise he might be associated with. Finally, wrote Albert Bigelow Paine in the official biography,
Clemens guaranteed failure by taking as partner a man
without money or business ability. The judgeship might
bring prestige, but a family could not survive on prestige
and a salary of two dollars a day when court was in session.
It was clear by now that he had miscalculated, that Florida
had no future; in the fall of 1839 John Clemens traded his

holdings for land and buildings in the nearby town of Hannibal, on the Mississippi. Hannibal was a river port, with good prospects; in the next ten years its population was to grow from a few hundred to nearly three thousand. An enterprising merchant or a shrewd real estate speculator might have won a fortune—but Judge Clemens was neither.

And "Little Sam," as they called him, during those Florida years? He survived, against everybody's expectations—survived even though, as he was told later, he had been a "sickly and precarious and tiresome and uncertain child." He escaped the cholera, dysentery, yellow fever, and malaria of the Mississippi Valley and survived the bleedings and purgatives of the doctors, who administered castor oil and molasses by the dipperful, and the home remedies of his mother, who believed in the water cure and regularly inflicted cold packs and cold showers on her frail son. In his first seven years, by family tradition, he lived mainly on medicines. Merely to live was an accomplishment for such a child, demonstrating unexpected toughness at a time when, according to a Hannibal paper, "one quarter of the children born die before they are one year old; one half die before they are twenty-one." The Clemenses were typical; three of their seven children died before reaching the age of ten. Little Sam survived, then; otherwise his history, like that of most small children, is the history of his family.

Father and mother were strongly marked, widely differing individuals, seeming not so much complementary as mismatched. They had in common mostly their pride of ancestry; John Clemens claimed descent from Gregory Clement, one of the judges who sentenced Charles I to death and thereby, Mark Twain later observed, "did what he could toward reducing the list of crowned shams of his day," while Jane Lampton believed that the Lamptons of America were somehow connected with the Lambtons of England, Earls of Durham. One relative wasted his life in trying to pursue a phantom claim to the earldom. From his example and from that reputed descent, no doubt often talked of in the family, would spring Mark Twain's long interest in claimants and pretenders, such as the King and the Duke in *Huckleberry Finn*. More immediately, and verifiably, both parents came from prosperous, slave-holding stock—there were already slave-owning Clemenses in Virginia in the late seventeenth century.

The word that came most naturally to Mark Twain in describing his father was "austere." Dignified, silent, scholarly for his time and place, proud of his ancestry— John Clemens set himself apart from his neighbors. He was "Squire" or "Judge" to them. "Once on the street someone slapped him on the back, and the family was horrified," a granddaughter remembered being told. It must have seemed extraordinary, that abrupt invasion of his reserve, for the event to be handed down in family history. As a father, he seems to have been conscientious but distant; within the family, Mark Twain was to recall, he was "stern, unsmiling, never demonstrated affection for wife or child . . . ungentle of manner towards his children . . . never punished—a look was enough, and more than enough." He was a disappointed man, constantly trying and failing to earn the income needed to live like a gentleman, at times barely able to support his family. Each of the many moves, from one settlement in Tennessee to another, from Tennessee to Missouri, from Florida to Hannibal, represented a failure. John Clemens was out of place in his world—too trusting, too visionary, too proud, and perhaps too unsocial, to succeed. He dreamed expansively, and Sam and Orion inherited that quality, but his dreams never materialized. His business history was a record of misplaced trust and mistaken calculations. Sam shared that quality, too; as "Mark Twain" he was to repeat his father's mistakes, on a grander scale.

Redheaded Jane Clemens—warm, spontaneous, impulsive—seemed her husband's opposite. Relations between them were correct, not affectionate; by her own recollection, she had accepted him in a moment of pique when her real lover had been too bashful to declare himself. The story dates from her extreme old age and cannot be confirmed, but her children found it credible. Her most distinctive quality, Mark Twain would remember, was her "strong interest in the whole world and everything and everybody in it . . . she never knew such a thing as a half-hearted interest in affairs and people." As a girl she had been a noted rider and had loved dancing: "Even in the last year of her life," her son Orion reported, she liked to show visitors "the beautiful step and graceful movement she had learned in her youth." She was a noted storyteller, speaking slowly, in a soft drawl. "Her happy flow of spirits," Orion wrote, "made her a popular favorite wherever she lived." Sam inherited more than his mother's red hair; as he grew older, he would show the same capacity for whole-hearted enthusiasm, and he would become a renowned storyteller, speaking in his mother's drawl.

She hated cruelty, whether to persons or animals, and befriended the helpless. Stray cats found a home with her—"They were out of luck and that was enough." Seeing a cartman beating his horse on the head with a whip handle, she took the whip away from him, then pleaded so eloquently for the horse that the man admitted he was in the wrong. Once, a "vicious devil of a Corsican, a common terror in the town" chased his daughter through the streets of Hannibal "with a heavy rope in his hand . . . declaring he would wear it out on her." No one dared to interfere, until Jane Clemens opened her house to the fleeing girl, then stood in the doorway and faced down the brutal father, who finally "said with a great and blasphemous oath that she was the bravest woman he ever saw, and so went his way."

Frail yet mischievous, Sam made his mother's life no easier. "He drives me crazy with his didoes, when he is in the house," she complained, "and when he is out of it I am expecting every minute that someone will bring him home half dead." More than once he nearly drowned; he never forgot the time when "the slave woman plucked me out of Bear Creek by the hair of my head when I was going down for the third time." He walked in his sleep, and he would run away—usually toward the river. At eight, he nearly died of measles; he had deliberately infected himself by sleeping in the same bed with a sick playmate. That seeming perversity in fact demonstrated the power of his imagination. There was an epidemic of measles, many children had died, the town was paralyzed with fear. As he remembered, "Every night a sudden shiver shook me to the marrow, and I said to myself, 'There, I've got it! and so I shall die.' Life on these miserable terms was not worth living," so he ended the unbearable suspense.

He began to spend his summers at John Quarles's farm. In recollection, it would become his great good place, a symbol of freedom and natural bounty. The house was friendly, no great mansion with white portico but a double log cabin, like the home of the Grangerfords in *Huckleberry Finn*, with living quarters and kitchen connected by a roofed passageway where in the summer the family could take their meals. The table overflowed with the abundance of the land, recorded in loving detail more than sixty years later in Mark Twain's *Autobiography*: "fried chicken, roast pig; wild and tame turkeys, pheasants, partridges, prairie-chickens; biscuits, hot batter cakes, hot buckwheat cakes, hot 'wheat bread,' hot rolls, hot corn pone . . . watermelons, muskmelons, cantaloupes—all fresh from the garden." On winter visits, by "the vast fireplace, piled high . . . with flaming hickory logs," the Clemens and Quarles children roasted apples, or scraped off and ate the sugary sap that bubbled out of the logs.

Outside were the slave cabins—John Quarles owned a half-dozen blacks. One of them, Old Uncle Dan'l, sometimes told stories by firelight; Mark Twain never forgot the "creepy joy which quivered through me when the time for the ghost story of the 'Golden Arm' was reached," and he made it a staple of his own repertory. There were home-made swings that "usually broke when a child was forty feet in the air," and a dusty road where snakes could be found—the rattlers to be killed, the harmless ones gathered for the teasing of mothers and sisters. As he grew older, the surrounding forest offered the excitement of turkey hunts at dawn or coon hunts at night, or the quieter plea-sures of gathering berries and nuts.

TOM SAWYER
DAYS

The frail boy grew stronger, and by the time he was
nine, as his friend and official biographer, Albert Bigelow Paine, wrote, "the Tom Sawyer days may be said to
have begun." On the Quarles farm and in Hannibal, young
Sam was living the childhood that inspired *Tom Sawyer* and
Huckleberry Finn, the early chapters of his *Autobiography*, as
well as speeches and sketches and passages in other books
till the end of his career. At first there seems no need to
retell the story of Sam Clemens's childhood—Mark Twain
has told it so well. But his matchless evocations of time and
place, of a kind of childhood that can never be lived again,
must not be taken as records of fact. They leave out much:
the father is absent, Tom Sawyer is an orphan raised by
his aunt. And much of what they narrate did not happen.
Mark Twain would always be autobiographical, but he

wrote autobiographical fiction and fictional autobiography. "When I was younger I could remember everything, whether it happened or not," he once remarked, "but now I am getting old, and soon I shall remember only the latter." But long before he reached old age, he could remember, intensely, the things that had not happened.

Of course, there can be no doubt that much of *Tom Sawyer* is taken from life: probably young Sam gave painkiller to the family cat, swindled his friends into whitewashing the fence, clobbered his younger brother for tattling, escaped a whipping by calling out to his mother to look behind her. He and his friends, like Tom and his gang, "used to undress and play Robin Hood in . . . [their] shirt-tails, with lath swords," in the nearby woods. He was mischievous and troublesome enough, he had a reputation as "the worst boy," and twenty-five years later a Hannibal acquaintance inquired "if you still climb out on the roof of the house and jump from third-story windows." The ritualistic fights with other boys must have happened, too, although if Sam won them as often as Tom did, it would have been through sheer fury, not by size and strength. The picturesque superstitions and folklore of *Tom Sawyer* and *Huckleberry Finn*—those too are authentic. Sometimes they are grotesque— *"Barley-corn, barley-corn, injun-meal shorts,/Spunk-water, spunk-water, swaller these warts!"*—more often ominous, threatening death by the howling of a dog, the cry of a whippoorwill, the ticking of a deathwatch beetle. They can bring the terror of ghosts, which "come sliding around in a shroud," says Huck, "when you ain't noticing, and peep over your shoulder all of a sudden and grit their teeth."

The geography of Hannibal and the surrounding region, of the town itself, of the river and its islands, of Holliday's Hill to the north and Lover's Leap to the south, of the nearby cave, became the geography of Tom Sawyer's St. Petersburg. But Tom's most dramatic adventures are imagined: Sam Clemens never witnessed his own funeral, never saw a man killed in a graveyard at midnight or testified at a trial for murder, never found hidden treasure, never was lost for days in a cave. *All* of the episodes showing the town's admiring attention focused on Tom are invented. *Tom Sawyer* is autobiographical fiction, drawn from memory of course, but memory shaped by imagination and desire.

It is misleading, then, to say, as his biographer, Paine, did and as Mark Twain himself did, that "Jane Clemens was the original of Tom Sawyer's Aunt Polly and the portrait is considered perfect." (For one thing, Sam's mother was just thirty-two at his birth, active and able, very different from Tom's elderly and ineffectual aunt.) Nor is it true that Nigger Jim "was" Uncle Dan'l, or that Huck Finn "was" a Hannibal playmate named Tom Blankenship— surely Huck "is" at least equally a reflection of the adult Mark Twain. Such claims seemed to lend authenticity, and Mark Twain liked to think of himself as a realist, but in practice he well understood that "by the privileges of our order we [writers] are independent of facts," and he used the privilege freely. Acknowledging that in *Huckleberry Finn* he had transformed the Quarles farm into the Phelps farm and moved it six hundred miles downriver, he adds that he "would move a state if the exigencies of literature required it." Like most books, also, *Tom Sawyer* derives in part from other books—the graveyard scene from Dickens's *Tale of Two Cities*, the hunt for buried treasure from Poe's "Gold Bug." And the relationship of Huck and Tom, with Huck playing literal-minded Sancho Panza to Tom's Don Quixote, must have been drawn from later reading of Cervantes, not from boyhood reality. Tom's courtship of Becky Thatcher seems to have originated in Twain's unpublished fragment written in 1870, concerning "Billy Rogers" and "Amy," which may, in turn, have been meant to parody David Copperfield's courtship of Dora Spenlow, or even Mark Twain's own impassioned, just-completed wooing of his bride, Olivia Langdon.

As for Aunt Polly, supposedly copied from life, her characterization seems to owe as much to Mark Twain's recollections of Mrs. Partington, a popular character in newspaper humor of the 1850s, as to the reality of Jane Clemens. Like Aunt Polly, Mrs. Partington raises a mischievous nephew, Ike, but is too softhearted to do her duty by him and punish him as he deserves. Both Ike and Tom are mischievous but not malicious; both successfully "work" their aunts, steal doughnuts, play tricks on cats, misbehave in church, feign sickness to avoid school, and find inspiration in such books as *Black Avenger*, or *The Pirates of the Spanish Main*. So close was the resemblance between the two women that Twain's economical publisher actually used an illustration of Mrs. Partington to represent Aunt Polly in *Tom Sawyer*. One of Mark Twain's favorite stories about his own mother, that in her tenderheartedness she would warm the water in which she was going to drown the kittens, was also borrowed from the Partington pieces.

Of all Hannibal's gifts, the river was best—"the great Mississippi, the majestic, the magnificent Mississippi, rolling its mile-wide tide along, shining in the sun; the dense forest away on the other side; the 'point' above the town, and the 'point' below, bounding the river-glimpse and turning it into a sort of sea," as Mark Twain would describe it thirty years later in *Old Times on the Mississippi*. There was picnicking, swimming, skating, boating, with the boat "borrowed" more often than not—Sam and his gang once stole a skiff for the whole summer, painting it red for disguise. After several near-drownings, Sam Clemens finally became the best swimmer in his gang. In the summer, boys could escape to the Eden of Glasscock's Island, washed away a few years later by the irresistible river, to camp and swim and dig for turtle eggs and go naked in the sun.

Sam came to know the river in all weathers and all seasons. Writing to his old comrade Will Bowen in 1870, he recalled the time when he jumped off the ferryboat into the stormy Mississippi to recover the hat that had blown off his head "& swam two or three miles after it (& *got* it) while all the town collected on the wharf & for an hour or so looked out across the angry waste of 'white-caps' toward where people said Sam Clemens was last seen before he went down." Skating one night with a single friend, "we heard some rumbling and grumbling and crashing." Realizing that the ice was breaking up, they headed for shore. "We flew along at full speed whenever the moonlight sifting down between the clouds enabled us to tell which was ice and which was water," pausing at every gap and waiting until some "floating vast cake" should make a bridge. Close to shore, there was another gap; thoroughly frightened, they started across too soon. Sam reached land safely, but his friend was drenched in the icy water and, once home, "took to his bed, sick, and had a procession of diseases," concluding with scarlet fever, which left him stone-deaf.

There was the excitement of steamboat arrivals, bringing the sleepy little town to life with the cry "S-t-e-a-mboat a-comin!"—the boat gorgeous with gilt and glass and gingerbread, flag flying bravely and tall twin chimneys belching thick, black smoke, a dramatic effect created by throwing carefully hoarded pitch pine on the fires as the town came into view around the bend. The steamboat was central to the lives of Sam and his friends; we may remember Ben Rogers, in *Tom Sawyer*, "impersonating the Big Missouri and . . . drawing nine feet of water," and simultaneously taking the parts of boat, captain, and engine bells. It was the dream of every boy to go on the river, to taste the glamor and excitement of its life. And a surprising number of them, including Sam Clemens, were to realize that dream.

But a boy's life could not be lived entirely in freedom, on the river or the farm. School and church, the institutions of culture, loomed forbiddingly; somehow the reluctant Sam had to conform to their requirements as best he could, since it was unthinkable that they should conform to him. On his first day at school, aged five, he broke a rule and was switched; the pattern of his schooling had been set. His older sister, Pamela, had won a certificate for "amiable deportment and faithful application," but Sam took no prize for either quality. To a restless and imaginative boy, school brought torturing boredom; it was a place where children "devoted . . . eight or ten hours a day to learning incomprehensible rubbish by heart out of books and reciting it by rote, like parrots," where they memorized and delivered hackneyed "declamatory gems" such as Byron's *"The Assyrian came down like a wolf on the fold,/And his cohorts were gleaming in purple and gold."* He excelled only in the weekly spelling bees, which offered the thrill of competition.

Discipline was arbitrary, often brutal—although as remembered in *Tom Sawyer*, the worst beatings never seemed to hurt. The second school that Sam attended was kept by a Mr. Cross. That wonderfully appropriate name inspired the boy's first known writing:

> *Cross by name and cross by nature—*
> *Cross jumped over an Irish potato.*

School taught him reading, writing, and arithmetic, and a smattering of history and geography; it exposed him to literature, generally moralistic; it sought to inculcate the virtues of industry, patriotism, and piety; it tried to make him a Model Boy—and failed utterly. His real education would come later.[1]

The Sabbath too brought boredom and fear, fear of damnation and hell rather than of the master's stick—a deeper, more spiritual, and longer-lasting terror. Sunday commenced with family worship, led by Jane Clemens, beginning "with a prayer built from the ground up of solid courses of scriptural quotations . . . and from the summit of this she delivered a grim chapter of the Mosaic Law." Then

came Sunday school, teaching Sam that bad boys went to
Hell and were likely to die early. Finally the Presbyterian
sermon had to be endured: "The minister droned along
monotonously through an argument that was so prosy that
many a head by and by began to nod—and yet it was an
argument that dealt in limitless fire and brimstone and
thinned the predestined elect down to a company so small
as to be hardly worth saving." That sermon was heard
by Tom Sawyer, but Sam Clemens must have suffered
through its counterparts. The Presbyterianism of the Mississippi Valley seems to have been a rigorous Calvinism, a
religion of "free grace and preforeordestination," as Huck
Finn puts it—demanding perfection while insisting on the
total depravity of the human race, giving to God the power
and the right, in His inscrutable wisdom, to save those
whom He chose to save and damn those whom He chose
to damn.

Religion permeated the culture of pioneer Missouri.
There might have been dissenting freethinkers—John Clemens might have been one—but they kept their heresy to
themselves. Besides the weekly ritual of family worship,
Sunday school, and sermon, with an evening service occasionally added as punishment for any extraordinary crime
that Sam might have committed, there was the frenzy of
the camp meetings, which were to reappear in *Huckleberry
Finn*, and of the periodic revivals in town. Not to share in
their enthusiasm was to be an outcast from Hannibal as
well as from Heaven. When Tom Sawyer recovered from
an illness and learned that during his sickness all his friends
had been "saved," "he crept home to bed realizing that he
alone of all the town was lost, forever and forever," and
that the raging storm outside was aimed at his sinful self:
"He covered his head with the bedclothes and waited in a
horror of suspense for his doom." The eye of God was
upon him and punishment would surely come, in this
world and in the next. Sam Clemens must have endured
such terrifying experiences; before his childhood ended, he

had learned to know the Bible, to fear God—the wrathful, implacable, all-seeing Calvinist God—and to feel guilt. That guilt might be unreasonable, exaggerated, completely without cause—but no matter. To be human was to be guilty.

There were lessons to be learned from the town as well, realities of class and race. Outwardly, as Mark Twain remembered, Hannibal might have seemed "a little democracy . . . full of Liberty, Equality and Fourth of July," but for all the civic piety and readings of the Declaration of Independence, it was a Southern town, and the "aristocratic taint was there." Class distinctions were clearly drawn, and the Clemenses, with more pride than property, suffering the periodic humiliations of forced moves and sheriff's sales, must have felt them painfully. At the top of the scale were the well-to-do professional men, wearing their tall hats and swallow-tailed coats, and owning land and slaves. By right of birth and education, John Clemens felt that he belonged to that class, but he could never earn the income needed to live as they lived. Below these "gentry," Hannibal had its respectable middle class, its workingmen, and its outcast poor whites, like Jimmy Finn, the town drunkard, or the disreputable Blankenships. Young Tom Blankenship, as Mark Twain remembered him, was "ignorant, unwashed, insufficiently fed," but goodhearted and independent, "the only really independent person . . . in the community—therefore happy and envied by other boys." Naturally his society was forbidden to boys of respectable families, and naturally "the prohibition doubled and quadrupled its value."

Beneath all whites were the blacks. Slavery was unquestioned; "the wise, and the good and the holy," Mark Twain recalled in his *Autobiography*, unanimously held that the institution was righteous and sacred, "the peculiar pet of the deity, and a condition which the slave himself ought to be daily and nightly thankful for." No one, at least to young Sam's knowledge, "seemed conscious that slavery was a bald, grotesque, and unwarrantable assumption." Doubters would have kept silent in any case; in the rural Missouri of the 1840s or 50s, to criticize slavery would have been to invite lynching. Denying the existence of God would have been safer. John Clemens apparently had no qualms about the institution; in 1841 he served on a jury that sentenced three abolitionists to prison terms of twelve years each for inciting slaves to escape. Mark Twain would observe, from his own experience, that it was a mistake to say that slavery made Southern whites hardhearted in general; it "merely stupefied everybody's humanity as regarded the slave." He had evidence for that in his own boyhood home. The Clemenses owned one slave—a girl named Jennie—during Sam's early childhood, and he remembered once seeing his father beat her with a bridle for insolence; Judge Clemens cuffed, too, the small black boy whom they hired from his master "for any little blunder or awkwardness," and occasionally gave him a lashing "which terrified the poor thing nearly out of his wits." Yet John Clemens was otherwise a humane man.

There were no great plantations nearby, and slavery as Sam knew it was of the "mild domestic variety." Yet the reality could not be avoided. Like every Southern town, Hannibal had its despised "nigger-trader"—he made a convenient scapegoat—and once Sam saw "a dozen black men and women, chained together waiting shipment to a Southern slave market." Harsh brutality was frowned on by decent whites but could not be prevented. Mark Twain would not forget "the slave man who was struck down with a chunk of slag for some small offense; I saw him die." Once the corpse of a slave, drowned while trying to escape and then "much mutilated" by his white pursuers, rose out of the river mud to terrify Sam and his friends. Although a reward was offered, one of the Blankenships had kept the man's hiding place secret all summer and occasionally brought him food—behavior that Twain must have recalled when he had Huck decide to help Nigger Jim escape.

The two races were in intimate, daily contact, and white and black children could, almost, be comrades. Mark Twain would remember that he "was playmate to all the niggers, preferring their society to that of the elect." But "complete fusion" could not occur; "color and condition imposed a subtle line"—subtle, yet a barrier that not even children could ever shut out of consciousness. Sam Clemens accepted slavery, as boys do accept the basic institutions of their society; he grew up with all the unquestioned prejudices of the Southern white and even served briefly in a Confederate militia unit at the outbreak of the Civil War.

Then, having left the South forever, he became aware, over the years, of his attitudes and worked to change them, doing his part to pay the debt that he came to feel every white man owed to every black man. He helped to finance the studies of a black artist in Paris and to pay the way of a black student through Yale Law School; he urged President Garfield to retain the black leader Frederick Douglass as marshal of the District of Columbia; he read and lectured in black churches; in his old age he composed "The United States of Lyncherdom," a searing indictment of the moral cowardice by which the decent majority permitted lynching. In "Which Was the Dream," a late fragment, he even created a black avenger, the mulatto Jasper, who inverts the relation of master and slave, mercilessly blackmailing a white man and forcing him to undergo every cruelty and degradation that Jasper has suffered from the white race in a lifetime. Mark Twain became, said his friend William Dean Howells, "the most desouthernized Southerner" that Howells had ever known. Yet childhood conditioning could not be completely overcome; he once confessed to Howells that he had hired George Griffin, the black butler at his Hartford mansion, because he could not bear giving orders to a white man, and in his dreams a dark-skinned woman would signify sexual abandon.

Life in Hannibal was uncertain, precarious; as the

townspeople must have been reminded every Sunday,
death could come at any moment, in the home or on the
street. The sick died at home, without drugs, often conscious to the end, and no family could escape the deathbed
ritual, with a ring of mourners around the sufferer, waiting
to make their good-bys and to hear the final words. The
Clemenses knew that experience three times during Sam's
childhood: with the death of nine-year-old Margaret from
"bilious fever," just before the move to Hannibal; of Benjamin, age ten, in 1842—Sam would never forget how his
mother had knelt beside the bed, holding his hand and
moaning "while the tears were flowing down her cheeks
unchecked"; and with his father's death five years later.

Violence was frequent, too, in that apparently peaceful
town. Young Sam saw things there he could never blot
from his memory. One evening, while John Clemens was
erving as justice of the peace, Sam entered his father's
ـmpty office and saw in the moonlight the corpse of a mur-
dered man stretched out on the floor, brought there to
await an inquest. As an adult, he told the story humorously: "I went out at the window, and I carried the sash
along with me; I did not need the sash, but it was handier
to take it than it was to leave it, and so I took it." But it
could not have been a joke then.

Murder could be committed on the streets and go un-
punished. The shooting of Boggs by Colonel Sherburn,
one of the most famous scenes in *Huckleberry Finn*, probably had its origin in the killing of Sam Smarr, a noisy but
harmless drunk, by William Owsley, a prosperous merchant whom Smarr had insulted. Owsley shot down the
defenseless man "in the mainstreet at noonday" and walked
away unmolested. Sam Clemens saw "the grotesque final
scenes—the great family Bible spread open on the profane
old man's chest." In his nightmares he himself "gasped and
struggled for breath under the crush of that vast book for
many a year." That detail was to appear in *Huckleberry
Finn*. A year later the murderer was tried and acquitted.

Hannibal was a Southern town, it acknowledged a gentle-man's right to protect his honor—and Owsley would have had his friends, who might have taken revenge on a jury that voted to convict. Violence, like slavery, was a part of Mark Twain's heritage and, again like slavery, would finally taint all his recollections of the South.

Things went badly for the Clemenses in Hannibal. Creditors pressed them hard, they moved frequently, there was a sheriff's sale in 1843 and another ordered in December 1846—but the sheriff found nothing left to seize. There might be recoveries, times when John Clemens could afford to buy a piano for his daughter or speculate, unsuccessfully, in silkworm culture or even build a new house, a cramped little dwelling with low ceilings and a ladderlike stairway on a lot twenty and a half feet wide, now preserved as Mark Twain's boyhood home. But the trend was downward. John Clemens kept store again, and again the store failed; land and buildings were lost; the slave girl was sold; Orion was apprenticed to a printer in St. Louis—much against his will, for he felt that he was a gentleman's son and deserved a profession, while printing was only a mechanical trade. Then Orion realized that he was following in the footsteps of Benjamin Franklin. Franklin records in his autobiography that as a young man he lived for a time on a diet of biscuits and water, and Orion decided to imitate his famous model. His mind "cleared amazingly," he felt, but biscuits and water did not make a Franklin.

The father's schemes seemed only to lead to more expense. In the winter of 1841–42 he made a long journey into the South, hoping to collect a debt. He took with him a new slave, Charley, apparently bought as a speculation, expecting to sell him for "whatever he will bring." Charley brought ten barrels of tar, the only return from the trip. The debtor was in difficulties, and John Clemens was too softhearted to press for payment, although he had traveled hundreds of miles through winter rain and snow to collect that debt. Reading his father's letters many years later, Mark Twain was struck by the contrast between his humanity toward the white man and the casual indifference of his reference to the slave, "as if he had been an ox—and somebody else's ox." The journey had been a costly failure. Orion would remember hearing his mother reproach her husband for the useless expense, and his father answering, "with a hopeless expression," that he "was not able to dig in the streets."

He tried to practice law, but cases were few; he worked as a clerk in another man's counting house; he served as justice of the peace "and lived on its meager pickings," as Mark Twain would recall. Meager they certainly were; in the Owsley case, Justice Clemens earned $13.50 for writing documents totaling 13,500 words, and $1.81 for swearing in twenty-nine witnesses. Each move marked a decline; the family had no fixed home. Once Orion returned from St. Louis without warning, late at night, went to the last address, where, according to family tradition, he silently climbed the stairs to his old room, undressed in the dark, and found himself in bed with two strange women—sisters of the new occupant. Final disaster came in 1846, when even the furniture was lost and the Clemenses were reduced to sharing quarters with another family for whom Mrs. Clemens cooked.

That calamity, family tradition held, "was inflicted upon us by the dishonest act of one Ira Stout." So Mark Twain tells the story in his *Autobiography*, explaining that his father had lent "several thousand dollars" to Stout. But that amount seems impossible; John Clemens could never have had several thousand dollars in cash at any time in his life. Paine gives a likelier version. Clemens "now adopted the one unfailing method of achieving disaster. He endorsed a large note for a man of good repute, and the payment of it swept him clean." This account is reinforced by another passage in Twain's *Autobiography*, according to which his father "did the friendly office of 'going security' for Ira

Stout, and Ira walked off and deliberately took the benefit
of the new bankrupt law" and so "lived easily and comfortably till death called for him," while the Clemenses were
ruined. Gentlemen did not hide behind bankruptcy laws.
Nearly fifty years later, facing far greater financial disaster,
Mark Twain, like his father, refused to take the shelter of
the law, circling the world on a lecture tour in order to pay
off every creditor in full.

Life in poverty, or under its perpetual threat, left Sam
with a lifelong horror of debt. But it did more than that: it
made him constantly aware of the need for money, of the
humiliating discrepancy between family pretensions and
family realities; forced him to prove his success and status
by extravagant spending, to yearn to be really rich, even
when he was already a wealthy man, and to indulge in ob-
sessive, ruinous speculating. He required absolute security,
and there could never be enough money to guarantee that.

Through all the family troubles there remained the tantalizing, frustrating hope of wealth from the Tennessee
Land. The last of John Clemens's few surviving letters,
written shortly before his death, appoints an agent for the
sale of the land and sets out terms. There was no sale. Mark
Twain would finally decide that the land had been a disaster for his family: "It put our energies to sleep and made
visionaries of us. We were always going to be rich next
year—no occasion to work." Always there were hopes, always disappointed; periodically there would be negotia-
tions, and occasionally offers, to be withdrawn or rejected.
Tomorrow, after all, there would surely be a better one.
Mark Twain would finally renounce all interest in the land,
although by using it in the plot of his first novel, *The Gilded
Age*, he became the only Clemens who ever profited from
it. But he could never free himself from the dream of sudden, overwhelming fortune; it might come through striking
it rich in the silver mines, or through a lucky speculation
in stocks, or by backing some invention that would sweep
the world, such as the automatic typesetter on which he

would squander hundreds of thousands of dollars. Always, riches would come in in some way quite unrelated to any actual vocation.

John Clemens was an unsatisfactory father. He failed as a provider, and at least once he failed in a more intimate and basic way to furnish the security that every child needs: he showed himself not only a distant father but a careless one. It happened when Sam was seven. The family was to make a visit to the Quarles farm; Jane and the other children left by wagon, Sam and his father were to follow on horseback, a day later. The next morning, while Sam slept, John Clemens saddled his horse and rode off, never thinking of his son until he reached the farm several hours later. A rescuer arrived in early evening and found the deserted child safe in the locked and empty house, but "crying with loneliness and hunger." Mark Twain would never make a joke of that story, but he did not forget it.

In March of 1847 John Clemens contracted pneumonia and rapidly declined. He died as he had lived. His son described the scene: "First instance of affection: discovering that he was dying, chose his daughter from among the weepers, who were kneeling about the room and crying— and motioned her to come to him. Drew her down to him, with his arms about her neck, kissed her (for the first time, no doubt,) and sunk back and the death rattle came." He said good-by to no one else, not even his wife. He spoke also of the Tennessee Land—"Cling to the land and wait." It was his only tangible bequest—an intangible one as well, with its never-to-be-realized prospects of wealth and status.

There was a gruesome sequel to his father's death, so shocking that Twain could never refer to it publicly and could not directly admit it even to himself. Late in life, he set down an entry in his notebook: "1847. Witnessed post mortem of my uncle through the keyhole." But he had no uncle; it was his father who died in 1847. In "Villagers of 1840–43," a late manuscript that he did not publish, Twain wrote a short sketch of his father, under the name Judge

Carpenter; following the account of his last moments comes a single, underlined phrase: "The autopsy." It seems, then, that the eleven-year-old Sam looked through that keyhole and saw the naked corpse of his father under dissection—a shameful, unforgettable violation of John Clemens's austere dignity.

Before that horrifying moment, Paine reports, another event occurred at his father's deathbed that would shape Sam's life. Overcome with guilt at the memory of all the times he had ignored or defied his father's wishes, the boy began to weep. His mother took his hand and led him to the bed: "It is all right, Sammy," she said. "What's done is done and it does not matter to him any more; but here by the side of him now I want you to promise me—"

He turned, his eyes streaming with tears, and flung himself into her arms. "I will promise anything . . . if you won't make me go to school! Anything!"

His mother held him for a moment, thinking, then she said:"No, Sammy; you need not go to school any more. Only promise me to be a better boy. Promise not to break my heart."

So he promised to be a faithful and industrious man, and upright, like his father.

That night Sam walked in his sleep. Wrapped in a sheet, he entered the room where his mother and sister slept, terrifying them until his mother spoke to him.

In 1920, in his influential study *The Ordeal of Mark Twain*, Van Wyck Brooks would attempt to explain much about Twain's personality and career through an examination of this story: "It is perfectly evident what happened to Mark Twain at this moment," he wrote. "He became, and his immediate manifestation of somnambulism is the proof of it, a dual personality"—split between a conscious allegiance to Victorian gentility, made manifest in wealth and outward respectability, and his rebellious creative instinct, the deepest element of his nature. The consequence would be a lifelong pursuit of money and a paralyzing fear of public opinion, leading to betrayal of his talent, artistic sterility, and final despair. And so, in Brooks's view, Mark Twain became a case study of an American artist destroyed by his environment, with its almost irresistible pressures toward conformity.

The theory has proved enormously attractive, supporting some widely held attitudes—artists *should* be rebellious, *should* violently reject their culture—and handily compressing a complex personality and immensely varied life within a neat dichotomy. It is still widely accepted. The title of the most recent biography, *Mr. Clemens and Mark Twain*, sums up the alleged duality. But the story of the oath is probably a fiction. It is found only in Paine and must have been told to his biographer by Mark Twain himself. Yet as Paine came to realize, those "marvelous reminiscences" often "bore only an atmospheric relation to history," being "built largely—sometimes wholly—from an imagination that, with age, had dominated memory." The story is contradicted by the only piece of concrete evidence available— Sam Clemens did not leave school for another two years. The sleepwalking, if it took place, proved nothing; Sam had walked in his sleep before, and sleepwalking is not necessarily a neurotic symptom. The scene is a Victorian cliché and reads like a product of Twain's imagination—a dramatically appropriate event that *ought* to have occurred. The story might also be a distorted recollection of a promise that Sam actually gave his mother when he left Hannibal a few years later, swearing not to drink or gamble until she released him from his pledge. It seems unlikely, then, that Sam ever took that oath, and the theory of Mark Twain's supposed duality was built upon an event that did not happen, an oath that was never taken.

APPRENTICE

The Clemens family was now reduced to Jane, Sam, and Henry—Orion was practicing his trade in St. Louis, sending part of his wages to his mother, and Pamela had left home to support herself by teaching music in another town. Sam's schooling seems to have ended in his fourteenth year, as it did for most American boys in the 1840s; before the end of that year he had been apprenticed to Joseph Ament, publisher of the weekly Hannibal *Courier*. The terms were standard: Sam would be taught the printer's trade, board with his master, and receive two suits of clothing a year. Although the "Tom Sawyer days" were not yet over, the serious business of life had begun.

No one knows for certain why Sam became a printer. There is no evidence that he had shown any literary inclinations; perhaps he simply followed in Orion's footsteps,

perhaps the printer's trade—connected with literature, hal-
lowed by association with Benjamin Franklin—seemed the
most gentlemanly possibility available.

The new life suited him. He survived the customary
hazing and soon graduated from office chores—building
fires, fetching water, sweeping out, and delivering
papers—to setting type. Food was sometimes scanty, forcing Sam and his fellow apprentices to raid the cellar for
potatoes and onions, which they cooked on the office stove,
and the promised suits turned out to be Ament's own
castoffs—the shirts gave Sam "the uncomfortable feeling
of living in a circus tent"—but the *Courier* office was not
an unhappy place. Sam never forgot one of the journey-
men, Wales McCormick, a young giant of seventeen or
eighteen, also dressed in Ament's old clothes, as much too
small for him as they were too big for Sam. He seemed to
Sam both comic and heroic, "a reckless, hilarious, admi-
rable creature," and in one of Twain's last fragments, a
dashing young printer named Doangivadam is a leading
character; "I don't give a damn" had been McCormick's
favorite exclamation. Above all, Sam Clemens admired and
Mark Twain would remember McCormick's "limitless and
adorable irreverence"—precisely the quality that would
shock and delight readers of Twain's *The Innocents Abroad*
twenty years later. Once the shop was printing a sermon
by a visiting revivalist; to save space, McCormick at one
point abbreviated "Jesus Christ" to "J.C." Sternly rebuked
by the minister for not giving the Savior's name in full,
he laboriously reset the entire sermon, printing the sacred
name, wherever it occurred, as "Jesus *H.* Christ."

Sam learned his craft quickly and well, becoming the
best worker in Ament's shop. A fellow worker remembered
Sam as "a little sandy-haired boy . . . mounted upon a little
box at the case, pulling away at a huge cigar or diminutive
pipe [he had been smoking since he was eight], who used
to love to sing . . . the expression of the poor drunken
man . . . 'If ever I get up again, I'll stay up—if I kin.' "

Printing had changed little in four hundred years. Except for the difficulties of language, Gutenberg could have set to work at once in the *Courier* office. From the cases of type—upper and lower, for capitals and small letters— Sam picked out one by one the individual letters, each cast in metal, and assembled them in a small metal frame called a "composing stick," adding spacers between words as needed in order to justify the lines. Speed, accuracy, and neatness of the printed page were the tests of skill. When the stick was full, the "compositor," as the typesetter was called, transferred the lines to the "galley," a kind of tray, to be proofread and made up into pages. Finally, the galley was inked and sent to the clumsy hand press to be stamped onto paper. That was manual labor, no part of the craft. For variety, Sam might set a popular song or favorite poem of the time, print it on a piece of cotton or silk, and send it to a girl. Every village had its newspaper, or newspapers; by the time he left Ament, Sam had learned a craft by which he could support himself anywhere in the country. That apprenticeship gave him a lifelong interest in the technology of writing; he became one of the first authors to use a typewriter and still later lost a fortune by investing in an automatic typesetting machine.

While he learned his trade, Sam was picking up an education of another kind, more valuable than anything he had learned in school. The newspaper office opened a contact with the world, not only through the news received but by the system of "exchanges" through which papers across the country reprinted material from each other. The country papers of the time were distinctly "literary"; they filled their columns with poems and essays excerpted from contemporary and classic writers, encouraged local contributions in both prose and poetry, and printed each other's most successful pieces. They could provide a literary education for the boy who wanted one. Mark Twain would pride himself on his mastery of English grammar and punctuation; he's more likely to have acquired those abilities in the printing office than in the schoolroom. One could begin to discriminate between good and bad writing, one could be unconsciously acquiring a style. More directly, setting in type the words of other writers might arouse the ambition to set one's own, as it had for Franklin, the patron saint of printers. Printing was a recognized road to literature in nineteenth-century America; Mark Twain, Whitman, Howells, and Bret Harte all worked at the trade. The printing office was said to be the poor boy's college; as the Hannibal *Gazette* put it, there was something in its atmosphere "calculated to awake the mind and inspire a thirst for knowledge." Sam began to show intellectual interests—influenced also, he told Paine, by picking up from the street a page torn out of a biography of Joan of Arc that fascinated him. (Almost fifty years later he was to publish *Personal Recollections of Joan of Arc.*) He read what histories he could find, he discovered the need for foriegn languages. French was not available (he would study it on the river later), but he did learn some scraps of German from the village shoemaker. His mind had awakened; he had become a reader and had begun a process of self-education that would continue throughout his life.

Life was not all work and reading. Sam still enjoyed playing pranks, sometimes dangerous, such as dropping a watermelon shell on his younger brother's head from a second-story window or, with some friends, prying loose the great boulder on Holliday's Hill. When it broke free, it nearly crushed one of the boys, then smashed a good-sized tree, leaped straight over a terrified Negro with his mule and cart on the road below, and wrecked an empty shed before burying itself in dirt at the bottom—or so he remembered it many years later. When he had finished his set task at the shop, usually by midafternoon, there would be time to join the other boys on the river or at the cave, or to wander with his sweetheart, Laura Hawkins, gathering wildflowers on the steep bluffs that overlooked the Mississippi. Adolescence had begun.

In Mark Twain's recollection, Hannibal was an Eden of sexual innocence, a place in which "there was the utmost liberty among the young people—but no young girl was ever insulted, or seduced, or even scandalously gossiped about. Such things were not even dreamed of in that society." That claim is impossible to accept if taken literally, yet it seems deeply revealing of both Sam Clemens the boy and Mark Twain the man. To him, as Dixon Wecter, one of his biographers, has remarked, femininity always meant either motherly, apparently sexless, older women or little girls like Becky Thatcher in *Tom Sawyer*, that "lovely little blue-eyed creature with yellow hair plaited into two long tails, white summer frock and embroidered pantalettes," who sat beside Tom at school. In his books he would usually limit himself to those types, at least when portraying white women, and while he did not actually regard his wife, Livy, as either a mother or a little girl in pantalettes, both attitudes can be traced in the complexity of his feelings toward her. In the loneliness of his old age he would be drawn again to the "innocence" of young girls. As for his adolescence, whatever his desires might have been, it seems safe to guess that his experience never went much further than picking wildflowers or exchanging sentimental notes and perhaps an occasional shy kiss with Laura Hawkins.

Yet sexual awareness existed, even among girls, as indicated by Becky Thatcher's fascination with the nude male figure in her teacher's anatomy book. For Sam himself, it sometimes took the form of intense sexual embarrassment, as revealed by his story of "playing bare." When fourteen, he was asked by his older sister, Pamela, to take the part of a bear in a fairy play to be performed at a party. Going to a supposedly empty room to rehearse, he did not know that two girls had hidden behind a screen when he entered. Stripping himself before putting on the heavy costume, Sam "growled and snapped and snarled," danced and strutted, did handsprings and stood on his head—until the

unseen audience revealed itself with giggles. Horrified, he
fled to the dark hall with his clothes and escaped. Returning late that night, he found a message pinned to his pillow:
"You probably couldn't have played bear but you played
bare very well—oh, very *very* well!" For weeks he could
not look any girl in the face, for fear that she might have
been behind that screen, and it was fifty years before he
learned the identity of one of the spies, a girl who had
seemed to him then the essence of chaste femininity:
"Dainty and sweet, peach-blooming and exquisite, gracious and lovely," as if "made out of angel clay and right-
fully unapproachable by just any unholy ordinary kind of
boy like me." There was evidence to shatter the myth of
feminine "purity"—that is, of sexual disinterest—but he
failed to draw the obvious conclusion that since the girls
had enjoyed watching the naked boy, they must have been
made of the same unangelic clay. The myth was necessary
to him, and he remained a believer until his death; he could
never associate sexuality with white women of his own
class who had any claim to be considered ladies. In his late
novel, *Pudd'nhead Wilson*, Roxy bears an illegitimate child—
but although blonde and beautiful, Roxy is also a slave,
and one-sixteenth black.

The range of the poetry he read was limited; much concerned with death and disappointed love. Popular songs,
too, he remembered, "tended to regret for bygone days and
vanished joys: Oft in the Stilly Night; Last Rose of Summer; The Last Link; Bonny Doon; Old Dog Tray . . . *Negro
Melodies* the same trend; Old Kentucky Home . . . Massa's
in de Cold Ground, Swanee River." He would delight in
Stephen Foster songs all his life, and in music he would
always prefer the melancholy. There were bookstores—
Hannibal might have been a raw country town, but it was
literate; and while they must have been small and poorly
stocked, they would at least have carried the latest Eastern
and British periodicals. Newspapers were filled with
quotations from or allusions to eighteenth- and nineteenth-

century authors, mostly English. Town favorites, Twain recalled, included "Byron, Scott, Cooper, Marryatt, Boz [Dickens]"; only one name on that list was American.

But if the official "culture" was largely alien and derivative, there was a native culture as well in the traveling entertainments going up and down the river, in the showboats, the circuses—one of them would be memorably recorded in *Huckleberry Finn*—and the minstrel shows, a startling novelty in the 1840s. The minstrel show fascinated Sam, with its contrast between the sidemen, burlesquing the dialect and appearance of the slave, dressed in extravagant rags, their faces blacked and their lips painted red until their mouths looked like slices of watermelon, and the Interlocutor, in formal dress and speaking a pedantically correct and stilted English — which would have seemed the height of gentility to many of his hearers. There were traveling "professors" of many varieties — phrenologists, ventriloquists, mesmerists. Sam volunteered to serve as a subject for a mesmerist and resisted the hypnotic spell for three performances. Then, envying the attention won by those who let themselves be "mesmerized," he pretended to fall into a trance: "Upon suggestion I fled from snakes, passed buckets at a fire, became excited over hot steamboat-races, made love to imaginary girls and kissed them, fished . . . and landed mudcats that outweighed me." He pretended to see visions, more lurid than any other subject's, and to receive telepathic communications; he even allowed pins to be driven deep into his arm and showed no distress. The pain was excruciating, but "to make the people laugh and shout and admire" seemed worth any suffering. His career as a platform entertainer had begun.

Remote as Hannibal was, it felt the impact of history. A route to the California goldfields passed through the town, and in 1849 the papers were filled with California news. Sam and his friends caught the fever; on summer Saturdays they would "borrow skiffs whose owners were not present," go down the river a few miles, and dig for gold. At least eighty townspeople went West. One of them was a younger schoolmate of Sam's, who left for the mines with his father. Watching that boy as he rode off, "sailing by on a great horse with his long locks streaming out behind," Sam burned with envy. Forty-niners crowded the Hannibal streets, bringing violence with them—violence that Sam Clemens invariably seemed to witness. There was the young man "stabbed with a bowie knife by a drunken comrade; I saw the red life gush from his breast." Late at night, another drunken emigrant went to an isolated house where a poor widow lived with her daughter, and stood outside it, shouting obscenities. The mother came to the door, carrying a musket loaded with slugs; she warned him to leave, counted to ten, and fired: "A red spout of flame gushed out into the night and the man dropped with his breast riddled to rags." Sam "went home to dream and was not disappointed." Each of those tragedies, he then believed, was a sign from Providence, directed expressly to him and warning of the dangers of sin and the need for instant repentance. And he did repent—in the night; he repented in terror and despair, and then his repentance would fade away in the sunlight. "From my youth up," he sardonically concluded when he told the story in his *Autobiography*, "I have been like the rest of the race—never quite sane in the night."

No Clemens went to California, but the gold rush did affect the family. When the editor of the Hannibal *Journal* joined the emigration, Orion seized the chance to start his own newspaper. In September of 1850, using borrowed money, Orion began publication of the *Western Union*, a Whig weekly. The Whig party was on the verge of extinction, but that allegiance to a dying cause was typical of Orion. However, for a time the venture looked promising. Within a few weeks, lured by an offer of $3.50 a week and board, Sam came to work for his brother. Pamela too returned, and the Clemenses were a family again. Orion's plans, as always, were ambitious; he promised subscribers that he would treat "politics, history, general literature, science . . . the mechanic arts." He actually published, for example, a condensed version of Dickens's *Bleak House*, which no doubt Sam read.[1]

But Orion was a hopelessly impractical businessman—visionary, absent-minded, impressionable, impatient with detail—and not likely to make a success of a country weekly with a few hundred subscribers who often paid in pumpkins or firewood. His real ambition was to be a lawyer and to speak in public every day; if that dream had been fulfilled, he believed, all his working hours would have been filled with bliss. But he found no bliss in being a country editor, once his initial enthusiasm had faded—his life would be made up of short-lived enthusiasms. The paper did not flourish, Sam's wage could not be paid, his board consisted of "bacon, butter, bread, and coffee." He did not seem to have improved his situation, but Orion would give him chances he might never have had with Ament.

A distinctively American brand of humor had begun to make its way onto the printed page, the most original literary form yet created in the United States, although nobody then thought of it as literary. Stories of shrewd Yankees and frontier brawlers, of Mike Fink and Davy Crockett, of rogues and confidence men, of brutal fights and practical jokes, often fantastically exaggerated "tall tales"—these were the models Sam would imitate. Reprinted from periodicals such as *The Carpet Bag* or the enormously popular *Spirit of the Times*, they filled the Hannibal papers, and he must often have set them in type. He was to work in this humorous tradition all his life.

On January 16, 1861, the *Western Union* printed "A Gallant Fireman," Sam Clemens's first known published writing. It is an anecdote so brief it may have been produced while he stood at the case, setting it into type as fast as he composed it. "A Gallant Fireman" tells of a pretentious and panicky apprentice who, when fire broke out next door to his master's shop, "gathered the broom, an old mallet, the wash-pan, and a dirty towel" and rushed into the street with them. Later, he declares that "if that thar fie hadn't bin put out, thar'd a' bin the greatest *confirmation* of the age!" Sam's impulse toward burlesque was already at work.

More than a year of silence followed. Then, astonishingly, Sam Clemens reached a national audience. *The Carpet Bag* published "The Dandy Frightening the Squatter," signed "S. L. Clemens," in its issue of May 1, 1852. "The Dandy" was a good deal more ambitious than "A Gallant Fireman," offering a miniature narrative with conflict and resolution in which poetic justice is inflicted on a braggart. When a Mississippi steamboat lands to pick up wood, one of its passengers, "a spruce young dandy with a killing moustache," decides to impress the ladies on board by terrifying a "tall, brawny woodsman" whom he sees leaning against a tree. He threatens the "squatter" with pistols and bowie knife: "Say your prayers! . . . you'll make a capital barn door, and I shall drill the keyhole myself!" The squatter looks calmly at him, then knocks him into the river. As the dandy sneaks off, the victor calls after him, "I say, yeou, next time yeou come around drillin' keyholes, don't forget yer old acquaintances!" In that conflict between a caricatured "civilization" and the frontier, expressed in part through contrasting dialects, a good deal of the mature work of Mark Twain is foreshadowed.

A week later the Philadelphia *American Courier* published "Hannibal, Missouri," signed "S. L. C." Its opening is an exercise in just the sort of sentimental nostalgia that Mark Twain would later delight in ridiculing: "Hushed is the war-cry—no more does the light canoe cut the crystal waters of the proud Mississippi."

Seeing those two pieces in print, Mark Twain told Paine fifty years later, "was a joy which rather exceeded anything in that line I have ever experienced since." But he did not follow up his success. Instead, he remained silent for several months, until Orion's paper, now become the Hannibal *Journal*, published "A Family Muss," a mock-heroic account of a row in a poor Irish family, signed "W. Epaminondas Adrastus Perkins." That was Sam's first pen name. He had no reason to hide his identity, he was simply accepting an established convention; *all* newspaper humorists of the time wrote under pen names, following a journalistic tradition dating back to the *Spectator Papers* of the early eighteenth century. Then Orion went off to Tennessee, hoping to sell the land, and left Sam to himself. He had his chance, and he took it; the September 16 issue of the *Journal* contained four pieces by him, three of them now signed "W. Epaminondas Adrastus Blabb." The longest and most successful of the "Blabb" items recounted a successful "sell," or swindle, carried out by a traveling showman who presents an exhibit entitled "Bonaparte Crossing the Rhine." The "exhibit" consists of a piece of bone about three inches long—the "bony part"—and a slice of skin— "rind." (This story of how a naive boy is taken in by a trickster who offers his victims mildly phallic humor in place of the promised content was to be echoed in the performance of the "Royal Nonesuch" by the King and the Duke in *Huckleberry Finn*.)

Another piece was a savage personal satire. Beneath a crude woodcut, carved by Sam with his jackknife, of a man with a dog's head, wading at night in a shallow stream, the *Journal* ran the following text: "'Local' contemplates Suicide . . . by feeding his carcass to the fishes of Bear Creek while friend and foe are asleep. Fearing, however, that he may get out of his depth, he *sounds the stream with his walking-stick*." The point of the joke lay in the fact that T. J. Hinton, local reporter for a rival paper, the *Tri-Weekly Messenger*, had left a suicide note after being disappointed in love, "but when found by an anxious friend was unheroically wading back in the shallows of Bear Creek." He was shown with a dog's head because he had written on the nuisance of barking dogs. The story was signed, "A Dog-Be-Deviled Citizen."

Hinton responded furiously in the *Messenger*; the unknown writer "had not the decency of a gentleman nor the honor of a blackguard," and his ideas were "of so obscene and despicable an order as to forever bar them against . . . even decent discussion." The next issue of the *Journal* ran two more caricatures of Hinton, with sarcastic comments. The *Messenger* denounced them as "the feeble emanation of a puppy's brain"—that "puppy" indicating that the young author had been identified—and there the matter dropped. Hinton could do nothing; it would have been ludicrous to challenge a boy of sixteen to a duel, and to carry on a war in the newspapers would only make him more ridiculous. Perhaps he realized also that he would get the worst of it. Sam had won the first of his journalistic feuds and had learned the power of satire; he had wounded and infuriated his opponent and left him helpless to reply. He had also been in the wrong, as he later confessed, "densely unconscious that there was any moral obliquity" in that unprovoked attack.

Guilt is often irrational. Sam felt none for the assault on Hinton, but he blamed himself bitterly, and without cause, for the horrifying fate of a tramp, burned to death in the Hannibal jail, where he was the only prisoner. Early on Sunday morning, fire was seen in his cell. The keys could not be found, the door could not be broken, and the horrified spectators could only watch and listen to the man's screams until he collapsed, asphyxiated by the smoke. The *Journal*'s story, no doubt written by Orion, supposed that the fire had been started by the victim, "an insane Irishman—made insane by liquor"—who had probably set his bedding on fire while smoking. Orion finished with a warning against whiskey, but to Sam the spectacle meant more than a pretext for a sermon. He had met the man on the street the night before, had given him matches for his pipe. Consequently, by a perverse but undeniable logic, he was

responsible for the fire. His "trained Presbyterian conscience" inflicted "hideous dreams" on him for months,
and after thirty years he could still picture the man "like a
black object set against a sun, so white and intense was the
light at his back." When he finally told the story, in *Life on
the Mississippi*, he gave his age at the time as ten. In fact he
had been seventeen, but a ten-year-old cannot so easily be
held responsible. The guilt, if any, may not have been entirely his own; writing to a boyhood friend in 1870, Twain
would refer to the time when "we accidentally burned up
that poor fellow in the calaboose." But if guilt was available, Sam Clemens, and later Mark Twain, would seize it
for himself; the Presbyterian conscience did not allow for
shared responsibility.

The *Journal* was sinking under its debts by this time, but
Orion made a last effort to save his struggling paper by
turning it into a daily. The change gave Sam new opportunities. In May of 1853, after several months of journalistic
silence, he burst into print with a whole set of new pen
names: Rambler; Grumbler; A Son of Adam; Peter Pen-
cilcase's Son, John Snooks. As Rambler, a pseudonym
made famous by Samuel Johnson almost a hundred years
earlier, he contributed a pair of saccharine, utterly conventional poems, "The Heart's Lament" and "Love Concealed": *"Oh, thou wilt never know how fond a love / This heart
could have felt for thee,"* et cetera. "Love Concealed," however, was not quite what it seemed; sentiment was turned
to burlesque by the subtitle "To Miss Katie of H——l."
Because it suggested either "hell" or "Hannibal," Sam
thought "H——l" "a perfect thunderbolt of humor."

As A Son of Adam, Sam gave advice on how to prevent
dogs from going mad in August ("Cut their heads off in
July") and on "How to check a runaway horse" ("Throw
an empty flour barrel at him. Green cotton umbrellas are
also good, but not always so accessible.") He printed jokes,
puns, conundrums, and hoaxes—a headline read TERRIBLE
ACCIDENT! 500 MEN KILLED AND MISSING!!— followed by an

explanation that the story was to be continued; the accident hadn't happened yet.

Realizing at last that in Sam he had an asset worth keeping, Orion gave him a column of his own. On May 23 "Our Assistant's Column" presented Sam feuding with a rival editor and a rival town, and parodying that hackneyed recitation piece, "The Burial of Sir John Moore." But recognition had come too late. By the end of May, Sam had gone and the *Journal* was advertising for an apprentice. He had mastered his trade, and there was nothing to hold him in Hannibal. Orion had never paid the promised wage, could give him nothing but poor food and shabby clothes; Sam had only his experience to show for two years of hard work. They had quarreled as well; associating with his incompetent, hapless older brother would always tend to produce uncontrollable exasperation in Mark Twain, and the chance to fill "Our Assistant's Column" could hardly compensate. And so, Orion would remember, "he went wandering in search of that comfort and that advancement and those rewards of industry which he had failed to find where I was—gloomy, taciturn, and selfish." Evidently the brothers shared a propensity for guilt. In losing Sam's "bounding activity and merriment," the *Journal* had lost its spirit. Orion did not get out an issue for a month, and in early fall he sold the paper. He blamed himself, but nothing he could have done would have held Sam much longer. He was grown, he was independent, and Hannibal was small; it was time for him to go into the world.

He returned to Hannibal after that only for brief visits. But in memory and imagination, the town never left him. It would reappear in book after book: as the often idyllic St. Petersburg of *Tom Sawyer*—where evil seems confined to Injun Joe; as the squalid river towns of *Huckleberry Finn*; as the harshly racist Dawson's Landing of *Pudd'nhead Wilson*; as the contemptible yet pathetic Eseldorf (Donkeytown, or Jackassville) of *The Chronicle of Young Satan*; and under its own name, but seen through a haze of nostalgia, in the *Autobiography*. It became for him the archetypal small town, sometimes heaven, sometimes hell—but on the whole, in his memory, the heavenly aspect would predominate. Writing in the 1890s, he boldly claimed that the Hannibal of his boyhood had been free from "the lust for money which is the rule of life today, and the hardness and cynicism which is the spirit of life today." It had been sentimental but not sordid; culture had been "soft, sappy, melancholy; but money had no place in it. To get rich was no one's ambition." To Twain, the Hannibal of his boyhood represented an age of innocence, an America of farms and villages still close to Nature, a country not yet spoiled by the California gold rush and by the Civil War and the industrialization, social strife, and political corruption that followed it.

Golden ages should never be given a date and a place— they are likely to dissolve under examination. John Clemens himself had craved riches, for his family if not for himself; that was why he had bought the Tennessee Land. European travelers, before the Civil War, invariably noted the prevailing money-lust and the general indifference as to *how* money was gained—Dickens's *Martin Chuzzlewit* provides satirical testimony.

But the point is not what Hannibal *was* but what Mark Twain's imagination made of it. It came to represent for him, and for his readers, a time of innocence, both personal and national. He could call the "St. Petersburg" of *Tom Sawyer* "a poor little shabby village," and such it undoubtedly was, but it seemed an Eden as well: "The locust trees were in bloom and the fragrance of the blossoms filled the air. Cardiff Hill . . . was green with vegetation, and it lay just far enough away to seem a Delectable Land, dreamy, reposeful and inviting." The town had less heavenly associations for him—with poverty and bankruptcy for the Clemens family, with slavery, violence, and death—that would shape his life and would also find expression in his work. There had been adulteries and unhappy marriages in Hannibal, there had been ne'er-do-wells, criminals, and lunatics, there had been cruelty, loneliness, frustration, despair. All of this Mark Twain knew, and much of it he recorded in "Villagers of 1840–43," a late manuscript published in 1869.[2] But in his greatest work he presented an idyllic portrait of his town because Hannibal was unforgettably associated with his boyhood—the single period of his life, he once remarked, that he would have considered living over again, and then only on condition that he should drown at fifteen.

JOURNEYMAN

Before Sam was allowed to go out into the world his mother required him to swear on the Bible that he would not "throw a card or drink a drop of liquor" until she released him from his pledge. By Twain's own testimony, he kept that oath "absolutely inviolate for seven years" before she set him free. There is no doubt this oath was really taken; Sam referred to it a few months later in a letter home, and in 1873 Jane Clemens was to demand that Orion—then forty-eight—take an oath never to make another invention, reminding him that "Sam took an oath before his mother, that oath saved him."

He worked in St. Louis a few weeks, to earn money, but his goal was New York, the metropolis of America, with its population of half a million or more, and the scene that summer of the first world's fair to be held in the United

States. Not yet eighteen, inexperienced, and alone, with two or three dollars in his pocket and a ten-dollar bill concealed in the lining of his coat, he entered the great city in late August, after an exhausting five-day journey by steamboat and railroad. He promptly found work in a printing house and began writing long letters home, detailing his way of life and the wonders of the city. He lived in a boarding house, rose at six and was at work by seven, where he took pride in his ability to meet metropolitan standards: "Why, you must put exactly the same space between every two words, and *every line must be spaced alike*." Nevertheless, he brags, his proof was the cleanest of all. Orion published his letter, "to encourage apprentices in country printing offices."

Everything in New York was on a grand new scale; his firm employed two hundred men, including forty typesetters; from his fifth-floor workplace he could look over the city and view the "forest of masts" beyond the Battery. He visited the fair in its Crystal Palace, a building of iron and glass resembling a giant greenhouse, but reported only that 6,000 people, more than twice the population of Hannibal, visited it daily. Writing to Pamela, he remembered his oath—"Tell Ma my promises are faithfully kept"—and adds reassuringly: "You ask me where I spend my evenings. Where would you suppose with a free printer's library containing more than 4,000 volumes within a quarter of a mile of me, and nobody at home to talk to?" He did not want his family to worry about him; everyone had heard tales of country boys going wrong in the city. The theater excited him; he saw the famous tragedian Edwin Forrest in *The Gladiator*, dying in the last act "in all the fierce pleasure of gratified revenge" and noted that "the man's whole soul seems absorbed in the part he is playing."

But his pay was poor—only four dollars a week in discounted banknotes. That left nothing after he had paid for his board and room and laundry, and no prospects of anything better offered themselves.

By October he was forced to retreat to Philadelphia, working nights and odd hours for the *Inquirer*, which paid in "sparkling gold," going to the theater or doing the sights in his spare time. He visited Franklin's grave and Independence Hall, feeling the appropriate awe; he found time for a midwinter journey to Washington, where Missouri's Senator Thomas Hart Benton and the original Franklin printing press, on display at the Smithsonian, drew his attention. "Mr. Benton," he wrote, "sits silent & gloomy in the midst of the din, like a lion imprisoned in a cage of monkeys, who, feeling his superiority, disdains to notice their chattering." The press interested him more deeply; the contrast between that primitive device, requiring two pulls of a lever to print every sheet, and the great steam presses of his own day, throwing off 20,000 sheets an hour, proved to him the superiority of his time.

If he wrote letters during the next several months, they do not survive. The northern winter was long, and the novelty of the East had worn off; he wanted to go to St. Louis before the Ohio froze and steamboat traffic stopped, but he did not have the money until late in the summer of 1854. Home, now, was not Hannibal, but Muscatine, Iowa, where Orion, Henry, and Jane Clemens lived, and Orion published the Muscatine *Tri-Weekly Journal*. Arriving by steamboat early one morning, Sam waited a few hours in a hotel, where he found a book containing portraits of the kings and queens of England, with the dates of their reigns. He memorized the information and thereby became interested in English history, an enthusiasm that eventually led him to write two novels, *The Prince and the Pauper* and *A Connecticut Yankee in King Arthur's Court*, and to invent a "history game," designed to teach history painlessly by encouraging memorization of the dates of kings and queens.

He had seen a good deal of the world for a boy of eighteen. He had proved that he could support himself wherever he chose, and he had kept on writing. In Philadelphia he had tried unsuccessfully to publish poetry of an "obituary sort"—the sort he would parody in Emmeline Grangerford's verses in *Huckleberry Finn*—but his letters home had constituted his real writing. Orion had printed three of them, and Sam expected publication: "I will try to write for the paper occasionally," he had promised. They are humorless and generally impersonal, written in clear, competent prose with occasional purple patches where heightened emotion seemed appropriate.[1]

His letters to Pamela are more revealing, especially in his vigorous assertions of self-reliance: "If you have a brother nearly eighteen years of age, who is not able to take care of himself a few miles from home, such a brother is not worth one's thoughts." And they are clearly the letters of a literary young man, who can quote Shakespeare and practice rhetorical flourishes, a serious young man bent on self-improvement, moralistic and rather shocked by the wickedness of the Eastern cities: "I never before saw so many whisky-swilling, God-despising heathens as I find in this part of the country. I believe that I am the only person in the *Inquirer* office that does not drink." He is conventionally moral, conventionally patriotic, conventionally prejudiced. Carpenter's Hall in Philadelphia, he writes, is "dear to every American, for within its walls, the first Congress of the United States assembled," and he is outraged by the number of "abominable foreigners" on the *Inquirer* staff and by the immigrant population of New York—the children are "vermin" and "brats." He is a white supremacist, too, remarking that "I reckon I had better black my face, for in these Eastern States niggers are considered better than white people."[2] Looking back in 1876 on the Sam Clemens of those years, Mark Twain wrote that he had been "a callow fool, a self-sufficient ass, a mere human tumblebug, stern in air, heaving at his bit of dung & imagining he is remodelling the world... Ignorance, intolerance, egotism, self-assertion, opaque perception, dense & pitiful chuckle-headedness—& an almost pathetic unconsciousness of it all. That is what I was at 19-20." And, of course, at seventeen or eighteen. That description, he concluded, "is what the average Southerner is at 60 today."

Muscatine offered adventure, of a kind—Mark Twain would not forget "Bill Israeel, who drew a butcher-knife gaumed with red ink on me once in a lonely place & made me apologize for some imaginary affront"—but no opportunities. Sam went to St. Louis, working as a printer and rooming with a young journeyman chairmaker who shared his liking for books. He made less use in his later writing of the nearly four years following his departure from Hannibal than of any other period in his early life, but in *Life on the Mississippi* he recorded a vivid memory from his stay at St. Louis. Antiforeign and anti-Catholic bigotry ran high in the 1850s. It was the time of the Know-Nothing party, founded on a "Native American" platform. When mobs invaded the Irish quarter of St. Louis, Sam and his roommate "saw some of the fighting and killings" and joined a militia organized to restore order. At about ten o'clock one night, "news came that the mob were in great force in the lower end of the town, and were sweeping everything before them." The militia marched, but the night was hot, Sam's musket was heavy, and "the nearer we approached the seat of war, the hotter I grew and the thirstier I got." Asking his friend to carry his musket, Sam dropped out of the ranks to get a drink, and did not return.

While Sam was in St. Louis, Orion had married—absent-mindedly boarding the coach after the ceremony without his new bride—and had abandoned Muscatine and the newspaper business to open a printing shop in Keokuk, Iowa, then a booming river port. In midsummer of 1855 Sam joined Orion and Henry at the Ben Franklin Book & Job Office, for a nominal wage of five dollars a week and board. It was a second choice. He had wanted to go on the river and learn the craft of steamboat piloting, and he had appealed for help to a distant, wealthy relative, James Clemens of St. Louis. But Clemens had done nothing; as he explained later to Orion, "I was then and am now of the opinion that your brother should stick to his present trade."

For the next sixteen or eighteen months, then, Sam Clemens stuck to his trade in Keokuk. It seems to have been a happy, uneventful time. He had felt the loneliness of Eastern cities; now he could make friends in the sociable atmosphere of a Midwestern town. He joined a singing class and a debating society; he was popular with girls but had no favorite, choosing to remain "a beau rather than a suitor, good friend and comrade to all, wooer of none."

At Keokuk he was known as a reader, always carrying a book—Dickens or Poe or some work of history—and had already formed a lasting habit of reading and smoking in bed until late at night. He also discovered that he had a talent for public speaking: at a printer's dinner celebrating Franklin's birthday, the Keokuk *Post* reported, "Sam Clemens was loudly and repeatedly called for and responded in a speech replete with wit and humor."

He began keeping a notebook—the first of forty-nine that survive. Neither a diary nor a literary journal, though at times it served both purposes, it contained French exercises, notes on his reading, experiments in writing, reminders to himself, a laundry list, an annotated chess game. In its variety and confusion it is an essay in self-discovery, offering unique insight into the mind of twenty-year-old Sam Clemens. The cover shows him experimenting with signatures—"Samuel L. Clemens," "S. L. Clemens," and simply "Clemens"—in different handwritings, each variation an experiment in identity, a role momentarily assumed. He had been studying a textbook of phrenology and took the trouble to copy long descriptions of the four psychophysical types recognized in the system: the sanguine, the bilious, the lymphatic, and the nervous.[3] Phrenology largely concerned itself with "reading" character from the bumps and hollows in the skull, but some phrenologists borrowed a theory of underlying "temperaments" from the ancient doctrine of the four humors.

Sam believed himself the sanguine type, possessed of a "burning, flaming, flashing temperament," marked externally by red or chestnut hair and "florid or sandy skin." Other physical details—"full ample chest... generally thick stout build"—did not fit, but psychologically the description seems remarkably apt. He conspicuously possessed "elasticity and buoyancy of spirit," "suddenness and intensity" of feelings, "impulsiveness and hastiness of character; great warmth of both anger and love." The sanguine type "is fond of change," "works fast and tires soon; runs its short race and gives over"; Mark Twain would make countless jokes about his own laziness, again and again he would abandon a manuscript when his enthusiasm died, sometimes returning to it years later, sometimes leaving it permanently unfinished.

To make the description fit more closely, he added two sentences, carefully imitating the style of the original: "It [the sanguine temperament] is very sensitive and is first deeply hurt at a slight, the next emotion is violent rage, and in a few moments the cause and the result are both forgotten for the time being. It often forgives, but never entirely forgets an injury." He observed himself accurately; that sensitivity, that sudden rage, and that memory for old injuries can often be seen in his later life.

Impulsiveness, restlessness, love of change, "elasticity and buoyancy of spirit"—these are the sanguine qualities, the same qualities that made him always seem so young, even in old age. When Twain began work as editor and part owner of the Buffalo *Express* in 1869, a reporter immediately recognized him as being of "what they used to call the 'sanguine' temperament." Here, at the outset of his career, we find the core of his final philosophy, his belief that "temperament" is inborn, fixed, irresistible. This belief, that he had discovered the unchanging essence of his nature, could easily have been a self-fulfilling prophecy, hardening tendencies into inexorable laws. If it were his nature to be impulsive, then what could he do but yield to the law of his being and act, immediately, on impulse? And every such choice could make an alternative choice in the future more difficult.

His need for change soon began to assert itself. Working for Orion brought the inevitable vexations; the business never produced more than a poor living and the promised wage could not be paid, a problem that Orion "solved" by making his brother a partner, with a share in the nonexistent profits; in his eagerness to get work, Orion always bid too low. The shop was mismanaged, exasperating Sam, who acted as foreman: "They throw all my plans into disorder," he complained, "by taking my hands away from their work. . . . I can't work blindly, without system." After a year, he must have felt that he had exhausted the possibilities of Keokuk and realized that in spite of the shop's brave name, he would never rise in the world, as Franklin had, while working there.

He invented a plan for escape that would have delighted Tom Sawyer—he would go to the upper Amazon to "collect coca [the plant from which cocaine is extracted] and make a fortune." He had read *Exploration of the Valley of the Amazon*, by Lieutenant William Herndon of the United States Navy. Buoyantly optimistic, Herndon claimed that the Amazon Valley was of "unrivalled fertility," producing "nearly everything essential to the comfort and well-being of man." In the eastern slopes of the Andes could be found "unimaginable quantities of silver, iron, coal, copper, and quicksilver," delicious fruits grew everywhere, the forests were filled with game and the rivers with fish. Even the climate was "salubrious." And all this wealth lay waiting to be developed by American enterprise. Sam read and believed. He was "fired with a longing to ascend the upper Amazon" and "to open up a trade in coca with all the world." To be credulous, enthusiastic, and impulsive—that, after all, was his temperament.

He found two partners, and for a moment the plan

seemed serious. In August, he reported to Henry, he and one of his companions "held a long consultation, Sunday morning, and determined to start to Brazil, if possible, in *six weeks*." As for money, he had "put 'feelers' out in several directions." Money was the problem, and, says Paine, money miraculously appeared. Walking down Main Street on a November day, "bleak, bitter, and gusty, with curling snow," Sam saw a bit of paper blow past, caught it, and found that it was a fifty-dollar bill. He advertised the find, and when no one claimed it, left Keokuk. But the only source for the story is Mark Twain's memory in old age; it is found in "The Turning-Point of My Life," an essay published a year before his death, and in Paine's biography. There is no mention of it in any surviving letter, and no such advertisement has been found in the Keokuk papers. Fifty dollars equaled ten weeks' wages for Sam, if his wages had been paid. The extreme unlikelihood of his picking up that much money off the street, exactly when it was most wanted, makes the tale seem more than doubtful— unless, like Paine, we attribute the find to "Fate or Providence or Accident—whatever we may choose to call the unaccountable." Sam might have found a smaller amount and magnified it in memory, or he could have begged and borrowed the money, a humiliating experience he might have preferred to forget, or there might have been no money at all, the entire story a fiction, another of the legends that have passed into Mark Twain biography.

Whatever happened, anticlimax followed. Sam Clemens did not go to the Amazon—he went to Cincinnati. Perhaps the scheme had been temporarily dropped, perhaps he needed to earn more money. Cincinnati was the western center of the book trade, and he found work easily. As he recalled in his *Autobiography*, he found intellectual stimulation as well. He encountered a man of ideas in his boarding house.[4] Among its "common-place people . . . full of bustle, frivolity, chatter . . . good-natured, clean-minded and well-meaning, but . . . oppressively uninteresting," was a self-taught workman named Macfarlane, who had worked out for himself an original, highly pessimistic philosophy. Three years before the publication of *The Origin of Species*, he had anticipated Darwin's theory of evolution and had reached a startling conclusion: evolution had proceeded on "an ascending scale toward ultimate perfection until *man* was reached; and... then the progressive scheme broke pitifully down and went to wreck and ruin!" In all the animal kingdom, said Macfarlane, only man "was capable of feeling malice, envy, vindictiveness, revengefulness, hatred, selfishness," only man became drunk and was personally unclean, only man made war and enslaved his fellow-creatures. Human intelligence merely degraded the race "to a rank far below... the other animals," since men used their intellects to advance themselves at other men's expense. To Macfarlane, humans were Yahoos, like the filthy and disgusting creatures in the last book of *Gulliver's Travels*. Ironically, those teachings, which seemed so boldly original, in fact repeated orthodox Christian doctrine concerning the nature of fallen man; young Clemens might not have recognized their underlying familiarity, but it surely would have made them more acceptable. It seems likely, then, that the foundations of Mark Twain's mature philosophy—his psychological determinism and his deeply pessimistic view of human nature and capabilities—had been laid down in his early twenties.

Sam found time for writing in Cincinnati, contributing a few letters to the Keokuk *Post* and signing them with a new pen name, Thomas Jefferson Snodgrass—the last name probably borrowed from that of a ludicrous literary man in Dickens's *Pickwick Papers*. Clemens's Snodgrass is a bumpkin in the city: he goes to the theater and thinks the action on the stage real; innocently holding a baby for a woman who promptly disappears, he is arrested as an "onnateral father." The letters were meant to form a series entitled "Snodgrass's Dierrea," and Mark Twain later preferred to forget them. But crude as they were, the Snodgrass sketches were his first experiments in a form that he would make his own, the humorous travel letter, and they were also the first writings for which he was paid.

But Cincinnati could be only a way station for Sam Clemens—he wanted travel and adventure, and he would not find them there. Restlessness returned with the spring. In April of 1857 he bought a ticket to New Orleans on the steamboat *Paul Jones*. Perhaps he still hoped to sail for the Amazon, but before reaching New Orleans he had apprenticed to Horace Bixby, one of the *Jones*'s two pilots.[5] His first career, as a printer, had ended. New starts were easy in Sam Clemens's America.

PILOT

Bixby had been reluctant to take Sam on at first, grumbling that "Cub pilots are more trouble than they're worth," and his terms were hard: one hundred dollars in cash and four hundred to be paid out of Sam's first earnings after receiving his license. He refused an offer of 2,000 acres of the Tennessee Land. Sam had no money, but the hundred dollars could be borrowed from Pamela's new husband, Will Moffett, a prosperous St. Louis merchant. If the act seems impulsive, the ambition was old, born in his Hannibal boyhood.[1]

The price was undeniably high—ordinarily cubs paid nothing at all, giving their service in return for their training—but there is no evidence that Sam ever regretted his bargain, and he was a man always ready to believe that he had been swindled. In thirty-five-year-old Horace Bixby he found a widely respected and highly competent master and a uniquely effective teacher. Bixby had started on the river at eighteen as an unpaid "mud clerk," and would stay on it almost until his death at eighty-three. (That he would always find boats to steer throughout the long decline in river traffic that followed the Civil War testifies to his skill and his reputation.) Most pilots held one license, but Bixby held three—for the Missouri, the Ohio, and the lower Mississippi. It was the lower river, from St. Louis to New Orleans, that Sam was to learn. There the traffic was heaviest, and year-round navigation often possible.

Sam Clemens came to the river at the right time. He would have two years to learn the craft and two years to enjoy the status of a licensed pilot before all peaceful traffic was ended by the Civil War—time enough to experience the profession thoroughly but not to delay seriously his development as a writer. He came when the steamboat business was at its zenith, only beginning to feel the competition of railroads, when lines of communication still ran north and south, when boats on the Mississippi and all its tributaries carried passengers and corn and cotton from all the Middle West and upper South down to the Gulf at New Orleans, bringing back foreign luxuries, staple goods, tools, and machinery, and in the process relieving the somnolent boredom of the river towns. Probably no one— certainly not Sam Clemens—foresaw that the era was so near its end. Steamboating had constantly grown on the Western rivers for at least thirty-five years, playing an indispensable part in the development of the Midwest. Technological progress had been surprisingly slow—the basic design of the Western riverboat hardly changed after 1830, and the travel times achieved between St. Louis and New Orleans in the 1840s were never significantly bettered— but the boats had grown steadily bigger and grander. There was nothing like them anywhere else in the world.

It was free enterprise at its most anarchic, with every boat for itself. There were no great corporations like those that would build the transcontinental railroads. The Mississippi remained uncontrolled and unimproved; in its whole length there was not a beacon light or a buoy. Safety regulations existed, spelled out by the federal government and insurance companies, but they were enforced haphazardly or not at all. Of course, the traffic was hazardous—the life expectancy of a Mississippi steamboat was about four years. Running aground was routine, hardly taken seriously, except for the time lost in unloading cargo so the boat could float free. Boats were destroyed in many ways; their bottoms were ripped out by snags or reefs or abandoned wrecks; they burned or blew up. The furnaces were always lighted and the engineers were often incompetent, the boats were wooden, and they carried inflammable cargo such as cotton, hay, and turpentine; the frequent boiler explosions started fires, and fires were usually uncontrollable. But to an imaginative young man, those hazards might only add to the "romance" of piloting.

The boats that Sam Clemens would steer were all of a pattern, though varying widely in size and luxury. They were flat-bottomed sidewheelers, up to 350 feet long. The flat bottoms reduced their draft; the side wheels, covered with gaily painted wheelhouses, provided more maneuverability than a single wheel at the stern. The shallow hold would be filled with cargo, while on the main deck the furnaces, boilers, and high-pressure engines shared space with more cargo, livestock, and deck passengers traveling cheaply. Higher still, the misleadingly named boiler deck, with cabins, ladies' "saloon," and the cavernous main saloon, or dining room, accommodated more genteel travelers. The degree of grandeur here could determine a boat's status. Sam's second boat, the *Crescent City*, had pretensions: when he "looked down her long, gilded saloon, it was like gazing through a splendid tunnel; she had an oil-picture, by some gifted sign-painter, on every stateroom door; she glittered with no end of prism-fringed chandeliers." Here, in the intricate carving of walls and ceiling and

wooden pillars, steamboat gothic reached its climax. Such
boats were inevitably called floating palaces, and palaces
they were in comparison with anything the average passenger was likely to see on land. "They tallied with the citizen's dream of what magnificence was, and satisfied it,"
Mark Twain would observe. Sophisticated travelers might
find such flamboyance cheap and showy, but steamboats
were not designed for them.

On the texas deck above, extending only part of the
boat's length, were the officer's quarters; in front of the
texas rose the twin chimneys—one engine for each wheel,
one chimney for each engine—sometimes reaching a hundred feet above the water. On the texas deck stood the pilothouse. In this glass-enclosed cage, the pilot stood behind
the great spoked wheel, communicating with the engine
room through bell ropes and speaking tube. On a bench
behind him, other pilots, traveling free to "look at the
river," might sit and talk shop. In that age of ineffable
gaudiness, not even the pilothouse was strictly functional.
Carved and fretted as though some lunatic carpenter had
run wild with a scroll saw, it might look from the outside
like a Turkish minaret, or a medieval turret. The interior
could be grand: "a sumptuous glass temple; room enough
to have a dance in; showy red and gold window-cur-
tains . . . a wheel . . . costly with inlaid work; bright brass
knobs for the bells," a leather-cushioned bench for visitors,
the inevitable stove and spittoons. There might even be "a
tidy, white-aproned, black 'texas-tender,' to bring up tarts
and ices and coffee during mid-watch." To Sam Clemens
at twenty-one, "this was unutterable pomp."

In this sanctum, the pilot reigned alone. The captain
might tell him where to land, but otherwise, once the boat
pulled out from shore, his authority was supreme. It was
that independence, above all, that Mark Twain would remember and whose loss he would regret—an independence
that a journalist or an author, dependent on editors and
public, could never possess. All men but the pilot "are

slaves to other men and to circumstances," he would write
to an old river friend a few years later; only the pilot
"comes at no man's beck or call, obeys no man's orders, &
scorns all men's suggestions."

On the pilot's skill depended the safety of boat, cargo,
and passengers; his income and prestige were correspond-
ingly high. He might earn from $150 to $250 a month—
"Two months of his wages would pay a preacher's salary
for a year," Mark Twain observed—with free board and
room. While a boat lay over at St. Louis or New Orleans,
discharging and taking on its cargo, the pilots had nothing
to do but draw their pay and "play gentleman up-town."
The profession offered responsibility, authority, income,
leisure, prestige. It's no wonder that Annie Moffett, Pamela's daughter, remembered "the stir caused by the announcement that Uncle Sam had decided to become a
pilot. It seemed to me as if everyone was running up and
down stairs and sitting on the steps to talk over the news."

When the *Paul Jones* headed upstream for St. Louis, carrying a cargo of axes, nutmeg, gunnysacks, rivets, scales,
linseed oil, buggy wheels, sugar, dried herring, coffee, co-
coa, wine, lemons, hardware, tinware, and earthenware,
Sam Clemens began his apprenticeship. It was a leisurely
voyage of nine days, punctuated with stops at river towns
and wood yards to pick up fuel cut from the limitless forests bordering the river, and even at individual farms and
plantations. A boat could land anywhere; it simply ran its
bow aground and threw a gangplank on shore, while the
lazily spinning paddlewheels held it in place against the
current.

"Learning the river" meant committing to memory the
names, shapes, and locations of innumerable reefs and
shoals and islands and points and bends, even of individual
snags, learning the passages that were safe under any conditions and the "chutes" that could be taken only when the
river was in flood. It meant learning the true shape of the
river, so the pilot could navigate by that knowledge

through fog or darkness, never mistaking shadow for solid shore. But that shape constantly changed as the river ate into its own banks. Landmarks vanished as new bars and shoals and snags appeared, islands might be washed away or joined to the mainland, river ports could be left stranded by "cut-offs" slicing through the bends of the river. The Mississippi could never be learned once and for all. The pilot must continuously renew his knowledge by experience, or by viewing the river from other boats when he had none of his own, or by talking shop with his fellows. The endlessly changing river provided an endlessly fascinating topic. Last of all to be mastered was the subtle art of "reading the river"—knowing intuitively that a snag or a wreck lay just below the surface, knowing whether a ripple indicated nothing more than a harmless "wind reef" or signalled a deadly, nearly vertical bar. But while knowledge was essential, it was not enough; the pilot needed also the confidence and courage to judge any situation and act instantly. Learning the river was an enormous task for any man, and almost impossible for Sam Clemens—impatient, absent-minded, easily distracted. It went against the grain of his nature; that he finally succeeded proves the strength of his ambition.

Learning began at once. Bixby, an impatient man, cursed out his new cub for his forgetfulness, then ordered him to "get a little memorandum-book" and write down everything he was told. That memorandum-book survives, a lined ledger book, no doubt borrowed from a clerk, filled with cryptic annotations concerning landmarks on the river and directions for navigating: "Island No. 10 . . . no bottom around it. Go in at ft of t—take mid. from bel. ft of fld. & keep out from l.h. shore till—S. on ft of I. h on Harris ugly dd. t." But no pilot could be constantly thumbing through a notebook; Sam had to transfer those facts to his memory. By the time the *Jones* reached St. Louis, he had already become a tolerably good steersman, and had commenced learning the river—but only half of it, since that was all he had seen on his alternating four-hour watches. He had also learned that a pilot could expect to be on duty twelve hours a day, often turning out of bed at midnight to stand a four-hour watch—facts that made the profession seem "not quite so romantic" but instead "very real and workmanlike."

There were many boats. After two trips on the ramshackle *Paul Jones*, Bixby and his cub moved in late May to the *Crescent City*, nearly twice as large as the *Jones* and more than twice as grand. Then Bixby went up the Missouri, leaving his cub on the *John J. Roe* in charge of its pilots, Zeb Leavenworth and Beck Jolly. The *Roe* was a friendly boat; it had a piano, and there was dancing on deck, and sometimes Sam Clemens entertained with a nearly endless song about an old horse named Methusalem. "It was a love of a steamboat," he affectionately recalled, "as slow as an island and as comfortable as a farm," and both pilots became his friends. He probably took only two trips on her, then left for the *Pennsylvania*—"a magnificent floating palace," according to the St. Louis *Evening News*. He would stay with the *Pennsylvania* until June of the following year. Between voyages, since a cub earned no wages, he guarded freight on the levee for three dollars a night, and on layovers in St. Louis lived at the home of his brother-in-law, Will Moffett. Jane Clemens now lived with her daughter, and in the Moffett household, with his mother, his sister, and his small niece, Annie, Sam Clemens enjoyed the only real home he would have between his departure from Hannibal in 1853 and his marriage in 1870.

He learned something more of the hazards of steamboating on the *Pennsylvania*. In December he may have been involved in, may even have been responsible for, a collision. The case went to court, Sam Clemens was called to testify, and the *Pennsylvania* was found at fault. If Sam had been a witness, then he must have been in the pilothouse, and in that case, as "cub," he would probably have been steering. But in any case, he suffered no penalties; perhaps cubs were allowed their mistakes. He soon learned the hazards of winter navigation. Sounding the channel in the *Pennsylvania*'s yawl in February, when the river was filled with floating ice, his boat was swept in to shore and it was impossible to row back. "Then the fun commenced," he reported to Orion: "We made fast a line 20 fathoms long, to the bow of the yawl, and put the men... to it like horses, on the shore. Brown, the pilot, stood in the bow, with an oar, to keep her head out, and I took the tiller. We would start the men, and all would go well till the yawl would bring up on a heavy cake of ice, and then the men would drop like so many ten-pins while Brown assumed the horizontal in the bottom of the boat. After an hour's hard work we got back, with ice half an inch thick on the oars." They tried sounding again, found the channel, and landed on an island to be picked up by the *Pennsylvania*. The next day and the next, conditions were even worse. The sounding boat was caught in the ice and drifted helplessly downriver, till it touched on a sandbar. There they waited four hours in rain and sleet to be picked up; the *Pennsylvania* had meanwhile run aground. On the third day, wrote Sam, he was "out in the yawl from 4 o'clock in the morning till half past 9 without being near a fire. There was a thick coating of ice over men, yawl, ropes and everything else, and we looked like rock-candy statuary."

Those months on the *Pennsylvania* were the unhappiest time in Sam's four years on the river. One pilot, George Ealer, was a genial man, a musician, a reader, and "a prime chess player," who admired Oliver Goldsmith and idolized Shakespeare, reading aloud by the hour while Sam steered. But Sam worked under William Brown—Bixby had gone on to another boat—and Brown was a petty tyrant, surly, stupid, and ignorant, who made the lives of his subordinates miserable with incessant faultfinding. Sam was his favorite target; no doubt Brown envied his bright intelligence and playful humor. His curses and angry explosions had to be endured, no matter how unjustified—a pilot held despotic authority over his cub. But one provocation proved intolerable: his abuse of Henry Clemens, Sam's younger brother, who had shipped as third clerk on the *Pennsylvania*.

As Mark Twain tells the story, Henry appeared on the hurricane deck one day and "shouted to Brown to stop at some landing or other, a mile or so below." Brown, who was slightly deaf, did not hear him. When the boat went past the landing, Captain Klinefelter came to the pilot-house to ask if Henry had delivered the order. Brown denied it, but Sam said *he* had heard it. Brown cursed him, and the episode seemed over. An hour later, Henry entered the pilothouse on another errand:

Brown began, straightaway: "Here! Why didn't you tell me we'd got to land at that plantation?"

"I did tell, Mr. Brown."

"It's a lie!"

I said: "You lie, yourself. He did tell you."

Brown instantly ordered Henry out of the pilothouse before attending to this insubordination. Then, as the boy left, "Brown with a sudden access of fury, picked up a ten-pound lump of coal and sprang after him." Sam jumped between them with a heavy stool; "knocking Brown to the deck with the stool, he then pounded the prostrate man with his fists until Brown "struggled free . . . and sprang for the wheel"—the *Pennsylvania* was heading downstream at full speed, unattended. Banished from the pilothouse, Sam refused to leave, mocking Brown's illiterate English until the pilot, who "was not equipped for this species of controversy," had been silenced.

There was a reckoning to come. Captain Klinefelter summoned the young cub into his own cabin, shut the door, and questioned him. Reluctantly, Sam admitted that he had fought Mr. Brown, had struck him with a stool, knocked him down, and pounded him. "I am deuced glad of it!" exclaimed the captain. "You have been guilty of a great crime; and don't you ever be guilty of it again, on this boat. *But*—lay for him ashore!" Relieved from duty, for Brown refused to work with him, Sam "knew how an emancipated slave feels," and passed his time at chess with George Ealer, or listened to him read "from his two Bibles . . . Goldsmith and Shakespeare."

That fight is the only known occasion in Clemens's adult life when he resorted to physical violence. The immediate consequence was that Sam left the *Pennsylvania* at New Orleans—and thereby probably saved his own life. Captain Klinefelter, who must have thoroughly disliked Brown, had proposed that Sam and George Ealer should pilot the boat to St. Louis, with Sam standing the daylight watches, but Sam refused—he did not feel ready. The *Pennsylvania* left without him, but with Henry still on board, while Sam traveled north as a passenger on the *A. T. Lacey*. Two days out, when the *Lacey* touched at a landing, "somebody shouted: 'The *Pennsylvania* is blown up at Ship Island, and a hundred and fifty lives lost!' "

The *Pennsylvania* had exploded at 6:00 A.M., June 13, seventy miles south of Memphis and three hundred yards from shore. Four boilers blew up, the blast and scalding steam instantly killing the firemen and most of the deck passengers. The whole forward part of the boat, including the texas deck and the pilothouse, was destroyed. Like many, if not most, such accidents, this one seems to have been caused by negligence and recklessness. According to testimony at the coroner's inquest, one boiler was known to leak badly and had to be watched constantly, and shortly before the explosion, the *Pennsylvania* had successfully raced one boat and was preparing to race another. The engineer had given orders to fire up to the limit to avoid being passed; the firemen, as one of them testified, "threw on pine-knots and coal till we got on a good head of steam and was running very fast . . . the fire was as strong as we ever made, could not be stronger."

"Without one minute from the time of the alarm, the boat was wrapped in flame," and many passengers were trapped. More than two hundred people were killed right away, and many others died later; it was the worst disaster to occur during Sam Clemens's years on the river. The body of Brown, the pilot on duty, was never found. Henry, apparently suffering internal injuries, had been blown into the river, then had swum back to the *Pennsylvania* before it caught fire, had been taken off in the flatboat, and was finally carried to Memphis with the others. There, Mark Twain wrote, "the physicians examined his injuries and saw that they were fatal."

While the *Lacey* steamed north, past wreckage and occasional floating corpses, Sam could only wait in suspense, hearing first that Henry was unhurt, then that he had been fatally injured. In Memphis he realized at once that his brother's case was hopeless. Entering the "great public hall" where the injured lay, he saw "two long rows of prostrate forms . . . and every face and head a shapeless wad of raw cotton." Mark Twain did not give details of his meeting with Henry in *Life on the Mississippi*—the memory must have been too bitter—but a Memphis reporter described the scene for his paper: "He [Sam Clemens] hurried to the Exchange to see his brother, and on approaching the bedside of the wounded man, his feelings so much overcame him, at the scalded and emaciated form before him, that he sunk to the floor overpowered." There was nothing to be done; Sam could only wait. Six days after the explosion, Henry died.

Writing to Orion's wife, Mollie, while Henry lay dying, Sam reverted to the faith of his childhood, or at least to its language. Henry was of the elect—"blameless," "unoffending," his "poor sinless brother"—while he himself belonged among the damned, a "lost and ruined sinner." Sam's "organization," Orion once explained, was "such as to feel the utmost extreme of every feeling. . . . Both his capacity of enjoyment and his capacity of suffering are greater than mine." Sam could remember losing a father and a young brother, but such deaths seemed in the nature

of things. They required no explanation; the death of
Henry did. To explain meant to place responsibility, and
grief was intensified by self-blame. By the same irrefutable
logic through which he had once held himself responsible
for the death of a tramp in the Hannibal jail—after all, the
man could not have burned himself up without the matches
young Sam had given him—he could be found guilty of
Henry's death. Would Henry have gone on the river at all if
Sam had not set the example?[2] Would he have clerked on the
Pennsylvania if Sam had not been there? And therefore was
not Sam responsible for everything that followed? In the
Calvinist universe, which was the universe of both the young
Sam Clemens and the older Mark Twain, there was no place
for accident. Besides, he said, advice he had given Henry in
case of disaster—to rescue passengers, then see to his own
safety—might have contributed to his brother's death. And
men congratulated him on his luck, because he had escaped
while Henry died!

In his old age he came to believe that his guilt had been
more direct. As Paine gives the story, no doubt as it was
told to him by Twain himself, Henry had rallied and the
doctor had pronounced him out of danger but left directions that he should be given one-eighth of a grain of morphine if he became restless during the night. Henry awoke,
and Sam asked the medical student who had been left in
charge to give his brother the morphine. "But morphine
was a new drug then; the student hesitated, saying: 'I have
no way of measuring. I don't know how much an eighth
of a grain would be.'" Henry seemed in pain, Sam insisted, and the student "ladled out... on the point of a
knife-blade, what he believed to be the right amount." It
was an overdose: "Henry immediately sank into a heavy
sleep. He died before morning." He would probably have
died in any case, Paine adds, "but Samuel Clemens, un-
sparing in his self-blame, all his days carried the burden of
it." The memory was so painful that Twain could never

bear to write of it and "was never known to speak of it but once."

Twain's *Autobiography* alters the story by omitting self-blame. Again the attending physician gives "a vast quantity" of morphine, "heaped on the end of a knife blade," with fatal results, but does so on his own initiative. Both versions are highly unlikely. Morphine was by then widely used to relieve pain, and any medical student or attending physician should have known how to administer it. There is no evidence that Henry began to recover; writing to Mollie, two days before Henry's death, Sam takes it for granted that his brother will die, and in *Life on the Mississippi* he observes that while the doctor in charge did everything possible, "as the newspapers had said in the beginning, his hurts were past help. On the evening of the sixth day his wandering fingers 'picked at the coverlet'. . . we bore him to the death-room, poor boy." In this account, written at the time, Henry was delirious before death, rather than dying in an opium-induced sleep. The later story, in both its versions, seems to be pure invention. Mark Twain found it necessary, both morally and aesthetically, to believe that he lived in a meaningful universe, that events had discoverable causes, and that responsibility—and therefore blame—could be placed.

He convinced himself that he had been given warning before the fatal event. His *Autobiography* describes a prophetic dream: Henry is lying in a metal casket, dressed in Sam's clothes; there is a bouquet of white roses with a red rose in its center on his breast. After Henry's death, the story goes on, he saw his brother in the "dead-room," lying in a metal coffin, dressed in one of Sam's suits; as he watched, "an elderly lady entered the place with a large bouquet consisting mainly of white roses, and in the center of it was a red rose, and she laid it on his breast." He offers a rationalistic explanation—that he had unconsciously "embellished" the details in many retellings—then rejects rational skepticism and asserts the reality of his experience, claiming that the "salient points" of the dream were images, which can be remembered better than words. There is external evidence for the dream's occurrence; Annie Moffett remembered that Sam had told the family of it, and "they were amused that he took it so seriously." The skeptic will add that dreams of death are frequent, that inevitably they will sometimes be fulfilled and in that case they will be remembered; nothing is more fleeting than the images of a dream, and in due time memory will certainly enhance, and create, "prophetic" details. Sam had grown up in a region still haunted by superstition, where it seemed only natural to believe that great disasters are foreshadowed by premonitions, omens, warning dreams. And so again his need to find pattern and meaning in existence was satisfied.

He had encountered love as well as death that spring. At twenty-two he had fallen seriously in love for the first time, with Laura Wright, the fifteen-year-old daughter of a Missouri judge. As the *Autobiography* tells it, on arrival at New Orleans he found that the *Pennsylvania*'s "stern lapped the fo'castle of the *John J. Roe*." Eager to see old friends and escape Brown's tyranny, he climbed on board the *Roe* and met Laura—"that instantly elected sweetheart out of the remotenesses of interior Missouri." For the next three days they were inseparable during their waking hours. Then "Zeb Leavenworth came flying aft shouting 'The *Pennsylvania* is backing out.' I fled at my best speed, and just as I broke out upon that great boiler-deck, the *Pennsylvania* was gliding past it." Making a desperate leap for her, Sam was hauled on board. "It is now forty-eight years, one month and twenty-seven days since that parting," he concludes, "and no word has ever passed between us since." Paine adds that Sam wrote to Laura, but received no reply—his letter did not reach her.

It is a touching anecdote, unspoiled by explanation, of youthful love thwarted by inexorable circumstance after a moment of happiness. To a considerable extent, it is a product of Mark Twain's creative imagination. There was a Laura Wright, and Sam Clemens loved her, but their acquaintance was longer than three days; she wrote letters to him, now lost, and he visited her home. The *Roe* and the *Pennsylvania* were never in port together during that spring; perhaps she had been a passenger on the *Pennsylvania*. The actual date of parting is given in a notebook entry for May 6, 1858: "This date, 1858, parted from L. Who said 'We shall meet again 30 years from now.' "

There may have been parental opposition; there must have been misunderstandings. Clemens believed that Laura's mother had intercepted his letters. In February of 1861 he visited Mme. Caprell, a New Orleans fortune teller and described the interview in detail in a letter to Orion. After remarking that Clemens had "written a great deal" and predicting that he would write more, although he would "continue upon the water" for another ten years, she advised him to marry "the girl you have in your eye," adding that the mother had "caused the trouble and produced a coolness which has existed between you and the young lady for so many months past." Neither of them "would break through this ice . . . You are both entirely too proud." She described Laura: "not remarkably pretty, but very intelligent, educated, and accomplished, and has property—5 feet 3 inches—is slender—dark-brown hair and eyes." However Mme. Caprell got her information, whether by pumping Sam (as he believed), by conversation with some friend of his, or through occult powers, she seems to have been correct. Sam comments only that "the young lady has been beaten by the old one . . . through the romantic agency of intercepted letters," adding that Laura thinks he is at fault and always will, for he is not going to be the first to speak. He had been in love, then, but not deeply enough to overcome hurt pride. He would remember her, even dream of her occasionally, but he does not seem to have suffered very severely from losing her.

Laura's romantic prophecy was not fulfilled; they never

met again. But in 1880 a Texas schoolboy, Wattie Bowser, wrote to Mark Twain and mentioned that his teacher, Laura Dake, had known Twain when they both were young. Laura Dake was the former Laura Wright. In his reply, Twain described the young Laura: "She was a very little girl, with a very large spirit, a long memory, a wise head, a great appetite for books...with grave ways, inclined to introspection." In another letter Wattie mentions a class discussion of Tennyson's *The Princess* in which his teacher recalled that she had once known a "romantic girl," who, like Tennyson's heroine, "had some wild ideas about 'being too lightly won' and when her Prince really came she said 'no.' She thought he would come and 'take her in a whirlwind'—but he went his way and she never saw him again." It seems likely that Laura herself was the "romantic girl" and Sam Clemens the prince: she knew her pupil was corresponding with Mark Twain, and she could easily have chosen that way to send an explanation and a message to her former lover. There was to be one more contact. Twenty-six years later, still teaching school, Laura herself wrote to Twain requesting him to ask his friend Andrew Carnegie for money, to help her care for her crippled son. Twain sent her a thousand dollars of his own.

In his grief over his brother's death, Sam appears to have stayed off the river for a month or more, thereby missing a yellow fever epidemic in New Orleans—his luck still held. He may have had a berth in late summer, followed by an enforced vacation for several weeks while the river was too low for any but the smallest boats, carrying the lightest cargo. Late fall and winter he spent on the *A. B. Chambers*; its captain remembered him as "a smooth-faced young fellow whose quiet and retiring manner did not prevent his being very popular with all his associates." On April 5, 1859, he received his pilot's license, testifying that Samuel Clemens, having been duly examined, was found to be "a suitable and safe person to be entrusted with the powers and duties of a Pilot of Steam Boats" and was licensed "to act as such for one year . . . on the Mississippi River." Two years of work, the most concentrated effort of his life, had brought their reward; at last he could practice his craft responsible only to himself and could enjoy the status and the income that it brought.

Details of his career as a licensed pilot are scarce; few letters survive, and *Old Times on the Mississippi* sums up two years with a paragraph: "In due course I got my license . . . intermittent work gave place to steady and protracted engagements. Time drifted smoothly and prosperously on. . . . I supposed—and hoped—that I was going to follow the river the rest of my days. . . . But by and by the war came . . . my occupation was gone." He seems to have found boats without trouble—the *Edward J. Gay*, the *City of Memphis*, the *Arago*, the *Alonzo Child*, and perhaps others. They ranged from small tramp steamers—the *Arago*—to new, first-class boats: the *Memphis* was described by a newspaper as "the largest and finest steamer ever at the St. Louis wharf." He spent much of 1859 on the *Gay*, captained by Bart Bowen, an old Hannibal acquaintance, and must have been at the wheel that September during a race in which the *Gay* left the *New Uncle Sam* behind after 375 miles. But Sam Clemens was not ordinarily a racing pilot.

By the spring of 1860 he was on the *City of Memphis*. To pilot such a boat, he proudly told Orion, was a distinction—she was "the largest boat in the trade and the hardest to pilot," and he could build a reputation on her, as well as "'bank' in the neighborhood of $100 a month." One night at New Orleans he ran the *Memphis* into another boat, but he had been following the captain's orders, and Captain Montgomery "shouldered his responsibility like a man." Sam had once felt awe for the experienced pilots, with their knowing talk and expensive clothes, who filled the guest bench of the pilothouse while they "viewed the river." Now, at twenty-three, he was one of those grandees himself, met with a "Why, how *are* you, old fellow—when did you get in?" when he entered the rooms of the Pilot's

Association, and he took an unabashed pleasure in the chagrin of "the young pilots who used to tell me, patronizingly, that I could never learn the river." In going to pay his dues, he rather liked to "let the d——d rascals get a glimpse of a hundred dollar bill peeping out from amongst notes of smaller dimensions, whose face I do *not* exhibit."

Prosperity and prestige had gone to his head—but he was young, he had passed through a laborious apprenticeship, he was already earning much more than his father or his brother ever had, and it's no wonder that he felt himself any man's equal and a good deal better than most. He claimed position as head of the family, and his claim was accepted. He sent money to Orion and to his mother and enjoyed the lordly gesture; once, when Pamela and Jane Clemens were "fussing about change," he sent them 125 quarters! He advised Orion, ten years older than himself, on how to conduct his life: he should write only good news to their mother, who worried about every trifle, and he should keep his plans to himself until they were consummated or he would be considered a "visionary." Sam praises heroic energy: "What is the grandest thing in 'Paradise Lost'—the Arch-Fiend's terrible energy. What was the greatest feature in Napoleon's character? His unconquerable energy!" He concludes, "I want a man to—I want *you* to—take up a line of action, and *follow* it out, in spite of the very devil." He quotes from Longfellow's "Psalm of Life":

In the world's great field of battle,
In the bivouac of life,
Be not like dumb, driven cattle—
Be a hero in the strife.

To himself, Sam Clemens had become a hero in the strife.

He was a man well established in a responsible, honored, and lucrative profession, and he met the requirements of his new role. He could now drink or play cards as freely as he chose; Jane Clemens, recognizing his status, had released him from the oath he had taken at seventeen. A pilot was, or could be, a gentleman; a typesetter could not. He had chewed tobacco since he was a boy; now he decided that the habit was ungentlemanly and abandoned it forever. A photograph of the time shows him in formal black, with bushy sidewhiskers increasing his apparent age—the famous moustache was not to appear for another four years. But if he was a gentleman, he was also young, enjoying his life. Those who knew him then remembered him as "well dressed—even dandified—given to patent leathers, blue serge, white duck, and fancy striped shirts." He liked the company of women, as he would all his life; in an affectionate, teasing letter to Belle Stots, a Keokuk friend, he refers lightly to his "flames." And he enjoyed flirtation and dancing; he rather proudly tells Orion that "Ma . . . was disgusted with the girls for allowing me to embrace and kiss them—and she was horrified at the schottische as performed by Miss Castle and me." His notebook mentions taking girls to the opera in New Orleans to hear Adelina Patti, and buying them strawberries in February. But there is no evidence either of any serious relationship with a woman or of any brooding over Laura Wright.

There had been no time for writing and little time for reading during his apprenticeship: "I cannot correspond with a newspaper," he told Orion, "because when one is learning the river, he is not allowed to do or think of anything else." As a licensed pilot he enjoyed more freedom. A notebook kept during the winter of 1860–61 contains not only the expected annotations about river conditions but French exercises and poetry. He writes whole pages of French phrases, he copies part of a satirical dialogue between two lawyers by Voltaire. Knowing French was a mark of gentility and of education, and the language was alive in New Orleans. In poetry, he displays a taste for vague, resounding melancholy:

Toll—toll—toll!
Way for a Mighty soul
Unbar the gates of night
Woe—woe—woe!
It passeth—So!

Mark Twain might have ridiculed that empty verse, but to Sam Clemens, at twenty-four, it represented the Sublime.

In a letter, he quotes at length from Dickens's *Martin Chuzzlewit*; he compliments Orion on his "quiet style," which resembles Goldsmith's *Citizen of the World* and Cervantes's *Don Quixote*. Those books, writes Sam, "are my beau ideal of fine writing." They were to have permanent effect. Ten years later, wishing to expose the brutality and injustice endured by Chinese immigrants in California, he would borrow Goldsmith's title and employ his formula of an intelligent Oriental visiting the West and sending his impressions home. The influence of Cervantes was to be still deeper, and longer lasting. We find it in Twain's devastating burlesque of medieval chivalry in *A Connecticut Yankee in King Arthur's Court* and in the relationship of Tom Sawyer and Huckleberry Finn (the most creative adaptation of *Don Quixote* in American literature), with Huck playing as an earthy, realistic Sancho, casting doubt on Tom's book-inspired fantasies of adventure but loyally realizing them. More generally, the influence of Cervantes can be seen in Mark Twain's unceasing ridicule of language or behavior that seemed highfalutin, pretentious, false.

Probably in 1859 or 1860 he read Thomas Paine's "infidel classic," *The Age of Reason*, "marvelling at its fearlessness and wonderful power." Paine applied reason and common sense to the Bible; in that light, he declared, "the story of Eve and the Serpent, and of Noah and his ark, drop to the level of the Arabian tales, without the merit of being entertaining." He attacked miracles, condemned the cruelties of the Old Testament Jehovah, denied that the Bible was in any sense God's word or that Moses had written its first five books. Those heresies could still shock or frighten a reader in the Mississippi Valley of the 1850s, but reading *The Age of Reason* again in his old age, Mark Twain "was amazed to see how tame it had become. It seemed that Paine was apologizing everywhere for hurting the feelings of the reader." He had gone far beyond Paine's "infidelity" by then, denying all Christian doctrine, including the immortality of the soul, asserting that man was a machine, totally determined in all his thoughts and actions, responsible for nothing. But the young Sam Clemens, who had never heard of Darwin or the Higher Criticism of the Bible, was seeing for the first time a reasoned challenge to orthodoxy.

He even displayed an interest in art, and in a letter to Orion rhapsodized for a whole page about a painting he had seen in New Orleans—Frederick Church's *Heart of the Andes*, a gigantic landscape, realistic to the minutest detail. Sam enthusiastically reports examining it through an opera glass, "for the eye cannot discern the little wayside flowers . . . and half-hidden bunches of grass and jets of water— you may count the very leaves on the trees."

He did more reading than writing; an engrossing, demanding profession left little time or energy for the labor of composition. Horace Bixby remembered that "Sam was always scribbling when not at the wheel," but that recollection seems colored by hindsight. During his years on the river, Clemens is known to have written only four short pieces. A pair of Gothic experiments, faintly reminiscent of Poe (one a story of murder and hideous revenge, another of a phantom pilot on a Mississippi steamboat), remained unpublished, but Annie Moffett recalled hearing the author read the ghost story aloud, "acting it out as he read. . . . As he read my grandmother touched his arm and said, 'Sam, look at Annie.' I stood in the middle of the room transfixed with horror and fascination." She may have been the first listener to be "transfixed" by her uncle's gifts as a storyteller.

He published two brief, humorous pieces, addressed to his fellow pilots. "Pilot's Memoranda," appearing in the Missouri *Republican* in August 1860, burlesques the usual style of river news. The *Arago*, an unpretending little tramp steamer, is recorded as having overtaken and passed an incredible number of boats—the *Skylight*, the *Twilight*, the *Daylight*, all fictitious, of course—and to have seen another boat—a real one—which had run aground and was lightening its cargo by shifting iron rails from one deck to another.

The other sketch, untitled, signed "Sergeant Fathom" and published in the New Orleans *Crescent*, was more ambitious, combining parody and personal satire. The victim was Isaiah Sellers, pilot and captain on the Mississippi since 1825—"the Oldest Pilot, full of strange lies & wordy brag," who occasionally wrote long-winded letters on river conditions for the New Orleans papers, parading his own supposedly unrivaled experience. The monument beside the captain's tomb, chosen by himself, sums up his self-image: a life-size Sellers at the wheel of a steamboat, with a map of the Mississippi spread out below. Such a character was ripe for satire, and Clemens comprehensively burlesqued his use of irrelevant details, his dogmatic assertiveness, his foolish complacency—"After 34 years of careful and constant observation, I am clearly of opinion that," was a typical Sellers opening; his "ever-flowing stream, without beginning, or middle, or end, of astonishing reminiscences of the ancient Mississippi"; and his fondness for predicting disastrous floods—"If the rise continues at this rate *the water will be on the roof of the St. Charles Hotel* before the middle of January." "Sergeant Fathom" can amuse a layman because it creates a character, and it is of interest for another reason—by his own account, Sam Clemens later borrowed the name Mark Twain from Sellers, who had used it to sign his newspaper letters. By the evidence of these pieces then, and of another that has been attributed to him on internal evidence, Sam Clemens continued to feel the desire, or the need, to write, but he clearly did not think of himself as a writer addressing the general public— he wrote occasionally, as an amateur, to amuse himself, or his family, or other pilots.

His humor was not confined to his writing. On board the *Chambers*, Captain Marsh recalled, Sam Clemens was "always joking but never smiled." And he was a practical joker. *Old Times on the Mississippi* recounts a particularly mischievous prank by a fellow cub, who freed a huge bear that had been chained to a lifeboat, terrifying passengers and crew. But a notebook entry, written years later, shows that Sam Clemens had been a partner in the mischief: "The bear that Bill Hood & I released 'for fun' & he took possession of the boat." A letter written from the *Arago* mentions that he has quarreled with the mate three times, "& intends to provoke a 4th by dropping a watermelon shell on his head."

Both Clemens and Captain Montgomery may have been dismissed after the collision involving the *City of Memphis*. At any rate, by August Sam was on the *Arago*, and in the fall he moved to the *Alonzo Child*, his last boat, where he was a copilot with Horace Bixby—surely a satisfying experience for Bixby's former cub. He came to grief at least once with the *Child*: on November 1, 1860, while "Running in the fog, on the coast [the river between New Orleans and Baton Rouge]" he "grounded [her] and had to wait twenty-four hours before the 'great' tide floated her off. And that dry bank spell so warped and twisted the packet, and caused her to leak at such a rate," that she had to be docked for repairs in St. Louis. That mischance was not held against him, though; he would pilot the *Child* until he left the river the next spring. A brief entry in a late notebook mentions driving the *Alonzo Child* into a stern-wheeler, but it seems likely that he was confusing the *Child* with the *Memphis*.

How good a pilot was Sam Clemens? Bixby, in a position to know, said that Clemens "never had an accident either as a steersman or as a pilot, except once when he got aground for a few hours in the *bagasse*." "Bagasse" literally meant the ground-up stalks of sugar cane, but Bixby would have been referring to the dense smoke produced when this refuse was burned. This accident must be the one that Sam described as occurring while "running in the fog." Bixby's statement cannot be taken literally, but running the *Memphis* into another boat had been done in obedience to orders, while going aground might hardly have counted as an accident. Clemens's record, then, was excellent for the time. He had narrow escapes: "Farris Landing below Wolf Island, where I went to sleep at wheel & came near getting into a snag," and "Place above Walnut Bend where I nearly ran into a bluff sandbar, steering on a cloud—Bob Kirkpatrick saved us." One night he pulled his boat into the shore to wait out a storm, then decided to look for a "smoother bank." The storm passed over harmlessly, but on the next trip upriver, Sam looked at the spot he had first chosen and saw that "half the trees on the bank were torn to shreds. We could not have lived 5 minutes in such a tornado." But every pilot must have had such escapes—if he was lucky.

Some dramatic pages in *Old Times on the Mississippi* describe Horace Bixby's successful navigation of the "intricate and dangerous Hat Island crossing," at night and in low water, past snags and reefs and a sunken wreck, while the pilothouse was full of visiting pilots. At the end, one of the onlookers pronounces an awed verdict: "By the Shadow of Death, but he's a lightning pilot!" That ultimate accolade was never awarded to Sam Clemens. Obviously his reputation was good; he could always find work, and he piloted some of the biggest boats on the river, but the evidence indicates that he was competent, not brilliant—"a good average St. Louis and New Orleans pilot," in his own assessment. Captain Marsh recalled that during the winter of 1858–59 Sam Clemens saved the *Chambers* by taking a yawl through the ice-choked river to fetch a flatboat of wood. That contrasts with Clemens's own self-denigrating version: "When we were taking that wood flat down to the Chambers, which was aground, I soon saw that I was a perfect lubber at piloting such a thing . . . so I resigned in Marsh's favor." But he does not really contradict Marsh's account; he simply emphasizes, characteristically, the part of the story that reflects no particular credit on himself. While not a great pilot, Marsh concludes, Clemens was "a man of good judgment and fearless, knowing his river thoroughly." That reinforces his own comment: "I always had good judgment, more judgment than talent."

A cautious pilot, a *safe* pilot, then—the quality stressed in Bixby's praise. Notebook entries from his final months on the Mississippi reinforce that impression: "Was a good deal of water inside Dead Man. Was probably 6 or 7 feet in Glasscocks—night—didn't try"; "Was probably enough water bet. bars at head Hurricane—had to go after woodboat—didn't try"; "Night—didn't run either 77 or 76 Towheads"; "Afraid of 82—had 3 fath in Gaines." To be a "lightning pilot," a man needed more than knowledge of the river, quick perceptions, instant decision and response; he needed also an absolute confidence in his own judgment, which required a certain lack of imagination, a refusal, or inability, to admit even the possibility of disaster. Sam Clemens could imagine disaster all too easily; more than twenty years later his nightmares still took the form of "running down into an overshadowing bluff, with a steamboat," which, he added, showed that his "earliest dread made the strongest impression . . . (running steadily down into the deep shadows of Selma Bluff & head of Hat Island)." It was the Hat Island channel that Bixby had triumphantly navigated. Sam Clemens could never be a lightning pilot; if he seemed fearless, as Marsh reports, then most of the time he successfully hid his fear.

A yarn reportedly told by an old riverman in a St. Louis barroom fifteen years later seems to prove that the fear was there. The narrator claimed that he had played an elaborate joke on Clemens, first scaring him with stories about steamboat fires started by burning cotton, then complaining about how carelessly their boat had been loaded, with cotton "right up to the furnace doors." That night the second clerk, who had been let in on the joke, hid behind a chimney and watched Clemens, alone in the pilothouse, go into a panic, "his hair on end, his face like a corpse's." He "pulled every bell, turned the boat's nose for the bank, and yelled 'fire!' like a Cherokee Indian." But there was no fire, though Clemens swore he had smelled burning cotton. And so he had—the joker had set fire to a wad of cotton and stuffed it into the speaking tube from the engine room to the pilothouse. The story is unsupported, but plausible; if true, it demonstrates not Sam's cowardice, but the power of his imagination.

Mark Twain would sometimes grow nostalgic over his piloting days. "I loved the profession far better than any I have followed since, and I took a measureless pride in it," he declared, and Paine believed that "the dreamy, easy, romantic existence suited him exactly." But that was sentimental retrospection—his nightmare gives better evidence. Piloting was not easy but continuously demanding, the romance was mostly in the recollection, and no pilot could afford to dream while on duty. Against the claim, in *Old Times on the Mississippi*, that he loved the profession far better than any other he had followed, we can set his remark in *Roughing It* that in the West he had known four years of the most vigorous enjoyment of life that he had ever experienced. There is no real contradiction; both statements are imaginatively true, dramatically appropriate— not to the historical Clemens-Twain, but to the central figure of each of those works, who is a *literary* creation. His remark to his friend Howells, that he "would quit authorizing in a minute to go to piloting, if the madam would stand it," has often been quoted. But that was a joke, made when he was in a creative euphoria, in the midst of writing the *Old Times* pieces. It is outweighed by Twain's own admission of a recurrent dream in which poverty forced him back to the river, to earn his living again by piloting: "I love to think about those days; but there's always something sickening about the thought that I have been obliged to go back to them; and usually in my dream I am just about to start into a black shadow without being able to tell whether it is Selma bluff, or Hat Island, or only a black wall of night."

Those four years on the river changed his view of himself, made him, for a time, a man of consequence. They formed an essential part of his equipment as a writer. "In that brief, sharp schooling," he would claim, "I got personally and familiarly acquainted with about all the different types of human nature that are to be found in fiction, biography, or history.... When I find a well-drawn character in fiction or biography I generally take a warm personal interest, for the reason that I have known him before—met him on the river."

REBEL

In the fateful presidential election of 1860, Sam Clemens cast his vote for John Bell of Tennessee, nominee of the short-lived Constitutional Union Party; standing for both union and slavery, Bell was the candidate for men who did not want to choose a side, and he carried most of the Border states. But politics did not interest Sam particularly—he was more concerned that autumn that he had lost $150 speculating in eggs at New Orleans; and he was no more prepared for civil war than were most of his fellow citizens. As late as March of 1861, only two months before the end, he renewed his pilot's license as usual.

Yet signs of the coming catastrophe were visible everywhere. In December the Memphis *Daily Avalanche* reported that Sam's old commander, Captain Klinefelter—known to be a Union man—had been "waited on" in New Orleans

by a committee "who gave him six hours to put his freight
out and leave the city," on pain of hanging if he disobeyed.
In late January of 1861, Louisiana seceded from the Union,
and Sam witnessed "Great rejoicing. Flags, Dixie, Soldiers." Mississippi had already set up batteries at Vicks-
burg and was stopping southbound boats for inspection.
He was piloting the *Alonzo Child*, whose owners and crew
were strongly Confederate. Learning on April 18 of the
firing on Fort Sumter, "we hoisted out stars and bars and
played Dixie," Mark Twain was to remember. The *Alonzo
Child* left St. Louis for New Orleans on May 2 and reached
it six days later. She did not return. (Two years later, the
Child, converted into an ironclad warship and renamed the
Arkansas, was to force its way through the entire Union
fleet—then run aground and be abandoned by its crew
when the steering gear jammed.) Sam Clemens went back
to St. Louis as a passenger on the *Nebraska*, leaving on May
13. He was never to pilot a steamboat again. The *Nebraska*
was the last boat to pass the Union blockade above Memphis, and at St. Louis the reality of war came home. A
cannon from Jefferson Barracks fired a warning shot. The
pilot ignored it: "Less than a minute later there was another
boom, and a shell exploded directly in front of the pilot
house, breaking a lot of glass and destroying a good deal of
the upper decoration." Although a passenger, Sam was in
that pilothouse. It was a command that could not be disobeyed; the *Nebraska* stopped for inspection. That was the
end; Union forces at Cairo, Illinois, stopped all southward
traffic, and on May 23 the "River Intelligence" column of
the Cairo *Weekly Gazette* read simply "Played out."

The time had come to take sides. For some the choice
was clear and easy, but it could not have been so for Sam
Clemens. His family had held slaves—but that had been
many years earlier, and his brother Orion was now an anti-
slavery man and had campaigned for Lincoln. He could
not simply follow his state, for Missouri was a border state,
divided within itself, and would soon fight a brief and

bloody civil war of its own. He wavered; he had been a
Union man in the fall, then a Rebel, and would end as a
Union supporter. Of one thing at least he was sure—that
he would not serve as a pilot on the Union river fleet; that
exploding shell had taught him the vulnerability of a glass-
enclosed pilothouse. He lived with the Moffetts in St.
Louis for two weeks or more, almost in hiding. As his
niece, Annie, remembered, "He was obsessed with the fear
that he might be arrested and forced to act as pilot on a
government gunboat while a man stood by with a pistol
ready to shoot him if he showed the least sign of a false
move." Even then his feelings shifted. One day he made
cockades for some boys marching down the street with a
Confederate flag, but soon after he became furious at seeing
a small boy, carrying a Union flag, set on by a gang who
captured the flag and set fire to it: "Uncle Sam rushed from
the house, rescued the flag, put out the fire and chased the
boys away." The eight-year-old who had lost the flag, he
said, "should have guarded it with his life!" Union forces
occupied St. Louis and other points, and on June 12 Governor Claiborne Jackson, a Confederate sympathizer, called
for the militia to repel the "invaders."

In his "Private History of a Campaign That Failed,"
published twenty-five years later as part of *Century Magazine*'s series of wartime reminiscenses, Twain described his
role in the struggle as he remembered it. Sam Clemens's
"soldiering" lasted about two weeks. Visiting Hannibal
soon after Jackson's call, he helped form a military company with some fifteen boyhood friends. They named
themselves the "Marion Rangers," after their county. Their
unit had to be organized secretly; Hannibal was under control of Union home guards. They elected their officers—
common practice in the early days of the war—and then
"toward midnight stole in couples and from various directions" to their rendezvous. Sam was elected second lieutenant, but that counted for little among men who had grown

up together, each one convinced that he was as good as any
of the others.

After a night march they were sworn into the Confederate service by Colonel Ralls, a veteran of the Mexican War,
in "an old-fashioned speech . . . full of gunpowder and
glory." The colonel belted a sword, which he had worn in
battle in Mexico, around the second lieutenant; "then we
formed in line of battle and marched four miles to a shady
and pleasant piece of woods . . . and took up a strong position, with some low, rocky, and wooded hills behind us,
and a purling, limpid creek in front." Promptly, "half the
command were in swimming, and the other half fishing."

The picnic atmosphere soon faded; it rained, there were
false alarms, panics, unnecessary retreats, all punctuated
by quarrels as the would-be heroes came to seem less and
less heroic to themselves, and the officers tried to order or
persuade the privates to cook, stand guard, or perform
other disagreeable duties. At moments of crisis, the whole
company, a little democracy, would hold a council of war.
The men obtained mounts for themselves, which made re-
treating easier. Clemens had a yellow mule named "Paint
Brush," but he was a bad rider and developed a saddle boil.
Then he sprained an ankle in leaping out of a barn when
the hay on which the Rangers had been sleeping caught
fire, and the war was over for him. The Rangers never fired
a shot at an enemy; Twain's account, at the conclusion of
"Campaign," of their killing a suspected Yankee scout
makes an appropriate climax, introducing the Rangers at
last to the reality of war, but it seems to be fictitious. Meanwhile, Governor Jackson had been driven to the Arkansas
border, Missouri was in Union hands, and Confederate
militiamen could go home without facing charges of
desertion.

So ended the military career of Samuel Clemens—brief
and inglorious, from the point of view of a Southern pa-
triot. Soon he would escape to the West and sit out the war
in safety. He was not alone. American literature for the

next generation or so would be created largely by men who found more pressing things to do than fight.[1] He had found that his Confederate sympathies, and his appetite for slaughter, were not as powerful as he had believed. He was a Southerner, and had no wish to fight against the South, but neither, perhaps, did he wish to fight for slavery. He may also have realized, as the protagonist of "Campaign" finally does, that what war actually meant was killing people who had never done him any harm.

Sometimes Mark Twain would recall his military experience with relative seriousness. "I was a *soldier*... once in the beginning of the war, and was hunted like a rat the whole time... Kipling himself hasn't a more burnt-in... familiarity with that death-on-the-pale-horse-with-hell-following-after, which is a raw soldier's first fortnight in the field—and which, without any doubt, is the most tremendous fortnight and the vividest he is ever going to see." More often he would dismiss it humorously, or contemptuously—he had been playing soldier on the Confederate side. The first version probably comes closest to the truth. No one was actually hunting Sam and his comrades; the danger was all imaginary—but for him, that meant that it could be infinitely magnified.

MINER

S am Clemens had resigned from the war, but in a bitterly divided Missouri what place could there be for a
healthy, single man of twenty-four who preferred to stay
neutral? Escape was the only answer, and his hopelessly
impractical older brother made it possible.

For once, Orion had been on the winning side and had
influence where it counted. He had campaigned for Lincoln, and his old friend Edward Bates, in whose office he
had once studied law, had become Lincoln's Attorney General. Orion was rewarded for his loyalty with appointment
as secretary of the newly formed Territory of Nevada, at
a salary of $1,800 a year. He had no money for stage fare,
of course, but Sam was eager to travel; Sam could accom-
pany him, as unofficial secretary to the secretary, paying
both their fares. Orion's wife and daughter would stay be-

hind in Iowa until a place could be prepared for them. To cross the continent by stagecoach, to see buffalo and Indians, desperadoes and Mormons, mountains and deserts, to reach the land of gold and silver—such a prospect for adventure would have tempted Sam Clemens even without a war at his heels, and after four years of piloting, he might have been ready for a vacation. He intended a three-months' holiday, he wrote later, "thinking the war would be closed and the river open again by that time."

The travelers reached St. Joseph, jumping-off point for the West, after a five-day journey up the Missouri by river-boat, which had been intensely boring to the ex-pilot—the boat "was walking most of the time," Sam wrote to his mother and sister, "climbing over reefs and clambering over snags . . . all day long." Sam bought their tickets, for $150 each, from the Central Overland and Pike's Peak Express Company, and they ruthlessly pared down their belongings to meet the twenty-five-pound luggage limit. Left behind were the solemn accouterments of Victorian gentlemen, stovepipe hats and swallow-tailed coats and patent-leather shoes. Instead, they dressed in boots and rough woolens.

On the morning of July 26, 1861, Sam and Orion left St. Joseph, sharing their coach with one fellow passenger and 2,700 pounds of mail, besides a volume of U.S. statutes and an unabridged dictionary to aid the new secretary in his duties. Sam also carried his total savings of eight hundred dollars. Eleven years later Mark Twain described their journey in *Roughing It*, capturing the glamor of staging as no other writer save Dickens has done. Through Kansas and Nebraska they followed the winding Platte, crossing hundreds of miles of open prairie at a steady eight to ten miles an hour, making a bed of the mailbags, stopping only to change horses or to allow the passengers to gobble a meal of "slumgullion" or condemned army bacon. There was a buffalo hunt while repairs were being made to the coach; an encounter with a pony-express rider, trav-

eling at almost double their speed ("a whoop and a hurrah
from our upper deck, a wave of the rider's hand . . . and
man and horse burst past our excited faces, and go winging
away like a belated fragment of a storm!"); a first meeting
with authentic Westerners, booted and spurred and mus-
tached, with six-shooters at their sides and bowie knives
in their boot-tops, "unspeakably picturesque." They felt a
delightful chill at conversing politely with a genuine desperado, a killer named Slade, who was later hanged by vi-
gilantes in Montana but was here a division superintendent
for the stage company; they witnessed a fight between their
conductor and a gang of drunken stage drivers; they were
thrilled by crossing the Continental Divide at South Pass
and to see midsummer snow; they passed a Mormon emigrant train, its members plodding on foot behind their
wagons, that had come as far in eight weeks as the coach
in eight days; they made acquaintance with sagebrush,
jackrabbits, and coyotes; they rested in Salt Lake City—
clean, prosperous, and industrious, but offering the scandal of polygamy and rumors of murderous Destroying Angels—where Orion paid an official visit to Brigham Young,
to learn his attitude toward secession.

Then they were off again—this time wisely taking their
own provisions. "Ham and eggs and scenery, a 'down
grade', a flying coach, a fragrant pipe and a contented
heart . . . It is what all the ages have struggled for." As the
coach rolled west from Salt Lake City, or plowed through
deserts of alkali and sand, with the passengers often walking behind to relieve the horses, the war must have seemed
very far away. They saw their first Indians—"treacherous,
filthy and repulsive," like all Indians, observed Mark
Twain in *Roughing It*. On August 14, the twentieth day
out, they reached Carson City, miniature capital of the new
territory. The emigrants had begun their transformation
into Westerners.

Their arrival was not propitious. A reception had been
planned for the new secretary, but when the welcoming

committee saw Orion and Sam climb down from the coach—"unkempt, unshorn—clothed in the roughest of frontier costume... dusty, grimy, slouchy, and weather-beaten with long days of sun and storm and alkali dust"—that committee melted away. The town itself seemed a capital in name only, with its few blocks of "little white frame stores" along the main street and its central plaza, "a large, unfenced, level vacancy with a liberty pole in it." The governor's "mansion" was only a one-story wooden house "with two small rooms... and a stanchion supported shed in front—for grandeur." Other officials of the new government boarded about the town, their bedrooms doubling as offices.

Everything in Washoe, as inhabitants of two or three years' residence called the Territory, seemed strange and new. Sam promptly set out to explore the country, already hoping to make his fortune. Within a day's walk of Carson, Lake Tahoe offered relief from sand and sagebrush. Its beauty was already celebrated, and its forested slopes held out a chance for riches—there was an insatiable demand for timber to shore up the tunnels in the silver mines of Virginia City. Sam and a friend clambered over Sierra Nevada ridges, reached the lake, and staked out a timber claim on what they called "Sam Clemens' Bay," in a place so beautiful that, he confided to Pamela, "whenever I think of it, I want to go there and *die*."

The two fortune seekers cut a few trees and built a brush hut on their claim to satisfy the law, then camped on the shore, eating and sleeping, smoking and talking, reading and playing cards, drifting over the lake in a rowboat, admiring the incredible clarity of the water and the beauty of the forested mountains surrounding it. Then their holiday ended disastrously; a campfire that Sam Clemens was supposed to be watching got out of control, burning over their claim and racing away up the mountainside. He described the fire in a letter to his family: "The level ranks of flame were relieved at intervals by the standard-bearers, as we

called the tall dead trees, wrapped in fire, and waving their
blazing banners a hundred feet in the air. Then we could
turn from this scene to the Lake, and see every branch, and
leaf, and cataract of flame upon its bank perfectly reflected
in a gleaming fiery mirror. . . . Occasionally, one of us
would remove his pipe from his mouth and say,—'Superb!
Magnificent! Beautiful!' " Environmental consciousness
hardly existed in mid-nineteenth-century America; twenty
years earlier, Henry Thoreau had accidentally set fire to
some woods near Concord, Massachusetts, had run to town
carrying the news, and then, instead of returning to fight
the fire he had started, sat on a hilltop to enjoy the spectacle. Sam's purely aesthetic response, then, demonstrates no
unique callousness. More interesting, because less expected, is the language of his description. This is not just
a son dutifully reporting events to his mother, but a writer
creating a scene. It is more self-consciously literary than
anything he had yet written.

He did not immediately give up hope of becoming a lum-
ber magnate, and he kept his faith in the new country. He
angrily rejected a suggestion from home that he should become a lawyer: "I have been a slave several times in my
life, but I'll never be one again. I always intend to be so
situated (*unless* I marry) that I can 'pull up stakes' and clear
out whenever I feel like it." There were fortunes to be
made—if "Cousin Jim" were there, he could make
$100,000 in six months. "Cousin Jim" was James Lamp-
ton, who would later inspire one of Mark Twain's most
successful characterizations—Colonel Sellers, the visionary
promoter of *The Gilded Age*, whose cry was always "There's
millions in it!" There was a good deal of Cousin Jim's su-
perheated enthusiasm in the character of Sam Clemens.
But he did not go back to Tahoe, beautiful as it had been;
as a rule, he disliked retracing his steps. Instead, he briefly
turned to mining, visiting the Esmeralda district on the
eastern slope of the Sierras to the south of Carson. He acquired fifty "feet," as the shares were called, in an undevel-

oped claim, generously offering a chance for wealth to his relatives. There were countless such undeveloped claims in Nevada; most of them stayed undeveloped.

Back in Carson City, he clerked for Orion while the legislature was in session, at a salary of eight dollars a day. But the prospect of striking it rich continually distracted him. Reading that the newly opened Humboldt district was "the richest mineral kingdom upon God's footstool . . . gorged with the precious ores," this sanguine twenty-five-year-old was unable to resist. "I would have been more or less than human if I had not gone mad with the rest," and Sam Clemens was abundantly human. In mid-December, with three companions, he left for the Humboldt, taking along a book of hymns, several decks of cards, a keg of beer, and Dickens's *Dombey and Son*.

The Humboldt might have been gorged with precious ores, but the Clemens party did not find them. Within a month Sam was back in Carson City, after being marooned for a week when the ordinarily insignificant Carson River flooded its banks—desert travel in midwinter had its surprises. In February, returning to the Esmeralda region, he found "everything frozen and covered in snow." There, financed by Orion, living in a tiny cabin in a barren canyon, he would seek both their fortunes for the next six months. There was no doubt as to which brother was in charge: "I am at the helm now," he explained to his family. "I have convinced Orion that he hasn't business talent enough to carry on a peanut stand . . . if mines are to be bought or sold, or tunnels run, or shafts sunk, parties have to come to me only. I'm the 'firm,' you know."

The brothers bought shares in such claims as the "Sam Patch lode, first extension east," the "Horatio Lode," the "Live Yankee Quartz Lode," the "Magna Charta Ledge." Surviving deeds show that they ultimately invested in more than three dozen ledges, acquiring "feet" with a nominal value of more than $5,000. That amount could never have been squeezed from Orion's meager salary or the remnants of Sam's savings, but feet could be traded, or acquired for labor or promises to pay. "Nobody had any money, yet everybody was a millionaire in silver claims," wrote an observer of Virginia City in its formative stage. "Sales were made . . . at the most astounding figures, but not a dime passed hands."

Clemens's letters show high hopes and fierce determination, only momentarily clouded by doubts. In January of 1862 he wrote to Molly that by the following July "some of our claims will be paying handsomely," and she could then join her husband and her brother-in-law in "'high-tone' style": "We could have a house fit to live in—and servants to do your work." He went on to outline his ideal of marriage, which required money enough to liberate his wife from household chores, freeing her to be his companion: "I don't want to sleep with a three-fold Being who is cook, chambermaid and washerwoman all in one."

He called on Orion for more money: "Stir yourself as much as possible, and lay up $100 or $150, subject to my call. I go to work tomorrow with pick and shovel. Something's got to come, by G——, before I let go here." He committed himself to success or lifelong exile as though the commitment itself would guarantee riches: "I shall never look upon Ma's face again, or Pamela's, or get married, or revisit the 'Banner State' until I am a rich man." There were lucid intervals when he could acknowledge his own "uncongealable sanguine temperament" and analyze his madness: "Don't you know that I have only *talked*, as yet," he cautioned Pamela, "but have proved nothing. Don't you know that I have never held in my hands a gold or silver bar that belonged to me?" And he never did. But in the next paragraph he optimistically calculated what he could accomplish if he only had a thousand dollars in cash.

Experience taught some painful lessons. The new miner learned that, for most prospectors, *nothing* that glitters is gold; that the assayer's report on a claim was likely to be based not on a representative sample of its ore but on the

richest fragment that could be found. He learned that picking, shoveling, drilling, and blasting out shafts and tunnels
on frozen mountainsides where snow lay far into the spring
was dismally hard work. He learned that miners could expect to be cold, hungry, and lousy, and that casual violence
was to be accepted as a condition of life: "Man named
Gebhart shot here yesterday while trying to defend a claim
on Last Chance Hill. Expect he will die."

On May 9 the Clemens Gold and Silver Mining Company, consisting of Sam Clemens and three partners, was
formed to work claims in the Monitor Ledge—"Money
can't buy a foot of it; because I *know* it to contain our fortunes." He was certain that if only "all spare change be
devoted to working the 'Monitor' and the 'Flyaway,' " then
within a year, or two at most, "all our wishes . . . so far as
money is concerned" will be satisfied. But meanwhile the
would-be silver king was "strapped," without even "three
days rations in the house." The Monitor claim was jumped
by armed men, and there was no legal way to get them
out, since by a quirk of the law the courts could not act
unless the claim-jumpers used violence against the rightful
owners: "The Clemens Company—all of us—hate to re-
sort to arms . . . but I think that will be the end of it, nev-
er-the-less." But there was no shooting; evidently the Clemens Company got there first the next day.[1]

As the season advanced, hope began to fade. A new tone
began to appear in the letters: "The work goes slowly—
very slowly on, in the tunnel and we'll strike it some day.
But—if we 'strike it rich,'—I've lost my guess, that's
all. . . . Couldn't go on the hill today. It snowed. It always
snows here, I expect." He considered clerical work in Orion's office—"How do the Records pay?" Despite his promise to Molly of riches by midsummer, he had not earned a
dollar in the mines. There had been expenses only, for tools
and provisions—freighted in by wagon or mule train and
ruinously expensive, for hire of men to work the claims,
for purchase of feet in other claims, and for paying assess-

ments to meet the cost of developing those claims. He
hated physical labor. He had had enough of continuous disappointment, of living on bacon and beans in a ten-by-
twelve-foot cabin with a leaky roof and a dirt floor. The
venture had produced nothing but debt and disillusionment and could no longer be carried on.

But first, as Mark Twain told the story in *Roughing It*,
his mining career reached its climax when for ten days he
held a fortune in his hands, and carelessly threw it away.
Clemens's partner, Cal Higbie, discovered that the silver
ore from the rich Wide West mine came from a "blind
lead"—that is, a vein with no outcropping on the surface,
which simply crossed the lead that the Wide West miners
had been following and was perfectly distinct from theirs,
making it public property. Taking the foreman of the Wide
West into partnership, Sam Clemens and Higbie staked
their claims and declared themselves millionaires. All night
long they planned their futures: first a triumphant return
to the "States," then brownstone mansions on Russian Hill
in San Francisco, with "French plate glass—billiard-room
off the dining-room—statuary and paintings—shrubbery
and two-acre grass plot—greenhouse—iron dog on the
front stoop—gray horses—landau—and a coachman with
a bug on his hat!" and finally a Grand Tour of Europe and
the Middle East.

To hold a claim, its locators were required to begin
working it within ten days, but the next morning Clemens
received news that an acquaintance was dangerously ill at
a nearby ranch, and that help was needed in the sickroom.
After leaving a note for Higbie telling him where he had
gone and urging his partner to begin the necessary work at
once, Sam hurried to the bedside. He spent nine days nursing the invalid, imagining the details of his mansion and
his travels, and "writing to my friends at home every day,
instructing them concerning all my plans and intentions."
On the tenth day he returned and saw a crowd gathered
around the Wide West diggings, but he didn't trouble to

investigate. Reaching his cabin, "the dingy light of a tallow candle revealed Higbie, sitting by the pine table gazing stupidly at my note, which he held in his fingers, and looking pale, old, and haggard. I halted, and looked at him. He looked at me, stolidly. I said: 'Higbie, what—what is it?' 'We're ruined—we didn't do the work—THE BLIND LEAD'S RELOCATED!' "

Higbie, too, had left the site ten days earlier, to search for the fabulous "Whiteman cement mine," leaving a note of his own telling Sam to start the required work. Being in a hurry, he had tossed it in through a broken windowpane and had failed to see Clemens's note. Meanwhile, the Wide West foreman had been called away to California "on a matter of life and death, it was said." Since no work had been done, the claim had been forfeited, and exactly ten days after it had been filed, "fourteen men, duly armed and ready to back up their proceedings, put up their 'notice' and proclaimed their ownership of the blind lead." And so a fortune was lost—"we would have been millionaires if we had only worked with pick and spade one little day . . . to secure our ownership." The story might seem like a "wild fancy sketch," Twain admitted, but he assured his readers that it was "a true history," verifiable by the evidence of witnesses and of official records.

Yet it almost certainly did not happen. No supporting evidence exists. Sam Clemens had been pouring his hopes and ambitions into his letters, yet no surviving letter mentions the episode, and they indicate that his partner at the time was Horatio Phillips, not Cal Higbie. Neither the Wide West mine nor its extension ever produced a fortune for anyone. The nugget of truth in the story can probably be found in a letter to Orion, written in late July, in which Sam promises to send a sample of decomposed rock that he had "pinched with thumb and forefinger from the Wide West ledge," adding that he and his partner had secured feet in a ledge that "perhaps is a spur from the W. W. shaft." The *Roughing It* story seems a composite, based on fact—the purchase of feet in a spur of the Wide West, the jumping of the Monitor claim by armed men—but highly elaborated. It provides a dramatic climax and conclusion for the narrator's mining adventures, and it seems true to the fantasies and fears of the miner. Tales of fortune narrowly missed, the miss growing narrower with every telling, must have been a staple of conversation around campfires and cabin stoves, and the fortune lost through negligence or slackening of effort at the critical moment was to be a recurring motif in Mark Twain's own experience, or at least in his interpretation of his own experience. Certainly no "true history," yet much more than a "wild fancy sketch," the story of the blind lead is intensely true to the spirit of the times, and to the psychology of Sam Clemens. He must have dreamed those dreams, traveled to those distant lands, furnished that mansion, often enough on freezing nights in his cabin.

Frenzied as it was, Sam Clemens's life during those months was not all prospecting and digging. He had found time for visits to the comparatively civilized Carson City and for pleasures of society—even for dancing. His style was unique; he was a humorist of the ballroom. As Higbie recalled, "In changing partners, whenever he saw a hand raised, he would grasp it . . . and sail off into another set," or he would apparently lose all hope of following the dance, shut his eyes and "do a hoe-down or a double-shuffle all alone." Soon most of the crowd would be watching and laughing.

He had even found time for writing, not just for notes to Orion demanding money or reporting on claims, but for deliberate composition. Three of his letters home had been published in a Keokuk paper; Americans back in the "States" wanted news from the West. The letters seem written for publication—particularly the last, which burlesques the popular literary convention of the Noble Red Man and which seems addressed not to the actual Jane Clemens but to a representative reader. Supposedly answering his mother's request to "tell me all about the lordly sons of the forest . . . sweeping over the prairies on their fiery steeds, or chasing the timid deer, or reposing in the shade of some grand old tree, lulled by the soft music of murmuring brooks," Clemens points out the discrepancies between sentimental illusions and actuality. Nevada was a desert, he said, and the literary Indian a fraud. He offers as reality "the warrior Hoop-de-doodle-do, head chief of the Washoes," coated with dirt and grease, wearing "a battered stovepipe hat . . . trimmed all over with bits of gaudy ribbon and tarnished artificial flowers." In fact, he had merely replaced one stereotype—the Noble Savage—with another—the filthy savage—which he unthinkingly accepted.

At some time during that spring he had begun contributing letters, signed "Josh," to the *Territorial Enterprise* of Virginia City, the leading newspaper of Nevada. None of them survives, but there were evidently several, and he recognized their possible value, instructing Orion on June 9 to "Put all of Josh's letters in my scrapbook. I may have a use for them some day." Tradition records that one was a burlesque Fourth of July oration, beginning "I was sired by the great American eagle and foaled by a continental dam." Evidently they amused *Enterprise* readers; in August the paper offered him a job.

The offer came just in time. That June he had told Orion that he was beginning to feel like a prisoner in jail: "I believe I have not spent six months in one place . . . since 1853." His restlessness would soon have driven him from Aurora in any case, but he had more urgent reasons for leaving. By the end of July his mining hopes had collapsed. Summing up his debts and his assets (he owed forty dollars, had forty-five in his pocket) and considering his prospects (how to live to October or November on "something over $100"), he reached the inevitable conclusion: "The fact is, I must have something to do, and that *shortly*." He had gone to work as a laborer in a quartz mill, breaking up ore with a sledgehammer and "screening the tailings"—shoveling up the dried sand left over by the refining process and throwing it against screens to remove pebbles before it was reworked. He lasted only a few days, but that was long enough to convince him that "of all recreations in the world, screening tailings on a hot day, with a long-handled shovel, is the most undesirable." It was a last resort, and a failure at that, but even then he would not think of going back to the river: "I never expect to do any more piloting at any price. My livelihood must be made in this country." But determination was not enough; he had been determined to strike it rich, after all. Surveying his Nevada career—"I had been a private secretary, a silver miner and a silver mill operative, and amounted to less than nothing in each, and now—what to do next?" Survival depended on the answer.

He asked Orion to offer his services to the Sacramento *Union*: "I'll write as many letters a week as they want, for $10 a week—my board must be paid." He was prepared to write two short letters a week for a Carson City paper, at five dollars a week. He hoped to become San Francisco correspondent for a Nevada paper and spend the winter in California. Then the *Enterprise* offered him work, not as correspondent from the mines but as a full-time reporter in Virginia City, at a salary of twenty-five dollars per week.

On August 7 he wrote to Orion that he had accepted, adding, "Now, I shall leave at mid-night tonight, alone and on foot for a walk of 60 or 70 miles through a totally uninhabited country." Much has been made of that walk: "He fasted and prayed a good while over the 'call,' " says Paine; "It meant the surrender of all his hopes in the mines, the confession of another failure." And so "he had gone into the wilderness, to fight out his battle alone." But going into the wilderness to search his soul was not Sam Clemens's way; he made his decisions by instinct and impulse. In fact he had already decided to accept. It's more likely that he meant to visit his ex-partner, Higbie—perhaps to join him in a last-ditch search for the "Whiteman cement mine," a guess that is supported by a letter of September 9: "For more than two weeks I have been slashing around in the White Mountain District, partly for pleasure and partly for business."[2]

REPORTER

One day in late September of 1862 Sam Clemens turned up at the *Enterprise* office to take up his duties as local reporter, or "city editor," to use the title he usually gave himself. By his own recollection, he seemed "a rusty-looking city editor . . . slouch hat, blue woolen shirt, pantaloons stuffed into boottops, whiskered half down to the waist, and the universal navy revolver slung to my belt."[1] He shook hands with Denis McCarthy, co-owner and business manager of the paper, "regarded him with a far-away look and said, absently and with deliberation: 'My starboard leg seems to be unshipped. I'd like about one hundred yards of line; I think I am falling to pieces. . . . My name is Clemens and I've come to write for the paper.' "

The Virginia City that he came to, nearing the climax of its first "flush times," was raw, rich, and violent. A straggle of tents and shanties only two years before, it was now a substantial town of wood and brick. The *Enterprise* building was one of its most impressive, appropriate for the most successful paper in the Territory. The population of nearly 15,000 was mostly male. Six thousand feet up on a desert mountain, Virginia, as the inhabitants generally called it, offered little to please the eye. Above it rose the bare ridge of Sun Mountain; below, the ground dropped away to the head of Six-Mile Canyon. It was a waterless landscape of sagebrush, bunch grass, and rock, varied by ore dumps and the occasional stunted pine. In the distance, on all sides, were mountains. A mile or so beyond, the highway ran through Devil's Gap to the smaller towns of Gold Hill and Silver City. Everything, from whiskey to mining machinery, was hauled in across the Sierras by ox or mule team. The mines were supplied and financed from San Francisco, paid dividends to San Francisco, and in San Francisco the lucky few would build their mansions. One lived in Virginia City in the hope of making enough to live somewhere else.

Jammed with freight wagons, ore wagons, and stage coaches, C Street ran across the lower slope of Sun Mountain. Along it were the main hotels and businesses, including the *Enterprise* in its solid brick building, and ornate saloons with mirrors and paintings and exotic woods. Above it lived the aristocracy of the town—mine owners who had not yet left for the Coast, mining superintendents, lawyers; below were the roominghouses of the miners and the red-light district consisting, said one disapproving observer, of "two rows of white cabins with gaudily furnished rooms at whose uncurtained windows the inmates sat, spider-like, waiting for flies"; lower still was a Chinatown offering opium dens and mysterious foods; and finally the huts of Piute Indians, living off the refuse of the whites. With frenzied energy, Virginia was transforming itself from mining camp to city; within a year after Sam Clemens's arrival, it would possess stock exchanges, gaslighted streets, three theaters—the largest of them seating 1,600 people, several newspapers, four churches, and forty-two saloons.

Beneath the city ran the great Comstock Lode, the richest body of ore ever discovered in America. The mines drove constantly deeper, the shafts already hundreds of feet down and the horizontal tunnels stretching for miles. Out of the shafts, at eight-hour intervals, poured thousands of miners who had been working by candlelight, risking death from cave-ins, fires, explosions, falling cages, and flooding, often with scalding-hot water at the lower levels. Now they were ready to drink and be entertained. There was no place here for the lone prospector; silver-mining was a large-scale industrial operation that could be carried on only by capitalists. But everyone, including reporters, could speculate in mining stocks. One could never forget the mines; dynamite blasts sometimes in the tunnels rattled windows above. Waste and extravagance were everywhere—one mine superintendent drove a coach and four with a harness of silver and gold-plated carriage lamps. The streets offered a never-ending show: "Auctioneers are shouting off the stocks of delinquent stockholders . . . hurdy-gurdy girls are singing bacchanalian songs . . . All is life, excitement, avarice, lust, deviltry, and enterprise." A shocking spectacle to a moralist—an exhilarating one to Sam Clemens.[2]

Thrown into this wide-open world without journalistic training, he promptly found his way. On his first day, as he recalled in *Roughing It*, he had trouble filling his quota, two columns of small type: "I wandered about town questioning everybody, boring everybody, and finding out that nobody knew anything." At last, finding "one wretched old hay truck dragging in from the country," he "multiplied it by sixteen, brought it into town from sixteen different directions, made sixteen separate items out of it." With the possibilities of hay wagons exhausted, "a desperado killed a man in the saloon, and joy returned once more."

Sam finished his first day's work with an inventive account of Indian attacks on a wagon train. Reading the paper the next morning, Mark Twain would remember, "I felt that I had found my legitimate occupation at last." Much of Twain's writing for the *Enterprise* has been lost, but that story may survive; on October 1 the paper carried an account of such an attack, unsigned but containing one characteristic simile—the sides of the wagons had been riddled by bullets and arrows until they were "like magnified nutmeg graters."

Outwardly, each issue of the *Enterprise* seemed indistinguishable from the other papers: the front page, in painfully small type, a composite of Mining Notices, announcements of Assessments Levied and Assessments Sold, and war news, with telegraphic dispatches from the various fronts. Inside, there was room for individuality. Lively, satirical, and irreverent, the *Enterprise* knew how to please its readers and succeeded accordingly; it ranked as the leading newspaper in the Territory and brought in more money from advertising each month than the owners knew how to spend. It was a young man's paper in a young man's town—William Wright, better known by his pen name of Dan De Quille, was the patriarch of the staff at thirty-four. It was a congenial place to work; camaraderie was strong, and after the paper had been put to bed, at 2:00 A.M. or so, printers and reporters might gather in the editorial room to drink beer, strum on broken-down guitars, and sing the love songs and war songs of the day.

Reporters for rival journals could be close friends, even as their papers denounced each other in their editorial columns. Sam Clemens and Wilson, a reporter for the *Union*, drank beer companionably together, "while the senior wranglers of the two papers befouled each other." The reporter was a privileged person, witness to everything, recipient of gifts, minor celebrity. Sam covered horse races, candy-pulls, dances, traffic accidents, fires, killings, legislative proceedings; he reviewed school exercises and perfor-

mances at the Opera House. He was invited to tour a mine
with his fellow reporters, "dangling down a dark shaft at
the end of a crazy rope with a candle between our teeth,"
to prowl through muddy tunnels "until the man up at the
bullet-hole that showed us a far-off glimpse of blue sky,
wound us up with his windlass and set us in the cheerful
light of the sun again."

Local and political reporting were comparatively
straightforward and factual, but only comparatively—Clemens remarked, while telling of one decision by a territorial court, that "its terms are darkly, mysteriously legal,
and I have not the most distant conception of what they
mean." Virginia City readers wanted to be amused as well
as informed. "The indifference to 'news' was noble," one
reporter of the time would recall. "Either Mark or Dan
[Dan De Quille] would dismiss a murder with a couple of
inches, and sit down and fill up a column with a fancy
sketch." Violence, unless spectacular, was too common to
draw attention. In *Roughing It* Mark Twain cites one
twenty-four-hour period in which "a woman was killed by
a pistol shot, a man was brained with a slung shot [black-
jack], and a man named Reeder was also disposed of permanently," first stabbed, then finished with a double-barreled
shotgun. Only the last item seemed worth reporting in
detail.

Dan De Quille was noted for his hoaxes, or "quaints,"
as he called them, including an account of a refrigerating
device, intended to cool desert travelers, that went out of
control and left its inventor a frozen corpse, sitting against
a rock at noon with frost on his beard and an icicle hanging
from his nose. Within two weeks of the publication of that
story, Clemens published his own "The Petrified Man,"
alleging that a petrified figure had been discovered and pronounced by scientists to have been dead for ten generations; nevertheless, the item continued, a local judge had
ordered an inquest, and a coroner's jury returned a verdict
of "death from protracted EXPOSURE." Clemens knew that

a good hoax should give itself away to the alert reader—
otherwise it is merely a lie—and he provided elaborate and
deliberately mystifying details concerning the corpse's position; these when analyzed, revealed that the petrified man
was winking and thumbing his nose. Nonetheless, at least
a dozen Western papers reprinted the story, and only two
San Francisco journals seem to have been sophisticated
enough to recognize it for a "sell." In *Roughing It*, Twain
would claim that it had been reprinted in the London *Lan-
cet*, a medical journal of great prestige. But that, too, was
a hoax.

Comic invective amused Washoe readers, and Clemens
promptly mastered the art. Of a Nevada politician—"He
is a long-legged, bull-headed, whopper-jawed, construc-
tionary monomaniac"; of a territorial law—"the Act was
born out of wedlock—was born in legislative vacation—
the bastard offspring of an emasculated governor and four
impotent Legislative officers!" Pretended feuds between reporters on different papers allowed a regular exchange of
humorous insults. Clemens nicknamed Rice, of the *Union*,
the Unreliable—consistently referring to him by that name
and describing his alleged laziness, boorishness, gluttony,
thievery, et cetera. Through it all, they remained friends.
In theory, Mark Twain subscribed to an ideal of crusading
journalism; "It is *your* duty," he scolded the editor of the
Carson City *Independent*, who had ignored accusations of
profiteering brought against the local undertaker, to "ferret
out" abuses of every sort and correct them. "What are you
paid for? What use are you to the community if you cannot
do these things?" But, in practice, he ferreted out no
abuses, spending his surplus energy instead in creative
play—inventing hoaxes and carrying on mock feuds.

He did serious work as well. In November and December, Clemens collaborated with Rice, his friendly rival, in
covering the territorial legislature, producing daily a large
amount of copy dealing with technical legislative proce-
dures and complex issues and doing it so thoroughly that,

at the end of its session, the legislature voted its thanks to the two for "their full and accurate reports of the proceedings." By his own account, at least, Clemens did not confine himself to reporting but became a political power as well. He had been "a mighty heavy wire-puller at the last legislature," he boasted to his mother and sister; "I passed every bill I worked for." In that tiny capital city, and in the little world of territorial Nevada, a man could quickly make himself known and felt.

Even in a legislative report, Clemens could be individual; he might observe that some visiting ladies "were well pleased with the night session . . . they enjoyed it exceedingly—in many respects it was superior to a funeral," or report, after a popular bill requiring local ownership of mines had been passed, that "Great excitement exists. Half the population is drunk—the balance will be before midnight." The Territory possessed a unique institution, the Third House, an unofficial body made up of politicians, lawyers, and newspapermen who met immediately after the legislature adjourned to burlesque its personalities and proceedings. When the Third House convened, Sam Clemens was elected its governor.

In just a few months Clemens had become a well-known journalist whose work had already been widely reprinted in California and Nevada papers, and a personality with a distinctive image had begun to emerge—a photograph taken at the time already shows a hint of the famous moustache. But something was lacking: " 'Joe,' he said to Goodman [his editor], 'I want to sign my articles. I want to be identified to a wider audience.' 'All right, Sam. What name do you want to use—Josh?' 'No, I want to sign them "Mark Twain." It is an old river term, a leads-man's call, signifying two fathoms—twelve feet. It has a richness about it; it was always a pleasant sound for a pilot to hear on a dark night; it meant safe water.' "

That Clemens wished to sign his work is easily understood; in using a pseudonym he was following the custom of the time. The pen name might be discarded as a writer's reputation grew, or it might be reserved for print with a clear distinction drawn between life and literature. At times it might usurp the writer's identity, his "true name" being known only to a few intimates. William Wright, his competitor on the *Enterprise*, was "Dan De Quille" even to his friends.

In Paine's account, derived from Twain himself, "That terse, positive, peremptory, dynamic" name was first used by Captain Sellers in his pompous letters on river conditions to the New Orleans *Picayune*. Clemens had parodied them under the name Sergeant Fathom, and that ridicule "broke Captain Seller's literary heart. He never contributed another paragraph." Hearing of Sellers's death, Clemens realized that the name had passed into the public domain, that it was precisely what he wanted, and that by adopting it he would pay "a sort of tribute to the old man he had thoughtlessly wounded."

There is an alternative story, found in various Western newspapers, which seems to have originated with a personal enemy of Clemens, who referred to him as an "aborigine from the land of sage brush and alkali, whose sobriquet was given by his friends as indicative of his capacity for doing the drinking for two."

Yet while Paine's version appears most circumstantial and convincing, it dissolves under analysis. Searches of the New Orleans *Picayune* have found no contributions signed "Mark Twain," and Captain Sellers did not die until the spring of 1864, more than a year after Clemens had assumed the name. Apparently, then, Clemens invented his pseudonym. But why then did he deny his own originality and fabricate an elaborate lie? Twain's earliest account, simply explaining that on the river "mark twain" meant a depth of twelve feet—safe water for a Mississippi steamboat—and making no mention of Captain Sellers, appeared in the *Alta California* of San Francisco in 1877, less than a month after that paper had printed a version of the two-drinks story and may well have been meant to refute a discreditable rumor. The Sellers story may have been invented later to add credibility through detail, and for the sheer pleasure of invention. With its constant repetition, Clemens could easily have come to take his own fiction as fact.

The new signature seems to have been first used on a letter from Carson City appearing in the *Enterprise* on February 3, 1863. It was a gossipy, humorous personal piece ridiculing his editor, Joe Goodman, and Rice the Unreliable. His routine reporting appeared without a by-line, but the sketches and letters that he increasingly contributed would be signed "Mark Twain," and when reprinted in other papers they would make the name known up and down the coast. Its rightness seems to have been instantly recognized. He promptly became "Mark Twain" to the Western public and "Mark" to most of his Western friends, just as Dan De Quille (William Wright) and Artemus Ward (Charles Farrar Browne) were "Dan" and "Artemus" to him. What to call him becomes a problem for a biographer. He would continue to be "Sam" only to his mother, sister, and brother, and to a very few of his oldest friends. Two of the three closest friends of his later life, the writer William Dean Howells and the Standard Oil magnate H. H. Rogers, called him "Clemens"—a choice reflecting their own formality. (But his letters to Howells were signed "Mark.") To the most intimate of them, Joe Twichell, his minister and Hartford neighbor, he would always be "Mark." To his wife, he would be "Youth" in private and "Mr. Clemens" in public. In business matters he was of course "Mr. Clemens"; to the reading public and the world at large he has always been "Mark Twain," and it's by that name that he will be referred to henceforth in this biography.

He had come to the right place at the right time: nowhere else could he have found the freedom and the encouragement to experiment and to explore his talent, to express himself freely and variously, that Virginia City and the *Enterprise* afforded him. Reporting for a San Francisco daily, he would learn a year and a half later, was a very different affair. In his few months with the *Enterprise* he had become known both as a writer and as a personality: in recognition of his success, the paper raised his salary to forty dollars a week. His earliest surviving fan letter, the first of thousands, dates from February 9, 1863, and is already addressed to "Mark Twain"—less than a week after his first recorded use of the name. By August of 1863 he could boast to his family of having "the widest reputation as a local editor of any man on the Pacific Coast"; by November a California critic had called him "that irresistible Washoe giant, Mark Twain," adding that "he imitates nobody. He is a school by himself."

In fact, his humor did have its similarities to the work of others; he had learned the art of hoaxing from Dan De Quille, and he was not the only Western humorist who found amusement in stinks, vomit, and blood. Yet as the nicknames imply—the "Washoe Giant," "the Wild Humorist of the Sagebrush Hills"—the public discerned a unique personality in both the man and his work. His favorite song, "I had an old horse and he died in the wilderness, died in the wilderness, died in the wilderness," continuing until listeners dragged him away from the piano, became a musical trademark. His drawl was universally known, if not universally admired. "Drawling stupidity, when well acted by an educated, intelligent man, is indeed comical; but when those features are the natural characteristics of an illiterate and by no means bright intellect, the mouthings of such a one it were a misapplication of terms to call wit," the Virginia *Evening Bulletin* once remarked.

It has been claimed by one historian of Virginia City that "Everyone on the staff [of the *Enterprise*] hated Mark Twain"—a wild exaggeration, but, undeniably, he was not the universal favorite that Dan De Quille seems to have been. Gentle and unassertive, De Quille was to bury his talent in Virginia City and finally die in poverty and obscurity; in drawing up a list of "blighted insignificants," Twain would one day include his name. No one hated De Quille, no one envied him—there was no reason to do either. But Mark Twain, quick-tempered man with a biting wit, obviously enjoying his own success, could easily arouse envy and dislike. He could make dull people uneasy; they never knew when he was joking and when he was in earnest, and they were likely to denounce him for frivolity or irreverence. His close friendships were longlasting but few, and only his relationships with De Quille and Goodman were to endure from his time in Virginia City. Easily provoked into explosions of profanity, he was a natural target of practical jokers; his fellow workers liked to steal his favorite candle just to hear him swear. Sometimes their pranks were more elaborate. Meerschaum pipes had been ceremoniously presented to various members of the *Enterprise* staff by their colleagues; Twain let it be known that he would like to receive one. A presentation was made, with appropriate ceremony, of a cheap imitation meerschaum, leaving him to discover the truth after a few days' smoking. To heighten the joke, he had been "secretly" told of the intended presentation, so that everyone concerned could enjoy his efforts to act surprised and his delivery of an "impromptu" speech of acceptance. Rice the Unreliable, so often insulted in print, took his revenge when asked to write Twain's column while he was sick. Under Twain's name he printed a humble apology to a long list of people whom Twain had insulted, including himself, and promising to offend no more.

There were other ways to play in Virginia City—drinking, dining, and theatergoing. After an evening at the Opera House to view the latest San Francisco attraction, Mark, Dan, and Joe would adjourn to a favorite saloon to analyze the performance, compare reactions, and work out the review that one of them would write. There were

chances to travel, there were visiting notables to be entertained, there was even sport. A certain Monsieur Chauvel,
a swordsman as well as a chef, opened a gymnasium behind
his restaurant, a place where boxing and fencing could be
practiced, and for an hour or two in the afternoon the place
would be taken over by reporters and editors. Mark Twain
enjoyed fencing—"he was fiery in attack, but in defense
would give ground when pressed"—but had no taste for
boxing. He preferred combat at a distance. Once, though,
he put the gloves on and received a black eye and bloody
nose. Angry and embarrassed, he left town for a few days
to avoid notice, but Dan De Quille wrote it all up for the
Enterprise, with a fantastically exaggerated account of his
friend's swollen nose and other injuries. When De Quille
took a painful fall from a horse, Mark Twain retaliated.
Comstock humor was not for the tender-minded.

Virginia was a man's town, and Clemens eagerly adapted
himself to it. Yet he considered himself, only half jokingly,
a model of propriety. "I *never* gamble, in any shape or manner, and never drink anything stronger than claret or lager," he assured his mother and sister, "which conduct is
regarded as miraculously temperate in this country." "Miraculously" was overdrawing it—a Nevada brewery advertised that its beer was "the best in the Territory, as we can
prove by 'Mark Twain,' who has sat in the brewery and
drank gallons and gallons of it"—but by the standards of
Virginia City, he was a temperate man.

And always there was work, for he was a busy reporter
as well as a fledgling humorist. There were new mines to
be written up and new discoveries in the old ones; there
was the rise and fall of mining stocks; there were fires and
parades; and the murders that were almost routine: in April
Twain ended a letter to his mother with "P.S. I have just
heard five pistol shots down the street—as such things are
in my line, I will go and see about it." He did, and added
a second postscript—two policemen, both friends of his,

had been shot and killed. The murderer was let off; murderers generally were in Virginia.[3]

He continued to seek out schemes for getting rich fast, buying stock in "wildcat" mines, located off the main Comstock Lode and highly speculative. In a fire at his rooming house, in the summer of 1863, a trunk belonging to Twain was "utterly consumed." It contained, by his own report, "a pair of socks, a package of love-letters, and $300,000 worth of wildcat stocks." Those love-letters may have been an invention, or they may have been the letters of Laura Wright. As for the stocks, that figure of $300,000 is a Twainian exaggeration, no doubt, but not necessarily extreme; the par value of wildcat stock usually bore no relation to its selling price, if it could be sold at all. A stock certificate survives, issued by the Sonora Silver Mining Co. and dated August 1, 1863, which registers "S. Clements" as owner of five shares with a nominal value of $5,000. The certificate is impressive—carefully engraved, elaborately lettered, handsomely illustrated with a cut of a miner pushing an ore car out of a mine tunnel into a steep, narrow valley. Those shares could not possibly have been worth $5,000; they might have been worth $500, or more probably $50, or quite possibly nothing. Almost certainly they were a gift, not a purchase. In the flush times, it seemed almost as natural to offer a man a few "feet" as to offer him a cigar. Such gifts were not entirely disinterested: "I pick up a foot or two occasionally for lying about somebody's mine," he remarked in a letter to his family. Actual lying might not have been required; it was publicity that counted, and a reporter could always find a way to praise the tunnel, or the machinery, or the gentlemanly manners of the superintendent.

In his letters Twain liked to make a display of a shrewd, amoral knowingness, paradoxically combined with careless disregard for his opportunities—an appropriate attitude for a Southern gentleman, which was how he sometimes saw himself. "I manage to make a living, but if I had any business tact the office of reporter here would be worth $30,000 a year—whereas if I get 4 or $5,000 out of it, it will be as much as I expect. . . . I managed to raise the price of 'North Ophir' from $13 a foot to $45 a foot, to-day, & they gave me five feet. I shall probably mislay it or throw it in my trunk and never get a dollar out of it." He was offered five feet in the "Overman" mine, going at $400 a foot, as a gift, but never took the trouble to collect it. A San Francisco paper had asked him to be its Nevada correspondent, "and if they will pay enough, I'll do it. (The pay is only a blind—I'll correspond anyhow.) If I don't know how to make such a thing pay me—if I don't know how to levy blackmail on the mining companies—who *does*, I should like to know?" That seems the remark of a corrupt and calculating man, but Mark Twain was neither, and there's no reason to believe that he ever tried to blackmail a mining company. In fact, he seems to have had no substantial, continuing income beyond his $160 monthly salary, although there must have been windfall gains from wildcat stocks.

The *Enterprise* allowed a good deal of freedom to its staff, and Twain found time for long visits to San Francisco during 1863. In May, with Rice the Unreliable, he arrived there for a stay of nearly two months. By this time Mark Twain himself was news. His going seemed important enough to deserve a notice in his own style: "Mark Twain has abdicated the local column . . . where by the grace of Cheek he so long reigned as Monarch of Mining Items, Puffer of Wildcats, Profaner of Divinity, Detractor of Merit, Recorder of Stage Arrivals, Pack Trains, Hay Wagons and Things in General."

That first visit was a joyous time. After the "sagebrush and alkali deserts of Washoe," San Francisco seemed like a paradise: "I fell in love with the most cordial and sociable city in the Union." Staying at the best hotel, drinking champagne and claret for dinner, taking "a sail on the fastest yacht on the Pacific Coast," watching the sea lions and dipping his feet in the surf at Ocean House, enjoying a modest celebrity ("I suppose I know at least a thousand people here") "doing" the city so thoroughly that "Thunder! we'll know a little more about this town, before we leave, than some of the people who live in it"—he "lived like a lord," making up, he said, for "two years of privation." He had been "sometimes flush, sometimes dead broke & in debt," but neither for long: "I was strapped the day before yesterday, but I'm on the upper side of the wheel again today, with twelve hundred dollars in the bank. I sold 'wildcat' ground that was given me, & my credit was always good . . . for two or three thousand dollars." The wheel would keep on turning, if stocks fell they would rise again, and money was made to be spent. That was Virginia City's attitude in its flush times, and that would be Mark Twain's attitude for life.

Back in Virginia in early July, he began contributing regular letters to a San Francisco paper, the *Morning Call* (the connection he had boasted of to his family), and found that he had not been forgotten in the two-month absence: "Everybody knows me," he bragged, "and I fare like a prince wherever I go, be it on this side of the mountains or the other. And I am proud to say that I am the most conceited ass in the Territory." Already he had won a higher standing in his new profession than he had ever had in piloting— he had been only "a good average St. Louis–New Orleans pilot," but he was considerably more than a good, average newspaperman.

He had acquired a new profession, and he was acquiring, in a sense, a new identity—he was gradually ceasing to be a Southerner. His Confederate sympathies had been superficial, a response to the political atmosphere surrounding him. In the West he found a very different political environment. The battlefronts might be 1,500 or 2,000 miles away and the war had little direct effect on anyone's life, but it was not forgotten. The papers were filled with war news, and from time to time wild rumors circulated of Confederate plots to detach the Pacific Coast from the

Union. Noisy sympathizers with the Southern cause could be found, but on the whole Nevada and California strongly supported the Union. In these surroundings Sam Clemens had quickly changed sides. Barely six months after his arrival, he had become a detached observer: writing to a friend, he notes that Union forces had "thrashed our Missourians like everything," and adds ironically, "They had to chase them clear down to Arkansas before they could whip them. . . . Take a Missourian on his own soil, and he is invincible." A few months more, and he had become a Union man. "We" now means the Northern armies and Union sympathizers: after a dismal series of defeats, he laments that "the very *existence* of the United States is threatened." There seems no reason to doubt the sincerity of his shift in sympathy. His Southern background would not have been held against him in Nevada; there were many Southerners in the mines. He had simply stopped thinking of himself as a Southerner; he was a Westerner now, as his work for the *Enterprise* would have reminded him daily. Of course he could not erase his background in a year or two; Southern prejudices and Southern conventions might still influence his behavior—dangerously, at times.

In September he was back in San Francisco for a month's stay. The city offered not only its climate and its metropolitan pleasures—fine restaurants, comfortable hotels, six theaters, and countless bars—but an audience several times larger than the tiny population of Nevada and opportunities for a writer that Virginia City could not match. It supported the *Golden Era*, the only literary or semiliterary journal of any pretensions on the Coast. A ragbag of a paper, mixing poetry with mining news, the *Era* published everybody. Beginning authors served their apprenticeships with it, and its office was an unofficial writers' club where the local practitioners and visiting notabilities might be met. San Francisco writers liked to think of themselves as "bohemians," artists and free spirits, consciously superior to reporters, and Mark Twain would soon become, briefly,

REPORTER • 123

a San Francisco bohemian himself. Meanwhile, he had established contact, and the *Era* began publishing his work that fall, longer pieces than the *Enterprise* could accommodate. They were likely to be experiments in language. Fascinated by the specialized jargons of fashion and sports reporting, Mark Twain simultaneously mastered and parodied them. In "The Great Prize Fight" he satirized the clichés of the sports writer and the violence of the sport. In "All About the Fashions" and "The Lick House Ball" he comprehensively burlesqued the language and the gushing enthusiasm of "society" columns and satirized the concept of fashion itself, seeing it as merely conspicuous display: "Mrs. J. B. W. wore a heavy rat-colored brocade silk, studded with large silver stars, and trimmed with organdy . . . a burnous of black Honiton lace, scolloped, and embroidered in violent colors . . . her head-dress consisted of a simple maroon-colored Sontag, with festoons of blue illusion depending from it: upon her bosom reposed a gorgeous bouquet of real sage brush, imported from Washoe. Mrs. W. looked regally handsome."

Mark Twain had succeeded instantly in his new profession, and for a year his reputation had continuously risen. Then, for a moment, he seemed to have destroyed his career. On October 28 the *Enterprise* published an account of "A Bloody Massacre Near Carson." The massacre was indeed bloody enough—a deranged husband had scalped his wife, then crushed her skull with an ax, killed and mutilated his oldest daughter with a knife, and finally beat out the brains of his six younger children with a club. Details were abundant and gory. The reporter named his source, a well-known citizen of Carson, theorized about the cause of the crime (the man was said to have been driven mad by his losses after investing in a shaky enterprise in San Francisco), and criticized California papers for not having exposed the fraud. A sensational scoop for the *Enterprise*, it must have seemed—but the entire story was a fabrication, another Mark Twain hoax.

Reveling in the "blood-curdling particulars," readers missed the physical and geographical impossibilities that Twain had carefully inserted, and overlooked his satirical intention of ridiculing Californian self-righteousness. Nothing else could have been expected; as Mark Twain realized too late, "we . . . never *read* the dull explanatory surroundings of marvellously exciting things." When he published a retraction the next day, headed "I take it all back," the shock and horror of his readers turned to outrage, intensified by the casual tone of the retraction. Other newspapers, in both California and Nevada, had reprinted the story; learning the truth, they denounced the "silly lunatic" and his "soul-sickening story," which had been "merely a LIE—utterly baseless and without foundation." The credibility of the *Enterprise* seemed in danger. When, a little later, it published a true story of a maniac who stabbed four men, there were papers that refused to be taken in by anything from that "fount of unreliability, the Virginia City *Enterprise*."

Mark Twain had misjudged his audience, his paper was suffering, and he himself writhed under the denunciation. "I am being burned alive on both sides of the mountains," he exclaimed to Dan De Quille, then sharing rooms with him, who remembered that "he could not sleep. He tossed, tumbled and groaned aloud." This "bit of a gale" would blow itself out, De Quille told him, but he would not be reassured. Believing that he had injured the *Enterprise*, he offered his resignation to Goodman, who refused it in almost the words of De Quille. Goodman and De Quille were right—the storm did blow itself out with no lasting damage to anyone, although Western papers would tease Mark Twain about it for years. If anything, his career had been advanced: the "Bloody Massacre" had made him notorious, and in the West notoriety could be as useful as fame—almost indistinguishable from it, in fact. But the whole episode, from his initial miscalculation of an audience's response to his exaggeration of the consequences, his guilt, and his suffering under criticism, was intensely characteristic.[4]

That winter—Twain's last in Nevada—was notable for its visitors. In December Artemus Ward came to town. The name is nearly forgotten, but in the early 1860s Ward (Charles Farrar Browne) was the most popular of all the "phunny phellows" in America. His written humor amused Lincoln, but it relied too much on puns and misspellings to survive; his art on the lecture platform enchanted audiences, but that of course has vanished. A few impromptu jokes keep their flavor. Asked by telegram what he would take for forty nights in San Francisco, he wired back "Brandy and water." At the height of a drunken banquet in Virginia City, he solemnly offered a toast: "I give you Upper Canada." Asked why—"Because I don't want it myself."

Mark Twain had written an advance notice in the *Enterprise*, composed in Ward's own style: "In his last letter to us he appeared particularly anxious to 'sekure a kuple ov horned todes; alsowe, a lizard which it may be persessed of 2 tales, or any komical snaix, an enny sich little unconsidered trifles, as the poets say, which they do not interest the kommun mind." On Ward's arrival, the *Enterprise* staff took him in charge, and there followed days of continuous celebration, of drinking and dining, pub crawling and sightseeing—from Chinatown to the depths of the mines. Somehow the paper kept on publishing. Six years later Twain recalled one of those dinners: "*Scene*—private room in Barnum's Restaurant . . . present, Artemus Ward, Joseph T. Goodman . . . and 'Dan De Quille,' and myself . . . empty bottles everywhere visible . . . time 6:30 A.M." "Thickly reciting" a sentimental poem about babies, Artemus was "interrupted every few lines by poundings of the table and shouts of "Splendid, by Shorzhe!" Finally, after applause, he invited "every man 'at loves his fellow man" to stand up and drink to the author: "On all hands fervent, enthusiastic, and sincerely honest attempts to comply. Then Artemus: 'Well—consider it stanning, and drink it just as ye are!'"

One early morning found Mark Twain "astride a barrel" on the porch of a saloon, with Artemus Ward feeding him mustard from a spoon and asking bystanders "if they had ever seen a more perfect presentment of a subjugated idiot." Twain retaliated in kind: "It was hardly fair . . . to get Ward hopelessly drunk, black his face with cork, and thrust him out before his waiting audience"—but no doubt the audience loved the joke. Washoe took Artemus to its heart; Governor James Nye appointed him "for the term of his natural life . . . 'Speaker of Pieces' to the People of Nevada Territory," and his going-away presents included a massive gold chain, a jug of whiskey, some shares in a wildcat mine, and a bowie knife said to have killed two men.

Mark Twain had been Ward's constant companion and became his friend. Ward singled him out, recognized his ability, offered to bring him to the attention of the editors of Eastern journals, suggested collaboration, even proposed a joint world tour. "I have promised to go with him to Europe in May or June," Twain wrote to his family. That project never materialized, but in February Twain was to publish two sketches in the New York *Sunday Mercury*, a popular weekly. Ward had urged him, Twain wrote, to "leave sage-brush obscurity, & journey to New York with him," but it had seemed better "not to burst upon New York too suddenly & brilliantly." That caution was justified. Twain would go East, and succeed, but only when he had already begun to build a national reputation. Meanwhile, although as a writer Twain had nothing to learn from Ward, the encounter had allowed him to measure his abilities against those of the most popular humorist of the time, had revealed exciting possibilities outside the narrow limits of Nevada and California, and had shown him some of the rewards that a successful humorist might receive.

The legislature convened in early January, and again Mark Twain covered the session. The Clemens brothers had become a power in the Territory. Twain was easily the best-known journalist in Nevada, perhaps in the entire West. Orion was at the climax of his career—"Governor Clemens" and "Your Excellency" now, during Governor Nye's frequent absences in California. His wife, Mollie, had joined him; with his minuscule salary augmented by official fees, Orion had built an impressive home, which, Paine writes, "became the social center of the capital, and his brilliant brother its chief ornament." When the Third House met, Twain was again elected "governor" and was called upon to deliver his Third Annual Message (there had been no first or second); the House voted also to have 300,000 copies printed, "in all languages." The message was delivered in the county courthouse and admission was charged, with proceeds supposedly going to the Presbyterian Church. "I got my satisfaction out of it," Twain told his sister, "a larger audience than Artemus had . . . the gratification of hearing good judges say it was the best thing of the kind they had ever listened to—& finally a present of a handsome $225 gold watch . . . inscribed 'To Gov. Mark Twain.' "

Late in February, Adah Isaacs Menken arrived in Virginia City. The most notorious actress of her day—known as The Menken for her idiosyncracies and vivid beauty—she had been three times married, wrote passionate, Whitmanesque free verse, and would in future years become the alleged lover of Swinburne and Dumas. She was to appear in her favorite vehicle, *Mazeppa*, notorious for one sensational scene: Mazeppa (played by Menken) was captured, stripped to her flesh-colored tights creating a bold illusion of nudity, and bound to the back of a "fiery steed" to die of exposure as it roamed the Russian wastes—while in fact galloping on a treadmill. Twain had seen and reviewed *Mazeppa* in San Francisco and wrote that the steed "went cantering up-stairs over the painted mountains . . . with the wretched victim . . . unconsciously digging her heels into his hams, in the agony of her suffering, to make him go faster," but nobody else seems to have noticed such details. The miners of the Comstock found *Mazeppa*'s climactic scene irresistible. Brass bands serenaded her on her arrival in Virginia City, she was escorted through mines and saloons, a bar of silver was presented to her, and the "Menken Shaft and Tunnel Company" was formed, its stock certificates showing the actress bound to her stallion. The *Enterprise* rapturously praised her "peerless" ability "as a speechless but eloquent delineator of human passions." Journalistic controversy inevitably resulted; when the *Union* condemned the "scandalous obscene exhibition," Joe Goodman, in his richest rhetoric, denounced the *Union*'s "venomous hate which stings because it is despised— a reptile revenge, which . . . would trail its slimy form over all that is good and lovely in this beautiful creation."

Mark Twain's response was equivocal. He spent much time in Menken's company, even submitting some of his work to her criticism, but he showed none of Goodman's unabashed delight in her freely displayed physical beauty. His printed remarks, satirical and slightly sniggering, and his elaborate circumlocutions in describing her costume, suggest a writer embarrassed and disturbed by his own sexual tensions. "Prudery is obsolete," wrote one of her San Francisco admirers, but for Mark Twain—that very Victorian bohemian—it never would be.

A restless, impatient man, Twain was growing discontented: "My dear brother," his devout sister Pamela wrote to him, "you talk of pursuing happiness, but never find it." She advised him to turn to Christ, but that was never a possible solution for Mark Twain. He had been with the *Enterprise* for eighteen months, he had just endured a desert winter, the visits of Ward and Menken had offered him tantalizing glimpses of a greater world. In March a "literary paper," the *Weekly Occidental*, had printed one issue in Virginia City. It was intended to carry the work of local writers, and Mark Twain was scheduled to appear, but the *Weekly Occidental* perished first. The cultural atmosphere of Nevada was apparently too thin, too dry, for a literary journal. "You couldn't expect that kind of a paper to be permanent here, could you?" Twain asked sarcastically. "Can a lark sing in a cellar? Can summer abide on Mont Blanc? Will flowers bloom in hell?" That failure must have been a sharp reminder of the limitations of his surroundings.

He suffered from simple restlessness as well; he had stayed too long in one small place. As he would recall in *Roughing It*, "I wanted to see San Francisco. I wanted to go somewhere. I wanted—I did not know *what* I wanted. I had spring fever and wanted a change, principally, no doubt."

Such wishes have a way of fulfilling themselves. His Nevada career was about to end—abruptly, farcically, embarrassingly. In mid-May Virginia and its neighbors had been caught up in a whirl of patriotic enthusiasm for the money-raising campaign of the Sanitary Fund, the Civil War equivalent of the Red Cross. A fancy-dress ball in Carson City, organized by ladies of the town, brought $3,000, but that wasn't enough. A rally in Virginia produced $3,500— still a poor showing. Then, along came Reul Gridley. Gridley had lost an election bet, and his penalty was to carry a fifty-pound sack of flour for a mile and a quarter with a brass band following, playing "Dixie." He carried the sack, "with the band and the whole town at his heels," Mark Twain noted. Then he sold the flour at auction, for the benefit of the Sanitary Fund.

The flour was gone, but why not auction the sack itself? It was done, the buyer paid—then he returned the sack to be sold again, and again, and again. All day it traveled through the smaller towns—Carson, Dayton, Silver City, Gold Hill—each one striving to outdo the others. The

brass band followed, and a newspaper reported that
" 'tone' was given to the procession by the presence of
Governor Twain and his staff of bibulous reporters, who
came down in a free carriage, ostensibly for the purpose
of taking notes, but in reality in pursuit of free whiskey."
Combining patriotism, competition, noise, and liquor, it
was the kind of occasion that Washoe delighted in. As the
procession reached Virginia City in the evening and filed
down C Street, "the town was abroad in the thorough-
fares." Then the bidding began, with mines, businesses,
and other organizations taking part, as well as individuals.
While Twain reported briefly to his office, the *Union* outbid the *Enterprise*. That was provoking; he had been instructed to go as high as a thousand dollars to keep his
paper ahead. "But we'll make them hunt their holes," he
bragged in a letter to his sister-in-law, Mollie.

Later that night, at the *Enterprise* office, Twain finished
his story. More than half-drunk, still smarting from having
been outbid, he added a sarcastic comment about the
fancy-dress ball at Carson, suggesting that the money
raised there "had been diverted from its legitimate course
and was to be sent to aid a Miscegenation Society somewhere in the East." Dan De Quille was sober enough to
ask, "Is this a joke?" and to inquire whether Twain meant
"to wound the feelings of the ladies of Carson." Answering
"No, of course not," Twain tossed the paragraph on the
table, and the two went out to dinner. While they were
gone, a copy boy carried the piece off for printing. It appeared the next morning in the *Enterprise*, along with a
half-disclaimer confessing that it was a hoax, "but not all a
hoax, for an effort is being made to divert those funds from
their proper course." The Carson ladies had been doubly
insulted, accused not only of misappropriating funds raised
for a charitable purpose, but—more shameful by the standards of the time—of encouraging intermarriage between
blacks and whites. The disclaimer, acknowledging that the

most damaging part of the accusation had been a conscious lie, yet implying that the rest was true, only increased their anger.

The ladies replied with an immediate and indignant denial, which the *Enterprise* refused to publish (it appeared several days later in the *Union*). As Twain confessed to Mollie, their letter had not been printed because it could not be answered. His position was intensely embarrassing: he had made false accusations, an apology was plainly due, yet to make a convincing apology would require explaining "that the affair was a silly joke, & that I and all concerned were drunk." The humiliation would be unbearable— "No, I'll die first." If the ladies would not accept his assurance that the publication had been unintentional, then let them "appoint a man to avenge the wrong done them, with weapons in a fair and open field.

"Mollie," he continued, "the Sanitary expedition has been very disastrous to me. Aside from this trouble... I have two other quarrels on my hands, engendered on that day, & as yet I cannot tell how either of them is to end." Those quarrels were with James Laird, publisher of the Virginia City *Union*, and J. W. Wilmington, a printer on the *Union*. Twain had tried to carry out his promise to "make them hunt their holes." In an editorial entitled "How Is It?" he had accused the *Union* staff of failing to make their pledged contributions. The *Union* answered with an angry editorial by Laird, denouncing Twain as a "vulgar liar," who "conveyed in every word... a groveling disregard for truth, decency and courtesy." The same issue carried a letter signed "Printer," proving that all pledges had been met and concluding that Twain, in his attack, had slandered "laboring men who gave their little mite willingly" and had "proved himself an unmitigated *liar, a poltroon and a puppy.*"

On May 21 Twain sent Laird a note demanding public retraction of both articles "or satisfaction." "Satisfaction" meant a duel. Virginia was more used to the barroom brawl with fists or knives, the impromptu gunfight, or the shot in the back, but the formal duel was recognized as the method by which gentlemen settled their differences (despite the fact that dueling—or even sending a challenge—was a criminal offense under Nevada law).

How could Mark Twain, who had ridiculed an encounter between his editor, Joe Goodman, and Tom Fitch of the *Union*, have involved himself in that barbaric ritual? Ferocious rhetoric was after all a commonplace of Nevada journalism, with papers regularly accusing each other of misrepresentation, corruption, even treason. But in this case bitter *personal* insults had been printed—insults that could not be mistaken for the kind of comic invective that Mark Twain and the Unreliable exchanged to amuse themselves and their readers.[5] Behind his challenge lay all his restlessness and discontent; his immediate irritation at having been outbid found release indirectly in the miscegenation sneer, and directly in the "How Is It?" editorial. His frustrated anger against himself and against the Carson ladies (a situation in which he could do nothing at all) vented itself against Laird. Twain could feel violent, unreasoning, unfounded rage—there are examples enough in his later life. Usually he expressed that rage privately; this time he had done it in public, and had gone too far to draw back without public humiliation and without violating his own concept of himself as a Southern gentleman. The "code of honor," after all, was part of his heritage, and he was still Southerner enough to obey its commands.

A whole day must have been given to writing and carrying letters, while the parties insulted each other. The situation turned into farce as the complications multiplied; Twain challenged Laird, who declined, referring him to Wilmington, the printer: Wilmington was ready, but Twain insisted on fighting Laird; Steve Gillis, Twain's second and a printer for the *Enterprise*, challenged Wilmington (who sensibly refused—he had no quarrel with Gillis), and a Mr. Cutler, husband of one of the Carson ladies, challenged Twain, who offered to meet him on the dueling ground. Gillis, a merciless practical joker, must have enjoyed the affair enormously—and probably did his best to goad Mark Twain into action. On May 24 the *Enterprise* published the entire Twain-Laird-Wilmington-Gillis correspondence, brimful of italics and indignation—no doubt to the amusement of its readers.

Anticlimax followed. On May 29 Twain and Gillis left for San Francisco by stage. There had been no meetings on the field of honor. In *Roughing It*, Twain would pass over his departure in a single paragraph, blaming it on his reluctance "to serve in the ranks after being General of the army." (He had been writing editorials during Goodman's absence.) Paine tells a different story, supplied by Steve Gillis. In this version, Laird accepted the challenge and at daybreak Gillis led his principal to the field. They arrived early, and Twain began target practice but could hit nothing; he closed his eyes when he pulled the trigger. Gillis seized the pistol to show him how to handle it, and shot off the head of a mud hen at thirty paces. At that Laird came in sight, attributed the marvelous shot to Twain, and retracted on the spot. The story is in the best tall-tale tradition, and completely false. Gillis had stolen his details from a humorous sketch by Twain himself, "How I Escaped Being Killed in a Duel," published in *Tom Hood's Comic Annual for 1873*.

A letter from Mark Twain to his brother on May 26 shows that no meeting took place. After asking for two hundred dollars, Twain tells his plans: "Steve & I are going to the states. We leave Sunday morning . . . Say nothing about it, of course. We are not afraid of the grand jury, but Washoe has long since grown irksome to us . . . We have thoroughly canvassed the Carson business, & concluded we dare not do anything either to Laird or Carson men without spoiling our chances of getting away." (Perhaps they feared the grand jury more than he admitted—they could not have flouted the law more openly. Long afterward Twain recalled that he left Nevada to escape the penitentiary.) He left suddenly and secretly to avoid prosecution, and also, without doubt, to avoid ridicule. As the Gold Hill *News* editorialized, Mark Twain had "played hell." He had made a fool of himself, with maximum publicity, in a small community.

The circumstances were humiliating and the departure unplanned, but he would soon have left Nevada in any case. Mark Twain was nomadic by nature and he was ambitious. Artemus Ward, the most popular humorist in America, had recognized him as an equal. It's impossible to imagine him following the example of Dan De Quille, who stayed in Virginia City for another thirty years, outlasting the silver and the *Enterprise* itself. In his brief stay he had found his vocation and had become "Mark Twain"; he had enjoyed a freedom to develop his abilities that he could have found nowhere else; and in the year and a half since taking his new name, he had become the best known, if not the best loved, humorist in the West.

BOHEMIAN

On June 8, 1864 The Sage-Brush Humorist from Silver-Land, as the *Golden Era* called him, settled into his favorite San Francisco hotel, the Occidental, expecting to enjoy a vacation while he sold his mining stocks. Then he planned a triumphant return to the "states," with $100,000 in his pocket—"enough to go home on decently," he recalled in *Roughing It*. That figure was surely inflated in recollection, but it's true in spirit; he dreamed grandly. To return poorer than he had been when he went West would have been to confess failure, a waste of three years. Reputation as a humorist, a reputation confined to California and Nevada, could hardly compensate. He might play the role of returned prodigal at times, with understanding friends, but it was the role he enjoyed, not the reality. Meanwhile, the flush times were over, stocks were falling, and he needed to support himself while he waited for the time to sell. Within a week he was at work for the San Francisco *Morning Call* as local reporter, *the* local reporter, at forty dollars a week.

The *Call* was a "one-bit paper," the cheapest in the city, with a weekly subscription rate of twelve and one-half cents; the *Alta California*, San Francisco's leading daily, was priced at a lofty four bits. Populist and racist, read mainly by the poor, and particularly by the Irish working class— it was nicknamed "the washerwoman's paper"—it slanted its news to accommodate the prejudices of its readers. Professionally, Twain had taken a backward step; there had been no compensating gain in salary, there were no more chances to pick up stray mining shares, and worst of all, there was none of the *Enterprise*'s freedom. His reporting was unsigned; the *Call* seemed to feel no need for "Mark Twain"—it simply wanted a pair of legs to cover the city.

The San Francisco that he came to might have seemed raw and crude to a critical eye—"a monument to California's march from barbarism to vulgarity," one Eastern visitor called it—but to its citizens it was the sophisticated metropolis of the Pacific Coast, boasting a population of 115,000, a variety of newspapers, theaters with productions ranging from Shakespeare and Italian opera to melodrama and minstrel shows, fine hotels and restaurants, dozens of churches and hundreds of saloons. It was a busy port as well. All this the new local reporter was expected to cover. He began his day with the police court, soon becoming familiar with its whores and drunks and petty thieves, and its fearsome assortment of smells. The higher courts made up his second regular beat, then he "raked the town from end to end" for news of accidents, fires, or the occasional earthquake, arrivals of ships, public meetings and orations, the rise and fall of stocks, the opening of a Chinese temple, or runaway beer wagons when nothing better offered.

Every evening he made the rounds of the theaters, never

catching more than one act of any performance. Then, as he would recall, "after being at work from nine or ten in the morning until eleven at night scraping material together," he would write it all up. "It was fearful drudgery, soulless drudgery . . . an awful slavery for a lazy man." Yet he found time for the occasional joke: once, seeing a policeman asleep on his beat, Twain borrowed a cabbage leaf from a vegetable seller and stood over the sleeping man, quietly fanning him until a crowd gathered; then he walked away. When his work was finally done, he often went out with Steve Gillis, who had taken a job as printer with the *Call*, to enjoy a few glasses of lager or a game of billiards, or to find a brawl that Gillis, a pugnacious little man, could pitch into, while Twain watched. More often, they would go to the rooms they shared, and Twain would read himself to sleep, usually with some book of history.

He kept his pen name in use at first with letters to the *Enterprise*, often reprinted in the San Francisco papers, and in late June and early July he published two pieces in the *Golden Era*: "The Evidence in the Case of Smith vs. Jones," drawing on his observation of evasive witnesses in the police court, and "Early Rising, as Regards Excursions to the Cliff House," a burlesque of sentimental rhapsodies over the beauties of nature. Expecting "the gorgeous spectacle of the sun in the dawn of his glory; the fresh perfume of the flowers still damp with dew; a solitary drive on the beach . . . and a vision of white sails glinting in the morning light," he finds only fog and cold and the "discordant barking" of seals, "writhing and squirming like exaggerated maggots" on their rocks. Then there was no time for anything but his work—not even for letters home.

There's no evidence that *Call* readers noticed a change in the reporting of local news, but other papers did; during that summer they reprinted *Call* items more often than they had before Twain arrived. Signed or unsigned, his writing remained distinctive. He made an item, "House at Large," out of seeing a house being moved—'Is there no law against houses loafing around the public streets at midnight?" His stories displayed striking imagery: in the police court, a large and angry black woman "rolled off the stand, and out of the Court Room like the fragment of a thunder cloud." An exhibit of bad portraits showed "no more life or expression . . . than you may find in the soggy, upturned face of a pickled infant, dangling by the neck in a glass jar among the trophies of a doctor's back office." He even indulged in stylistic experimentation: "As sinks the aged man quietly into the grave, so silently settle the old wharves into the Bay, leaving a wretched, wracked aspect to remind us of the instability of earthly things."

In his police reporting he often adopted an amused cynicism, avoiding the bathos and moral melodrama common in the newspapers of the time. After reading in a rival paper a passage like this, describing a prostitute found dead in an alley—"Now at the close of her pilgrimage on earth she yields up her life, without one friend near her to receive her last words, and nothing to cover her with but a few tattered rags and the broad canopy of Heaven"—how refreshing it must have been for the reader to encounter Twain's cool astringency: "Mollie Livingston and two friends . . . none of whom are of at all doubtful reputation, cast aside their shifts to engage in a splendid triangular fist fight in Spofford Alley about seven o'clock yesterday." Somehow, even in routine reporting, he personalized his work. As a contemporary admirer put it, instead of presenting mere literal fact, Twain achieved a different reality—"the poetic truth, the jocular truth."

Still, Twain was restless and dissatisfied that summer; he and Gillis moved five times in four months. Twain lacked the hustle his employers insisted upon; he disliked walking, was dilatory in covering his beat, and "so tortuously slow" in writing copy that the editor, George Barnes, considered him "the most useless of local reporters." Much later, when Mark Twain had become a national celebrity, Barnes liked to tell stories demonstrating his incapacity:

" 'Mark,' said the managing editor to him, one day, 'there is a riot going on among the stevedores along the city front. Get the facts and make a column.' 'Ya-a-s,' he responded with his inimitable drawl; 'but how can I get them? There's no street railway down that way. You wouldn't want a fellow to walk a mile to see a couple of 'longshoremen in a fight, would you?' "

Steve Gillis later testified that "Mark was the laziest man I ever knew in my life, physically. Mentally, he was the hardest worker I ever knew. . . . I never knew Sam Clemens without a book to study." Twain's frequent self-accusations of laziness were a staple of his comic repertoire, and they were also based on his own understanding of "work": reading, writing, and later lecturing were not work, because they required little physical effort and were often enjoyable. By that standard, a fourteen-hour day reporting for the *Call* was definitely work.

In September he took a salary cut to be excused from evening work, and with the time gained began contributing to the "new literary paper," the *Californian*. He had quit the *Golden Era*, he explained to his family, because "it wasn't high-toned enough," while "the *Californian* circulates among the highest class of the community, and is the best weekly literary paper in the United States." Best of all, "the paper has an exalted reputation in the east, and is liberally copied from." He planned a book as well, perhaps a collection of short pieces, possibly an account of his life in the mining camps; in any case, on September 28 he wrote to Orion that he would soon be asking for the "files"—scrapbooks of his newspaper work—in order to "begin on my book." But he was not yet really ready to write a book. He turned toward writing—as opposed to reporting—as an escape from the *Call*, and because an early, victorious return to the "states" was now out of the question. After going into debt to keep his Hale & Norcross mining shares, he had been forced to sell at a loss. He took revenge in print. In late August he wrote two bitter pieces for the *Call* on the dishonesty and extravagance of mining companies, particularly Hale & Norcross. Years later, he would remember that he had bought his shares for a thousand dollars, held them while their value rose to seven thousand, and had finally sold them for three hundred. The figures are believable, and the performance would be typical of Twain's career as a speculator—he always bought dear and sold cheap, or not at all.

The contributions to the *Californian* began immediately, at twelve dollars apiece, making him the highest-paid contributor. Bret Harte, at twenty-eight the most promising young writer in San Francisco, with the possible exception of Mark Twain himself, was editing the paper, while also serving as secretary to the superintendent of the U.S. Mint. By a lucky chance the *Call* shared its building with the mint, and for all the differences between them—Harte was a fop and something of a snob, formal in his dress, genteel in his prose, cynical in his morals—he and Twain recognized each other's talents. To Twain, Harte's essays for the *Californian* seemed "worthy to take rank among Dickens's best sketches," while at their first meeting, Harte recognized the uniqueness of Mark Twain: his "head was striking" with its curly hair, aquiline nose, and bushy eyebrows. "His dress was careless, and his general manner one of supreme indifference to surroundings and circumstances." They did not become intimates, as Twain and De Quille had been, but they established a friendship that was to endure uneasily for eleven years, while they leapfrogged each other on the way to fame, then sour as Harte began his long slide back into obscurity.

By Twain's own testimony, Harte became his teacher, who "trimmed and trained and schooled" him and changed him "from an awkward utterer of coarse grotesquenesses to a writer of paragraphs and chapters that have found a certain favor in the eyes of even some of the very decentest people in the land." But what Harte taught him is not easy to guess. His formal prose, his sentimentality tempered with irony, bears no resemblance to Twain's writing, then or later. Perhaps it was more a matter of attitude than style. What Mark Twain seems to have acquired from Harte and the *Californian* was a consistently satirical tone—the *Californian*'s contributors recognized the crudity and naiveté of Western culture and felt a superiority to their surroundings. His weekly sketches were usually burlesques, ridiculing sentimental novels, operatic performances and operatic reviewing, the banality of the daily press. He began to identify himself with the self-consciously sophisticated *Californian* writers rather than with his fellow reporters.

He had commenced a journalistic feud, Nevada style, with Albert Evans ("Fitz Smythe"), a humorless, moralistic writer for the *Alta California*. Tall and lean, sporting a long, pointed moustache and a heavy beard beneath his broad-brimmed hat, Evans was an absurd, quixotic figure as he rode his horse through the streets of the city, an ideal subject for ridicule. But even that diversion could not compensate for the drawbacks of reporting for the *Call*. In *Roughing It* he tells another story of opportunity missed (he might have collected an enormous commission by going to New York to help sell a silver mine) adding that the disappointment caused him to lose all interest in his work. Again, by his own account, he had lost a fortune through "native imbecility . . . it was the 'blind lead' over again," and like the story of the 'blind lead,' it seems to have been mostly an invention.

Mark Twain was growing more and more unhappy with his paper. According to one friend, he found his stories "sadly slashed, and clipped, and decapitated, until he became persuaded that 'what they wanted of him principally was his legs.' " Worse still, his work was censored. The *Call* refused to print his account of a brutal, unprovoked attack on a Chinese laundryman. As he told the story six years later, some "Brannan Street butchers set their dogs on a Chinaman who was quietly passing with a basket of clothes on his head; and while the dogs mutilated his flesh, a butcher increased the hilarity of the occasion by knocking some of the Chinaman's teeth down his throat with half a brick." His editor explained that the *Call* could not afford to offend its readers by printing such a story; it was the paper of the Irish poor, who hated the Chinese. That episode, and no doubt others like it, burned itself on Twain's memory. (In 1870 he was to publish a bitterly ironic series of articles, "Goldsmith's Friend Abroad Again," on the persecution of the Chinese in California, and the *Call* would remain for him "that degraded 'Morning Call,' whose mission from hell & politics was to lick the boots of the Irish & throw bold brave mud at the Chinaman.")

Mark Twain was not yet a liberal in matters of race, even by the standards of the time. He and Gillis once amused themselves by throwing bottles from their room onto the tin roofs of Chinese shanties below; in his reporting he casually referred to blacks as "niggers," and he opened one *Call* story with: "A case of the most infernal description of miscegenation has come to light . . . a mixture of white and Chinese." But the sight of brutality revolted him, and when the impulse moved him, he could defy the racial proprieties of his day; an eyewitness described him once walking down Montgomery Street, the Wall Street of San Francisco, arm in arm with a black journalist, Peter Anderson of the San Francisco *Elevator*.

In early October he left the *Call*, or was invited to resign, as he later remembered. It was a clear case of incompatibility; he took no interest in the work his employers expected of him, and they found him unsatisfactory. He had complaints enough about the paper, but they might all have been summed up in this: the *Call* would not let him be Mark Twain.

The two months that followed would remain a dark time in his memory. He had hated his job, but its loss meant another humiliating failure. He had gained his freedom, but he had no prospects and was in debt. In *Roughing It* he would dramatize his poverty; he "did not earn a penny," he "became an adept at slinking," he "slunk from back street to back street," he shunned familiar faces, and finally at midnight slunk to his bed. He had one dime in his pocket and would not spend it, fearing that the sense of being "entirely penniless, might suggest suicide." In fact, he was not quite workless or penniless—he wrote ten sketches for the *Californian* that fall, at twelve dollars each—but he was in genuine difficulty. In his dejection, he may even have considered going back to the river. He is reported to have told a friend, John McComb, that he had done his last newspaper work and had taken an appointment as a government pilot at three hundred dollars a month. But McComb replied, "Sam, you're making the mistake of your life. There's a better place for you than a Mississippi River steamboat," and by his arguments saved Mark Twain for literature. It's hard to believe that Twain had actually applied for a position as a military pilot on the wartime Mississippi, but that he was sometimes tempted, and that he talked about the possibility, seems likely enough.

Those pieces for the *Californian* would have amused its readers, but they were not likely to raise his reputation significantly or improve his circumstances. Only three of them retain any interest: "Lucretia Smith's Soldier" (a parody of sentimental wartime fiction in which Lucretia devotedly nurses her wounded lover back to health—and when his head is unbandaged, discovers that he is the wrong man); "The Killing of Julius Caesar Localized" (a report of the assassination allegedly taken from the *Roman Daily Fasces*, parodying "sensation items" in the daily papers, complete with "a little moralizing here and plenty of blood there"); and "Daniel in the Lion's Den—and Out Again All Right" (in which the reporter ventures into the San Francisco Exchange, masters its arcane language and learns the secrets of bulls and bears, decides that a broker *can* be saved, and admires the Exchange president's fluency—"the words flowing in a continuous stream from his mouth with inconceivable rapidity, and melting and mingling together like bottle-glass and cinders after a conflagration.")

Association with the *Californian* writers—who thought of themselves as *writers*, not journalists—had begun to change his view of himself; for the first time, he became part of a literary circle. The need to produce weekly sketches was essential to his development. He had written no long, humorous pieces for the *Enterprise*; now he was required to work with longer forms, to experiment with styles and techniques of humor. Most of his work for the *Californian* was still reporting, in a sense, but highly imaginative reporting—less limited by fact, more closely approaching the "jocular truth."

But he was in no position to realize the value of those new opportunities; the realities of his life pressed him hard. Disappointed, poor, and in debt—again, he needed to escape, and again the perfect escape offered itself. "By and by, an old friend of mine, a miner [it was Jim Gillis, Steve's brother], came down from one of the decayed mining camps of Tuolumne, California, and I went back with him." Paine writes of trouble with the police: Steve had been arrested for brawling, Twain stood bail for him, Steve jumped bail, and Twain felt it wiser to leave town. But no record of Gillis's arrest can be found, and while the story is plausible, it is unnecessary. Mark Twain had reasons enough to get away from San Francisco.

On December 4 he reached the cabin shared by Gillis and his partner, Dick Stoker, at Jackass Hill in the Sierra foothills, the "mother-lode" region. It was dirt-floored but stocked with books—"Byron, Shakespeare, Bacon, Dickens, & every kind of first-class literature," Twain noted—for Gillis was a reader. In *Roughing It*, he is presented as "one whose dreams were all of the past, whose life was a failure, a tired man . . . without ties, hopes, interests, waiting for rest and the end." But that is sentimental cliché; Gillis was no ancient recluse waiting for the end but a vigorous man of thirty-five, a humorist and a gifted storyteller; with the winter rains setting in, there would have been time enough for stories. Two of his fantasies, no doubt elaborated, were to appear in Twain's books: "Dick Baker's Cat," concerning Tom Quartz, a cat that becomes expert in gold mining, in *Roughing It*; and "Jim Baker's Bluejay Yarn," a fable of talking birds, in *A Tramp Abroad*.

His new comrades initiated him into the minor art of pocket mining. The pocket miner might search for weeks or months before discovering his "pocket" of nuggets, which would bring him a few hundred or a few thousand dollars—pocket mining made no millionaires—allowing him to pay off his debts and enjoy a spree in San Francisco before going back to the hills. The miner would find a promising slope, take a shovelful of dirt, and wash it in a pan. If the pan showed "color," he would move to one side and wash another pan, continuing until he discovered a fan of gold particles that he could follow up the hill, panning as he went, until he found the pocket from which the gold had washed down. There he would dig, and if he were lucky, up would come "a spadeful of earth and quartz . . . all lovely with soiled lumps and leaves and sprays of gold." It seems a sort of mining likely to attract Mark Twain, with a chance of quick results and with no tunnels and shafts to excavate.

Bad weather brought frequent leisure, and Twain began keeping a notebook, apparently for the first time since he had left the river. From it, that winter at Jackass Hill and at Angel's Camp, where he and Gillis moved for a few weeks to try their luck, can be reconstructed. A week of bad weather and bad food: "Angels—rainy, stormy— Beans & dishwater for breakfast at the Frenchman's; dishwater & beans for dinner, & both articles warmed over for supper." He took notes on local characters: "Old Mrs. Slasher—Englishwoman 45 years old—married merchant of 38—wears breeches—foulmouthed b—h." He practiced his rudimentary French and recalled a Missouri anecdote: "In a country cabin in Mo.—Traveler asks 3 boys what they do—last & smallest 'I nusses Johnny, eats apples, & totes out *merde*.' " Even in the privacy of his notebook, he could not bring himself to write *shit*, although it is the forbidden word that gives point to the story. Yet the notebook also contains an exercise in scatological humor, a burlesque lecture on the "Great Vide Poche [Empty Pocket] Mine," in which the speaker, after describing the extraordinary mixture of limestone, grindstone, soapstone, and brimstone found in the mine, concludes that the owners have "got the world by the ass, since it is manifest that no other organ of the earth's frame could possibly have produced such a dysentery."

Storytelling helped kill time. "Mountaineers in habit telling same old experiences over & over again in these little back settlements," Twain noted, and he recorded one of them in his notebook: "Coleman with his jumping frog— bet a stranger $50—stranger had no frog, & C got him one—in the meantime filled C's frog full of shot & he couldn't jump—the stranger's frog won." That story, he wrote Gillis five years later, "heard while we sat around the tavern stove," had been "the one gleam of jollity that shot across our dismal sojourn in the rain and mud of Angel's Camp." Playing billiards in the tavern, they would quote their favorite line: "I don't see no p'ints about that frog that's any better than any other frog," or while Gillis and Stoker panned on a hillside, Twain might remark, "I don't see no p'ints about that pan o' dirt that's any better'n any other pan o' dirt." His elaboration of that story would soon carry his name across the country, although at the time he thought only that he "would have been glad to get ten or fifteen dollars for it."

But Angel's Camp and Jackass Hill had offered an escape from his problems, not a solution—at least not an immediate solution. On February 20 Mark Twain started back to San Francisco. "Left Angel's with Jim & Dick & walked over the mountains to Jackass in a snow storm—the first I ever saw in California," his journal notes. "The view from

the mountain tops was beautiful." He had found no gold,
but the familiar story of a fortune missed—through his
own carelessness, as usual—recurs. As Paine tells the story,
Twain and Gillis were at work on a promising lead, with
Twain carrying water and Gillis washing the dirt. The
"color" grew steadily better, but a cold rain was falling and
"Clemens . . . shivering and disgusted, swore that each pail
of water was his last." Finally he refused to go on. Tearing
a page from his notebook, Gillis wrote and posted a notice
of claim beside the last, still unwashed, pan of dirt. Soon
after, Twain left the city. Meanwhile, the rain had washed
away the earth from the abandoned pan, and "exposed a
handful of nuggets—pure gold." Two passersby saw the
gold, waited for the thirty-day notice to expire, then followed the lead to its source and took out "some say ten,
some twenty, thousand dollars." It almost certainly did not
happen. The sole authority appears to be Jim Gillis, who
liked a good story and might have adapted this one from
Twain's own apocryphal yarn of the blind lead. The con-
clusions are suspiciously alike.

"Home again—home again at the Occidental Hotel,"
Twain wrote on February 26, "find letters from Artemus
Ward asking me to write a sketch for his new book . . . Too
late—ought to have got the letters three months ago."
Nothing seemed to have changed. He had done no writing
(except in his notebook), he had earned no money, his debts
were unpaid, and he still had no regular position. He had
solved none of his problems. In *Roughing It* he briefly explains that he returned penniless, was too lazy to work on
a morning paper and could not find a place with an afternoon one, "was created San Francisco correspondent of the
Enterprise, and at the end of five months . . . was out of
debt" but again lost interest in his work: "my correspondence being a daily one, without rest or respite, I got unspeakably tired of it." In fact, the *Enterprise* contributions
seem not to have begun until fall; until then he was probably earning no more than fifty dollars a month from his

work for the *Californian*. Twain's memory of that year and
the preceding fall must have reinforced the lessons of his
childhood, teaching him that there could never be enough
money, leading him to search constantly for some source
of wealth more secure than writing. Ironically, all his
schemes and speculations failed—*only* writing could be depended on.

Poverty oppressed him, but his writing shows few signs
of the debts and anxieties that weighed down his life. Burlesque continues to dominate. "Advice for Good Little
Boys" and "Advice for Good Little Girls" parodies the
moralizing of the Sunday school: "You ought never to take
anything that don't belong to you—if you can not carry it
off." A few months later he would expand on the subject
in "The Christmas Fireside For Good Little Boys and
Girls," a piece in which germs of *Tom Sawyer* can be seen
as he tells "The Story of the Bad Little Boy That Bore a
Charmed Life": "Once he climbed up in Farmer Acorn's
apple tree to steal apples, and the limb didn't break and he
didn't fall and break his arm, and get torn by the farmer's
great dog, and then languish on a sick bed . . . and repent."
Humor can be startling in its violence: "I sawed off my
Johnny's under-jaw . . . It afforded instant relief; and my
Johnny has never stammered since." Language can be
slangy and crude—"Young bucks and heifers taste each
other's mugs" as the lights are turned down at a spiritual-
ist meeting—but always it is individual: a new hair style is
"like a kidney bean covered with a net"); a showy new hearse
is a "gorgeous star-spangled-banner bone-wagon." "A
magnificent funeral car," Albert Evans had called it.

He reviewed visiting performers of note, preferring popular artists to classical. In "Enthusiastic Eloquence" he
praises the banjoist Tommy Lee at the expense of Louis
Gottschalk, classical composer and concert pianist. "The
piano may do for love-sick girls," he comments, but for
"*genuine music*—music that will . . . break out on your hide
like the pin-feather pimples on a picked goose . . . just

smash your piano, and invoke the glory-beaming banjo!"

"A Voice for Setchell" praises the art of a successful comedian—Twain had "experienced more real pleasure, and more physical benefit," he said, "from laughing naturally and unconfinedly at his funny personations . . . than I have from all the operas and tragedies I have endured." Albert Evans, speaking as the voice of gentility, had attacked Setchell as "a low comedian," admired by men in the habit of attending "entertainments not frequented to any great extent by ladies." But Mark Twain offers as defense the laughter of the crowds who flocked to the theater: such criticism "can always be relied upon as sound, and not only sound but honest." That argument would justify his own humor, in crowded lecture halls or on the printed page of his best-selling books.

Current news could always provide material. When the *Evening Bulletin* published a story on the difficulties being met in filling the pulpit of San Francisco's Grace Cathedral—the minister most recently invited had been offered $3,000 more by his New York congregation—Twain intervened, with a mock correspondence between himself and the three ministers named in the report. He kindly offered to raise the offered salary and even to write their sermons, playing the role of helpful innocent and contrasting his naive realism with the hypocrisy of the ministers—both the distinguished Easterners, who had comfortable situations already and must watch their investments, and the "swarm of low-priced back-country preachers," eager "to sacrifice their dearest worldly interests and break the tenderest ties that bind them to their rural homes, to come and fight the good fight in our stately church."

On October 8, 1865, the Bay Area experienced a major earthquake. Twain published an "Earthquake Almanac" in the *Dramatic Chronicle*: "Oct. 23—Mild, balmy earthquakes. Oct. 24—Shaky. Oct. 25—Occasional shakes, followed by light showers of bricks and plastering." In the New York *Weekly Review* he offered a fuller account, describing a minister who "ran like a quarterhorse" from his church, while his wife and children and congregation sat bravely through the quake, and "the wife of a foreign dignitary" who set a new style in earthquake costume, rushing out of her bath into the street, wearing nothing but a towel around her neck—a costume which, if generally adopted, "would go far toward reconciling some people to these dreaded earthquakes."

A bohemian, a jester—to San Francisco he presented an image of carefree irresponsibility. Little evidence survives to indicate what lay beneath; he kept no more notebooks in California. He associated regularly with Harte and the other *Californian* writers and his earlier friends from the *Golden Era*, but unfortunately none of them set down their reminiscences of him. He might be teased in print about his drinking, or be accused by Evans of drunkenness or of frequenting low women, but such charges were part of the rough humor, or rougher warfare, of Western journalism. There is no reason to believe that Mark Twain was either an alcoholic or a lecher. His bohemianism may have gone little further than keeping literary society, eating at cheap restaurants, drinking a little, and earning a small, irregular income.

He only rarely went to church, but when he did he remained faithful to his upbringing, regarding himself as a "brevet Presbyterian" by virtue of having been "sprinkled in infancy," and consequently entitled in the afterlife to "the substantial Presbyterian punishment of fire and brimstone" rather than any "heterodox hell of remorse of conscience." There is a bitter irony in that declaration—few men suffered more from remorse of conscience than Mark Twain did, long after he had stopped believing in the orthodox hell of fire and brimstone. But, he continued, the heterodox hell was preferable after all, "because eternity is long, and before a man got half through it he would forget what it was he had been so sorry about. Naturally he would then become cheerful again." That cycle of remorse, forgetting, and returning cheerfulness is familiar enough, but it was a good deal more frequent in Mark Twain's life than in most.

He was drifting, barely supporting himself—a decision, a commitment, and an effort of will were needed to extricate him. "I have a religion, but you will call it blasphemy," he told Orion. "It is that there is a god for the rich, but none for the poor." He talked of suicide: "If I do not get out of debt in three months—pistols or poison for one—exit *me*." (He would recall later that he had actually put a pistol to his head in 1866, "but wasn't man enough to pull the trigger"—but that dismal fall of 1865 seems a likelier time.) He sums up their situation with "I am utterly miserable—so are you." Orion had lost his secretaryship, and now, with a wife to support, was even poorer than his brother. But Twain does not despair; he has solutions to offer. Apparently Orion had preached a sermon, and Twain tells him, "There was *genius*—true, unmistakable genius—in that sermon of yours." If he had heard it seven or eight years earlier, he adds, it might have "saved" him—but he is "beyond the reach of argument now."

Clearly, Orion is called to preach, and he should obey the call—let him think of the glory of "snatching an immortal soul in mercy from the jaws of hell!" Twain confesses that he had had only two powerful ambitions in his life: "One was to be a pilot, & the other a preacher of the gospel." He achieved the first but not the second, because, he said, "I could not supply the necessary stock in trade—*i.e.* religion." Nevertheless, he too has his vocation: "a 'call' to literature, of a low order—i.e. humorous." "It is nothing to be proud of," he adds, "but it is my strongest suit," and therefore it is his duty to stop meddling with affairs for which he was "by nature unfitted" and turn his attention to "seriously scribbling to excite the laughter of God's creatures. Poor, pitiful business!" He proposes a bargain: let each of them accept his destiny, let Orion "go hence to the States & preach the gospel," and he, Twain, "will drop all trifling, & sighing after vain impossibilities, & strive for a fame—unworthy & evanescent though it must of necessity be."

How could Mark Twain have felt a "powerful ambition" to preach, when he entirely lacked religion? Tom Sawyer might have had that ambition—to stand before a great congregation, swaying its emotions at will, snatching souls from the jaws of hell—and there was much of Tom Sawyer in Mark Twain. He knew himself well enough to realize that; writing to his thirteen-year-old niece, Annie Moffett, a month later, he facetiously remarks that while becoming a minister had been his highest ambition, he "never had any qualification *but* the ambition," adding that if he had Orion's chance, he "would make the abandoned sinner get up and howl." To pass on the desired vocation to Orion was to fulfill the dream vicariously; a year later he would realize it in his own terms by commencing a successful career as a humorous lecturer.[1] He would often refer to his lecturing as "preaching," and perhaps that was not quite a joke.

Those disparaging comments on the trade of humorist are more puzzling; they seem to support the thesis, first set out by Van Wyck Brooks more than sixty years ago in *The Ordeal of Mark Twain*, that he became a humorist against his will. Yet except for his straight reporting, Twain had written nothing but humor, even when writing without pay, purely for his own satisfaction, and his reporting was humorous whenever the subject allowed. Certainly he was justified in claiming that he had a "call" to the writing of humor. His judgment that such writing constituted literature "of a low order" is in part a rhetorical strategy designed to persuade Orion by glorifying his supposed vocation in contrast to Twain's own humble calling. It represents also a mood of self-disparagement that often overcame him—and other humorists must have felt the paradox of "seriously scribbling to excite the *laughter* of God's creatures, particularly in circumstances as dismal as Twain's had been. The condemnation is modified when he adds that the humorous talent "is a mighty engine when supplied with the steam of *education*—which I have not got, & so its pistons & cylinders & shafts move feebly . . . and are useless for any good purpose." He would labor all his life, unsystematically but continuously, to give the engine of his talent that necessary "steam" of education.

There seems a flat contradiction between the work and the public image, and the private personality. Yet we should avoid the stereotype of the tragic clown, and we need not assume that either Twain's despair or his humor must have been false. His view of the world—a continuous, amused perception of incongruity, of the discrepancies between convention, or ideal, or pretense, or supposition, and reality—was essentially humorous. To use his own term, that way of looking at life, combined with his verbal gifts, constituted his "call." The letter is a product of depression, and his depressions, as he well knew, were genuine and deep, but also brief. The essence of Mark Twain's temperament was its extraordinary mobility; he could no more be continuously despairing than he could be continuously laughing. And even in that moment of gloom, he was anticipating a fame that would be more than "evanescent." He concludes with a postscript advising Orion to "shove this in the stove—for if we strike a bargain I don't want any absurd 'literary remains' & 'unpublished letters of Mark Twain' published after I am planted."

That anticipation was justified; his work was becoming nationally known. As he had foreseen, some of the *Californian* pieces had been reprinted in the East. In September the New York *Round Table* had observed that "the foremost among the merry gentlemen of the California press as far as we have been able to judge is one who signs himself 'Mark Twain.' " He might hope, said the *Round Table*, to "one day take rank among the brightest of our wits." That praise may have influenced him to accept his "call"; it had been reprinted in the *Dramatic Chronicle* on October 18—

his letter to Orion is dated one day later. It was "only now," he had admitted in that letter, "when editors of standard literary papers in the distant east" gave him "high praise" that he began to believe "that there might be something in it"—that is, not only that his talent was real, but that it offered him a career. And more praise would follow; in November the New York *Weekly Review*, a journal of considerable prestige, had introduced his "The Great Earthquake" as a "contribution from the sprightly pen of MARK TWAIN, one of the cleverest of the San Francisco writers."

Mark Twain now set to work "in dead earnest" to write himself into prosperity and fame. He contributed a daily San Francisco letter to the *Enterprise*, for a hundred dollars a month, he wrote squibs and reviews for the *Dramatic Chronicle*, a kind of daily entertainment newsletter, distributed free at hotels, and the distant ancestor of today's San Francisco *Chronicle*. His contributions began with a paragraph ridiculing Evans, who had solemnly written that the steamer *Colorado* "arrived from Panama after the quick passage of twelve days and twenty-four hours." The *Dramatic Chronicle* pieces paid another forty dollars, and on the combined income of one hundred and forty dollars a month, he could live and begin to pay off his debts. Most important of all, it was probably at this time that he wrote the sketch that would at once raise him beyond any comparison with other "merry gentleman of the California press"—"Jim Smiley and His Jumping Frog," better known under its later title, "The Celebrated Jumping Frog of Calaveras County," published November 18, 1865, in the New York *Saturday Press*.

The "Jumping Frog" was a long-delayed response to Artemus Ward's request for a contribution to his forthcoming book; its publication had been delayed, and Ward had urged him again. Bret Harte later claimed credit for having persuaded Twain to write it. By his account, Twain had dropped into his office soon after returning from the mines:

"... he remarked upon the unearthly laziness that prevailed in the town he had been visiting ... He said the men did nothing all day long but sit around the bar-room stove, spit, and 'swop lies.' ... He went on to tell one of those extravagant stories, and half-unconsciously dropped into the lazy tone and manner of the original narrator," and Harte immediately advised him to write it up for the *Californian*. Harte's story may well be true in part—it's likely enough that Twain told the anecdote around the town after coming back from the mines—but the "Jumping Frog" was probably not composed until several months after Harte and he had spoken about it, and it was not written for the *Californian*. Twain's own account is different: while lying on a hotel bed "one dismal afternoon ... about determined to inform Artemus that I had nothing appropriate ... a still small voice began to make itself heard. 'Try me! Try me! O, please try me! Please do!' It was the poor little jumping frog."

The story of the jumping frog was simple enough: a miner, Jim Smiley, owns a frog, matches it in jumping contests with other frogs, and it always wins. A stranger appears, doubts the superiority of Smiley's frog ("I don't see no p'ints about that frog ... "), a contest is arranged, the stranger surreptitiously fills the champion frog with buckshot until it can't raise itself off the ground. The trick is discovered too late; the stranger has left, with his winnings.

Twain's problem was to find a way of elaborating the simple anecdote he had heard at Angel's Camp, whether by complicating the action or the method of telling the story. In the end he did both; giving brief histories of two other remarkable animals belonging to Jim Smiley, and (more important) using two narrators. The first is a gentleman, his language painfully genteel, his diction formal, his sentences carefully structured: "I called on good-natured, garrulous old Simon Wheeler, and inquired after my friend's friend, Leonidas W. Smiley ... and I hereunto append the result." Simon Wheeler, on the other hand, is an illiterate backwoodsman, his vocabulary is simple and concrete, his sentences are loose and repetitious, and his mind seems to work purely by association—"Rev. Leonidas W. H'm, Reverend Le—well, there was a feller here once by the name of *Jim* Smiley, in the winter of '49—or maybe it was the spring of '50—I don't recollect exactly, somehow, though what makes me think it was one or the other is because I remember the big flume warn't finished when he come to the camp... "

Earlier humorists had used uneducated characters to tell their stories, often in their own words, but had always carefully demonstrated their own superiority to their material. They were gentlemen. In the "Jumping Frog," condescension has disappeared; the stilted diction of the gentlemanly narrator seems absurdly pretentious; slow, fat Simon Wheeler gets the better of the encounter. Twain had mastered the American vernacular; captured the effect of oral storytelling in written prose. He was to write nothing to equal "The Jumping Frog" until *Tom Sawyer*, nearly ten years later.

The story reached New York too late to be included in Ward's book, so Ward sent it on to the New York *Saturday Press*, and it appeared in the issue of November 18. By December 10 the *Alta California*'s Eastern correspondent, "Podgers," could write that it "had set all New York in a roar... I have been asked fifty times about it and its author, and the papers are copying it far and wide. It is voted the best thing of the day." The delay in publication had been fortunate; the appearance of the "Jumping Frog" in the *Saturday Press* allowed the reprinting that gave it an enormously wider circulation than it might have had in Ward's book—a "wretchedly poor one," in Twain's opinion. Podgers's report did not reach San Francisco until January 10, but Westerners had already had the chance to judge for themselves; the *Californian* had published the "Jumping Frog" on December 16.

Within a few weeks of his agonized letter to Orion,

Twain's prediction of fame had come true—he had become a minor national celebrity. The *Saturday Press* had carefully introduced the author to its readers, explaining that "Mark Twain" was "the assumed name of a writer who has long been a favorite contributor to the California press, from which his articles have been so extensively copied as to make him nearly as well known as Artemus Ward." Twain was delighted, of course, but a little sorry his first fame had come for *this* story: "To think that after writing many an article that a man might think tolerably good, those New York people should single out a villainous backwoods sketch to compliment me on."

"A villainous backwoods sketch"—the reasons for his discontent can be found in those words. Written largely in the vernacular, the piece was simply not *literary*, by the standards of his time. But the public judged better, and eventually Twain accepted the verdict. A year and a half later he reported with pride that James Russell Lowell—poet, critic, and humorist—had pronounced the "Jumping Frog" to be "the finest piece of humorous writing ever produced in America." Lowell's opinion became Twain's own; in 1869 he echoed it in a letter to his fiancée, Olivia Langdon, and he made the jumping frog his trademark.

He must have needed his new fame to help him bear the frustrating, infuriating failure of a promising scheme he had developed for disposing of the Tennessee Land. He was "tired of being a beggar—tired of being confined to this accursed homeless desert," he complained to Orion, and a sale would have allowed him to go back to the "states" without seeming to be a failure. He had arranged to go East and collaborate with a friend, Herman Camp, a mining man with business connections, in selling the land—and perhaps to capitalize on the success of "The Jumping Frog" while it was still fresh. He records in his *Autobiography* that Camp offered to buy the land himself for $200,000, intending to "import foreigners from grape-growing and wine-making districts in Europe, settle them

on the land, and turn it into a wine-growing country." But
Orion, in a spasm of temperance, vetoed the project: "he
would not be a party to debauching the country with
wine." Again the motif of the fortune lost—this time with
some foundation. Whatever the offer might have been, Orion's interference is proved by a letter of Twain's written
the following spring: "I am in poverty and exile now because of Orion's religious scruples." Twain was left permanently disillusioned, not only with the Tennessee Land but
with the practical ability of "that worthless brother of
mine, with his eternal cant about law & religion, getting
ready in his slow, stupid way, to go to Excelsior."

Not only had a chance at wealth been lost through Orion's obstinacy, but Twain's circumstances did not begin to
match his new reputation. He was still in debt, still earning
at most a hundred forty dollars a month, still chained to
the drudgery of daily correspondence for the *Enterprise*—
for Mark Twain, any obligation soon became drudgery. He
could enjoy writing enormously, as long as it was volun-
tary, but "the spur and burden of the contract" soon became unbearable. He may even have spent a night in jail
that winter; in January, his old enemy Albert Evans wrote
that the stink of San Francisco's slaughterhouses was like
"the horrible density . . . which prevails in the Police Court
Room when the Bohemian of the Sage-Brush is in the dock
for being drunk overnight." But the accusation may have
been a lie; lacking wit, Evans had no weapons against Mark
Twain but slander and crude insult.

Yet Twain's journalism remained surprisingly good-
natured, as he indulgently commented on spiritualism,
"the new wild-cat religion"; admired the current fashions—"what handsome, vari-colored, gold-clasped garters
they wear now-a-days"; solved the mystery of why Albert
Evans's horse "always looks so dejected and indifferent to
the things of the world"—it was fed on old newspapers; or
related how the most notable liars of history, beginning
with Ananias, had appeared to him in a dream in order to

Samuel Clemens's birthplace, in Florida, Missouri. "Recently some one in Missouri has sent me a picture of the house I was born in," he once wrote. "Heretofore I have always stated that it was a palace but I shall be more guarded now."

Samuel Clemens, apprentice printer, age fifteen. "One isn't a printer ten years," he said much later, "without setting up acres of good and bad literature and learning—unconsciously at first, consciously later—to discriminate between the two."

Mark Twain at his boyhood home, in Hannibal, Missouri, May 1902. From his memories of Hannibal (that "half-forgotten Paradise") sprang Tom Sawyer and Huckleberry Finn.

*Four generations photographed June 18, 1882. Mark Twain's
mother, Jane Lampton Clemens (left), with her daughter Pamela
Clemens Moffett (right) and her daughter Annie Moffett
Webster (standing), behind her daughter Jean Webster,
who is holding a doll.*

Mark Twain, steamboat pilot, about 1859 or 1860. "I loved the profession far better than any I have followed since, and I took a measureless pride in it," he wrote. "The reason is plain: a pilot, in those days, was the only unfettered and entirely independent human being that lived in the earth."

*Orion Clemens as Secretary of the Nevada Territory in the
1860s. Remembering his brother, Twain wrote, "His day was
divided—no, not divided, mottled—from sunrise to midnight
with alternating brilliant sunshine and black cloud."*

Olivia Langdon, 1872. On a ship in the Bay of Smyrna, Charlie Langdon happened to show Twain, his friend, a miniature portrait of his sister. "From that day to this," Twain was to write many years later, "she has never been out of my mind."

BROOKLYN ACADEMY OF MUSIC, FEB. 7th

*Tickets at 244 Fulton St. and
172 Montague St.*

Poster promoting a lecture by Mark Twain. The Celebrated Jumping
Frog of Calaveras County *made Twain so well known that his name was
considered superfluous to this placard depicting the author astride a frog.*

praise Evans for the quantity rather than the brilliance of
his lies and to accept him into their order. He could allow
a go-getting cemetery keeper to expose himself in a few
lines, instead of blasting the man with invective: "Everybody says so—everybody says mighty few graveyards go
ahead of this. We are endorsed by the best people in San
Francisco. We get 'em, sir, we get the pick and choice of
the departed."

He was not so gentle in his dealings with the police; in
his letters to the *Enterprise*, regularly reprinted in the San
Francisco papers, he bitterly attacked their corruption, in-
competence, and brutality. He virtually accused them of
murder for shoving a prisoner with a fractured skull into a
cell and leaving him to die there, unattended—"Had not a
gentleman just said he stole some flour sacks? Ah, and if
he stole flour sacks, did he not deliberately put himself outside the pale of humanity and Christian sympathy by that
hellish act?"

He had had enough of the bohemian life in San Francisco and was working hard to escape. He published more
pieces in Eastern periodicals, he talked of joint projects—
collaboration with Bret Harte on a book of sketches, or on
a volume of parodies of California poets ("We know all the
tribe . . . and understand their different styles, & I think we
can just make them get up & howl."). Neither book materialized. He planned a more ambitious work, dropping hints
where they might be useful. In January a San Francisco paper reported that "that rare humorist, 'Mark Twain,' whose
fame is rapidly extending all over the country . . . has commenced the work of writing a book. He says that it will treat
on an entirely new subject." Twain himself confided to his
mother and sister that he planned a book, the subject of
which was known to no one but himself, and that part of it
would have to be written in St. Louis. That final remark im-
plies that the subject was to be his experience on the river.
Here, apparently, is the concept of *Old Times on the Mississippi*,
not to be written for another eight years. More than a year

earlier, he may have been considering a primitive version of *Roughing It*. He was not yet ready to write either book, but the fact that he had conceived one, and possibly both, of them indicates that his literary career was a good deal more self-determined, less haphazard, less subject to chance and casual suggestion, than it sometimes seemed.

CORRESPONDENT

In January of 1866, the steamer *Ajax* had undertaken her maiden voyage from San Francisco to the Sandwich Islands, as the Hawaiian Islands were still called, carrying a select party of passengers. Mark Twain had been invited, had refused because of his commitment to the *Enterprise*, had promptly regretted his refusal, and before long had persuaded the Sacramento *Union*, then the leading newspaper in the West, to send him to Honolulu as a traveling correspondent, with instructions to stay for a month and "ransack the islands, the great cataracts and volcanoes completely, and write twenty or thirty letters" for twenty dollars each. Telling his family about it in a letter, he casually added that if he comes back to San Francisco—he must have been thinking of going on around the world—he expects "to start straight across the continent by way of the

Columbia river, the Pend d'Oreille Lakes, through Montana and down the Missouri River." The world seemed to open before him. To travel and to write—no assignment could have suited his talent and his temperament better.

He embarked on the *Ajax* on March 7, supplied by friends with brandy and cigars and letters of introduction. There was some rough weather during the eleven-day voyage, but he proved a good sailor, enjoying his new freedom and the novelty of shipboard life. In his first letter to the *Union* he commented on "the strange new sense of entire and perfect emancipation from labor and responsibility coming strong upon me." But he was no idler; he used his time to learn what he could about the islands and eagerly absorbed the lore and language of the sea—technical jargons always fascinated him. He noted the gap between romance and reality, advising young men "who yearn to become bold sailor boys" against shipping out as firemen: "The fireman stands in a narrow space between two rows of furnaces that flame and glare like the fires of hell, and shovel coal four hours at a stretch in an unvarying temperature of 148 degrees Fahrenheit. . . . Steamer firemen do not live, on an average, over five years." He again began keeping a journal, from which he drew the raw material of his *Union* letters, and commenced a lifelong habit of composing maxims: "Never refuse to do a kindness unless the act would work great injury to yourself, and never refuse to take a drink—under any circumstances."

After an eleven-day voyage, he landed in a Honolulu about the size of Virginia City, a town in which any white man encountered was likely to be either a missionary or a whaling captain. It had been Christianized some forty years earlier by New England missionaries, Twain noted, and their pervasive influence made it "the most excessively moral and religious town that can be found on the map of the world." Still independent, the Hawaiian kingdom was an absurd and delightful place, a sort of Pacific Ruritania, with all the trappings of monarchy: bemedaled, dark-skinned royalty, a nobility, a legislature, household troops and servants, king's yeomanry, governors of the various islands, marshals and sheriffs—all supported by a total population of about 60,000. Pomp mingled with arcadian simplicity; the king might sometimes be found sitting on a barrel on a wharf, fishing. Life, even among the whites, seemed easy and slow: "No careworn or eager, anxious faces in the land of happy contentment," Twain noted in his journal. "God! What a contrast with California and Washoe."

He could admire that tropical indolence, but he resisted it. He took his assignment seriously, and his time was filled with writing, study, and sightseeing. Into his notebooks went jottings on Hawaiian history, politics, and economics, on scenery, on native customs and legends, on the language—all to reappear in his letters to the *Union*. He planned an ambitious itinerary, taking in the six major islands, but in a four-month stay managed to visit only Maui, Hawaii, and Oahu. By land one traveled on horseback or muleback (Twain was a hopelessly bad rider) and by sea on tiny schooners at the mercy of contrary winds and calms. Ransacking the islands in a month, as he had proposed in his ignorance, was a clear impossibility.

Outwardly, it was a "civilized," Americanized Hawaii that Mark Twain saw, a chaste and modest Hawaii in which the hula could be performed only in private, by special license. The reality was rather different; one of the "strong characteristics" of the natives, he observed, was that "the women *will* fornicate"—but that comment stayed in his journal. He could envy the relaxed existence of the whites, but the remnants of native life and culture made no appeal to his imagination. He was no Gauguin, surrendering to a pagan spell, but a Victorian American, a "brevet Presbyterian," alternately prudish and coarse. In his letters he occasionally titillated his readers with voyeuristic titles—"Venus at the Bath," "The Shameless Brown." He could refer in his notebook to the "soft voices of native girls—liquid, free, joyous laughter," but in general he seems to have been more shocked than tempted, contrasting "white virtue" with "native licentiousness." He might concede the unselfishness and good nature of the Hawaiians, but they remained "savages" and "barbarians" for him—dirty, lazy, and adulterous. In his notebooks, though not in his printed letters, they were sometimes "niggers." Not only their culture but their race seemed on the verge of extinction. Since Captain Cook's "discovery" of the islands not quite ninety years before, an array of European diseases, from syphilis to whooping cough, had reduced the population by at least five-sixths. Twain described riding over what must have been a burial pit dug for victims of some epidemic and later uncovered: "... ground so thickly strewn with human bones that the horses' feet crushed them... at every step."

Toward the natives he was condescending; toward the missionaries, his attitude was more complex. He could be sharply satirical, observing that "the missionary—I should say (preacher) feature of insincerity & hypocrisy marks the social atmosphere" of Honolulu, and commenting "More missionaries and more row made about saving these 60,000 people than it would take to convert hell itself." But those remarks were left in his notebooks; in print he carefully balanced praise and criticism. He cracked jokes at the missionaries' expense—"How sad it is to think of the multitudes who have gone to their graves in this beautiful island and never knew there was a hell!"—but on fundamental issues he was on their side. Paganism was outside the range of his sympathies; self-evidently, it was better to be Christian than heathen, to be civilized than savage. At times the simple reality—the extinction of a culture and near-extinction of a people—impressed him: "S. Islanders never intended to work. Worse off now with all religion than ever before. Dying off fast. First white landed there was a curse to them." (Thirty-five years later, in "To the Person Sitting in Darkness," he was to charge that missionaries were pioneers of Western imperialism.)

After four weeks of intensive touring in Oahu, he sailed for Maui. There he spent late April and most of May "riding backwards and forwards among the sugar plantations—looking up [at] the splendid scenery and visiting the lofty crater of Haleakala." It had been "a perfect jubilee. . . in the way of pleasure," a tropical idyll, his first true vacation since his visit to San Francisco in June of 1863. "I have not written a single line" he confided to Mollie, "and have not once thought of business, or care. . . . Few such months come in a lifetime." Not a single line for publication, he meant, for he was busily filling his journal. Later, to his *Union* readers, he casually observed that he had had "a jolly time" and "would not have fooled away any of it writing letters under any consideration whatever." Plainly, the *Union* was a more sympathetic employer than the *Call*.

Travel was slow and difficult, over narrow trails to remote villages and isolated sugar plantations. Except in Honolulu and at Kilauea, hotels did not yet exist. Mark Twain could simply ask for accommodation at the home of any white man and pay for his lodging with jokes and stories, or simply with news of distant America. To sober missionaries he must have seemed a fantastic figure, wearing a long, badly fitting "duster" when he rode that was constantly slipping off one shoulder or the other, swaying back and forth in the saddle, talking "foolishly" in his exaggerated drawl—sometimes they took him for drunk, or crazy. His profanity could be startling; one missionary's daughter, aged five, was so shocked that she stuffed cotton in her ears to shut it out. They spoke of him as "the Moral Phenomenon," he solemnly assured *Californian* readers after his return, but we are not required to believe him. Visiting a rich sugar plantation on Maui, belonging to a family that included two pretty daughters, he wrote to his mother that "if I were worth even $5,000 I would try to marry that plantation." Evidently he was susceptible. He went to dances and card parties, and often rode out with one planter's sister-in-law, a "mighty fine looking" young lady, who thought that once he came near proposing. But he could not—as the planter observed, "He hadn't a red cent, not even decent clothes." He was only a newspaperman, earning twenty dollars a letter, and in debt, and there was still the island of Hawaii, with its crater Kilauea (already a major tourist attraction) to be inspected.

So he went back to Honolulu, sailing from there for Hawaii on the schooner *Emeline*—"about as long as two street cars and about as wide as one," he informed his readers. As for his cabin, "One might swing a cat in it, perhaps, but then it would be fatal to the cat to do it." But there was room for himself and his carpetbag; he traveled light. It was an uncomfortable voyage; the *Emeline* was crowded not only with native passengers, their dogs, chickens, and fleas, but also with cockroaches and rats. But he felt compensated for his sufferings when he stepped out on deck in bright moonlight, "to see the broad sails straining in the gale, the ship keeled over on her side, the angry foam hissing past her lee bulwarks, and sparkling sheets of spray dashing high over her bows and raining upon her decks."

The island of Hawaii itself met his expectations. He toured strenuously, traveling two hundred miles by muleback during his three weeks on the island. He bought the mule for ten dollars, he reported in a *Union* letter, paid four dollars to have it shod, and finally sold it for fifteen: "Up to that day and date, it was the first strictly commercial transaction I had ever entered into and come out the winner." Reaching the great volcano of Kilauea, he wrote that at night the crater floor, seamed with cracks through which molten lava glowed, resembled "a colossal railway map of the State of Massachusetts done in chain lightning on a midnight sky." But two hundred miles on the back of a mule had been too much; he returned to Oahu with an incapacitating case of saddle boils: "They kept me in my room, unclothed, and in persistent pain, for two weeks." There would be no more travel; he would remain on Oahu until his return to the mainland.

Meanwhile, his letters to the *Union* were finding their readers. They were informative, often stuffed with statistics and commercial advice, sometimes directly addressed to the California capitalist—"you" will do this or require that in order to do business with the islands—but they reached a wider audience. The *Union* had expected him to "write up sugar," he remembered long afterward; he did so, and "threw in a lot of extraneous matter that hadn't anything to do with sugar." But he could hardly have written anything without doing that, and if the *Union* had not wanted "extraneous matter," it would not have hired Mark Twain. The letters constitute a general report on island scenery and life, with emphasis on the humorous, the incongruous, and the picturesque. They mark a clear advance in his writing; there is greater stylistic variety than in anything he had yet done. He can practice the conventional sublime: "If these mute stones could speak, what tales they could tell . . . of fettered victims, writhing and shrieking under the knife." And he can also write spare and precise description. A coconut palm against a cloudy sky: "The slender stem was a clean, black line; the feathers of the plume—some erect, some projecting horizontally, some drooping a little and others hanging languidly down toward the earth—were all sharply cut against the smooth gray background."

He invents a companion, "Brown"—thus fictionalizing rather than merely reporting his experience, and so taking a long step toward transforming journalism into literature. Brown is a slangy, ungrammatical vulgarian who despises sentiment and "poetry"; when seasick, he induces vomiting by having Mark Twain recite an old Hannibal schoolroom classic, "The Assyrian came down like the wolf on the fold." Brown plays Sancho Panza to Twain's Don Quixote, deflating the pseudopoetry of hackneyed descriptions—

"on the far horizon, a single lonely sail"—and restoring a tone of comic realism by insisting on the realities of heat and dirt and stinks, of "'santipedes" and missionaries. He offers an alternative that the reader may accept or apply as a corrective to the genteel prose and the sentimental and conventional views of "Mark Twain," who also functions in these passages as a fictional character.

The last few weeks in Honolulu were the most important, if not the most pleasurable, of the Hawaiian journey. Mark Twain scored a notable scoop when he interviewed survivors of the American clipper ship *Hornet*; the *Hornet* had burned at sea near the Galápagos Islands, and its crew had reached Oahu after a forty-three-day voyage in an open boat. He sent the first story to the mainland, after writing all night to catch a schooner sailing for the mainland at 9:00 A.M.; it filled the front page of the *Union* and was widely reprinted.

And more important, he met and established a friendship with Anson Burlingame, the American minister to China. In late June, Burlingame and General Robert Van Valkenburgh, minister to Japan, stopped in Honolulu on their way to their posts. With Burlingame was his eighteen-year-old son, Edward, who had read "The Jumping Frog." The party learned that Mark Twain was in Honolulu, called on him in his room, and asked to read more of his work. (He must have brought a scrapbook along.) It was novel, and surely satisfying, to be sought as a celebrity by people of such position, to be told, by the minister to Japan, that "California is proud of Mark Twain, and some day the American people will be, too, no doubt."

But it was Burlingame's approval and advice that mattered most. Rising from poverty and obscurity, he had managed to attend Harvard Law School, had gone into politics and made a name for himself in Congress, then gained a wider reputation as minister to China, simultaneously defending Chinese sovereignty against European encroachments and encouraging the imperial government to westernize itself. Then forty-five, a diplomat of international stature, a mature and sophisticated man of the world—his approval mattered enormously. He gave practical help, arranging for the bedridden Twain to be carried on a cot to the hospital where the *Hornet* crew were recovering, and questioning them while Twain took notes. There were lighter moments—"We just made Honolulu howl," Twain bragged in a letter to Will Bowen, adding that "I only got tight once, though. I know better than to get tight oftener than once in 3 months. It sets a man back in the esteem of people whose opinions are worth having."

The influence of Burlingame can be seen in that last remark. With his age, his prestige, and his experience, he had an authority that made his advice acceptable. As Twain would remember, it was "Avoid inferiors. Seek your comradeships among your superiors in intellect and character: always *climb*." Paine gives an amplified version of Burlingame's advice, beginning "You have great ability; I believe you have genius," and adding "Refine yourself and your work." It was advice, Twain said, that he had never forgotten. Twentieth-century critics have seen this episode as proof of his surrender to the "dominant force" in his America, "the business community." By its standards, superiority in intellect could only be measured in terms of financial success, while "character" meant "the traits that would inspire confidence in a banker." The implication seems clear; wittingly or unwittingly, Mark Twain had sold out.

But it is not necessary to draw that conclusion, nor to read back into the 1860s the modern doctrine that the artist *must* be alienated from, and hostile to, the "business community." Certainly Twain appeared to follow Burlingame's counsel in making decisions and forming relationships that would shape his life and his career: in his marriage to Olivia Langdon, in his choice of Hartford, Connecticut, for his home and of William Dean Howells, the man in America best qualified for the position, as his literary mentor. Yet the effect of those actions on his writing would be at worst neutral and often demonstrably good. He *did* need to "refine" himself, and still more his work—refinement is not necessarily castration—and to "climb" by association with superior persons. It is the word, not the action, that seems objectionable. Burlingame's advice made conscious a principle he had already begun to follow: he had learned the pilot's craft from the best teacher on the river; he had worked for the *Enterprise*, the foremost newspaper in Nevada; he had written for the *Californian*, which had the highest literary reputation of any periodical in the West; he had established friendships with Bret Harte, the outstanding talent in San Francisco's literary coterie, and with Artemus Ward, the most popular humorist in America. Mark Twain can appear the most impressionable of men—but he carefully chose the influences to which he would submit.

In mid-July, recovered from his saddle boils, he embarked for San Francisco by sailing ship. It was a leisurely, twenty-five day voyage. He passed the time by working on a magazine article based on journals kept by *Hornet* survivors, playing childish games with other passengers, even leading the choir at Sunday services; "I hope they will have a better opinion of our music in Heaven than I have down here," he observed. Singing hymns did not signify conversion; it was done as a favor to a shipmate, a minister named Franklin Rising, who had been a Virginia City friend. They were often together; there was no other congenial company on board ship. "He tried earnestly to bring me to a knowledge of the true God," Twain would recall, and "in return, I read his manuscripts and made suggestions for their emendation." It was not quite a fair exchange; presumably Mr. Rising altered his manuscripts, but Mark Twain did not change his life. Once, Twain's memory turned back to Hannibal days. Under the heading "Superstitions," he listed in his notebook half a dozen cures for freckles and warts, or preventives of witchcraft—material of a kind that would eventually go into *Tom Sawyer*.

He never returned to the islands, but he never forgot

them, either. That visit provided the favorite topic of his early lectures, and twenty years later he began, and perhaps completed, a novel with Hawaiian setting and characters.[1] It was not the surviving traces of pagan sensuality that attracted him—he was too much the Missouri puritan for that—but the sheer tranquillity. For him, Hawaii would always be "that far-off home of profound repose . . . where life is one long slumberless Sabbath, the climate one long delicious summer day," offering an image of perfect, unspoiled beauty and a symbol of repose, of respite from the "raging, tearing, booming nineteenth century." But Mark Twain was a child of that raging, booming century; he often longed for escape, but he could not be a dweller in Lotus-land.

"Aug. 13—San Francisco—Home again. No—*not* home again—in prison again—and all the wild sense of freedom gone. The city seems so cramped, & so dreary with toil & care & business anxiety. God help me, I wish I were at sea again!" That journal entry showed the inevitable reaction of return, intensified by memory of the freedom and consideration he had enjoyed in the Islands, and by thought of the decisions he must soon make. There were compensations, though; when he went to Sacramento to collect his pay, the *Union* met his demand of a three-hundred-dollar bonus for his *Hornet* story—a hundred dollars for each column it had filled. That figure was high for the time and place, but it was paid without question. The *Union* was pleased with his work, and so was the public; his reputation had grown. It had grown nationally as well; that spring *Beadle's Dime Book of Fun* had printed, without authorization or payment, three of his sketches—Mark Twain was now worth pirating.

He had no commitments, his future lay open. He hoped to make a book of his Sandwich Island letters, and he planned a return to the "states." Then he meant to travel, to visit Anson Burlingame in China, where Burlingame could offer him "facilities that few men can have there for seeing and learning," and go on to the world's fair in Paris. But he needed something to do immediately. Piloting entered his mind; the war was over and the Mississippi was open. In a letter to Will Bowen, two weeks after his return, he praised the profession, observing that pilots were "the only real, independent & genuine gentlemen in the world," and remarked that if he were two years younger he would go back and learn the river again. Two years younger—but he was only thirty. What else prevented him from returning to the beloved craft? "It is too late now. I am too lazy for 14-day trips—too fond of running all night and sleeping all day." Nothing but his own lack of desire restrained him. As a delightful memory, as a subject for reminiscence, and later as material for literature, piloting was invaluable—but not as a present reality.

There were always the newspapers, and no doubt any daily on the Coast would have been glad to list Mark Twain on its staff. But after months of freedom, how could he submit to the routine of daily journalism? How, on the other hand, could be bear to go back to the shabby existence of a free-lance bohemian? He finished the *Hornet* article and mailed it to *Harpers*, which promptly accepted, publishing it in the December issue as "Forty-Three Days in an Open Boat," by "Mark Swain." He hoped to make a book of his letters for the *Union*, but that would need time. There was a faster way to capitalize on the popularity of the letters, and he took it—he would lecture, while the public was still interested in Mark Twain and in the Sandwich Islands. His letters had been reprinted by the *Golden Era*, the *Californian*, and various newspapers, and were still running in the *Union*.

Lecturing offered the chance of making a good deal of money more easily and quickly than anything else Twain could have done. He had already spoken successfully in public, and his Hawaiian letters would provide abundant material. He hesitated, consulted friends, then gambled, hiring the largest hall in the city and setting admission at fifty cents and one dollar—daringly high prices. His advertising was raucous and original. Posters promised "A SPLENDID ORCHESTRA, A DEN OF FEROCIOUS WILD BEASTS, MAGNIFICENT FIREWORKS" and "A GRAND TORCHLIGHT PROCESSION." Small type below informed readers that "The orchestra is in town but has not been engaged," the wild beasts "will be on exhibition in the next block," the fireworks were "in contemplation," and the torchlight procession "may be expected; in fact the public are privileged to expect whatever they please." In place of the standard announcement that "The program will begin at ——," the posters concluded with an inspired variation: "The trouble to begin at 8 P.M."

Once committed to appear, Twain recalled five years later, he was "the most distressed creature on the Pacific Coast." "I thought of suicide, pretended illness, flight. . . . I wanted to face the horror alone and end it." Going to the empty theater, he waited backstage for an hour and a half. "Then I heard a murmur, it rose higher and higher, and ended in a crash, mingled with cheers. . . . Before I well knew what I was about, I was in the middle of the stage, staring at a sea of faces, bewildered by the fierce glare of the lights, and quaking in every limb. . . . The house was full, aisles and all! The tumult in my heart and brain continued a full minute before I could gain any command over myself." He had spoken in public before, but never had so much ridden on the outcome.

The lecture was in fact a triumph, the hall was packed, the elite of San Francisco were in attendance. If the lecturer had been momentarily paralyzed by fright, his hearers never realized it. They had come expecting to be entertained, ready to laugh or to be moved, and they responded freely, cheering and clapping even before Twain could speak. And they were not disappointed. According to one member of that first audience, "His slow deliberate drawl, the anxious and perturbed expression of his visage, the apparently painful effort with which he framed his sentences, and . . . the surprise that spread over his face when the audience roared with delight or rapturously applauded the finer passages of his word-painting, were unlike anything of the kind they had ever known." That deadpan delivery was calculated; two years earlier he had declared that "the first virtue of a comedian . . . is to do humorous things with grave decorum and without seeming to know that they are funny."

The papers the next day compared him to Artemus Ward—and found him superior; he offered solid content as well as jokes, and his performance was free from obvious straining for effect.[2] He shared Ward's practice of ludicrous exaggeration, but he was a satirist as well, displaying "shrewdness and a certain hearty abhorrence of shams." And if this might have been expected from the Wild Humorist of the Sagebrush Hills, the audience was quite unprepared for his eloquent description of Kilauea. There seems to have been only one dissenting voice; an anonymous reviewer in the *Golden Era* found that "the uniformity of praise is disgusting. They are all afraid of you, Mark; afraid of your pen."

Twain's profit, after meeting all expenses, came to more than four hundred dollars, equal to almost three-months' income from his writing for the *Enterprise* and the *Dramatic Chronicle*—and all this, applause and cash, for an hour and a half on the stage. Mark Twain would spend a significant part of his life on the lecture circuit for the next thirty years, turning to it whenever he wanted to make money quickly, in substantial amounts. But it was not only the money that drew him. He loved the platform itself, the laughter and the applause, the exultation of mastering an audience—no literary success could equal those satisfactions. He might have hated the rigors of preparation and travel, and sworn off lecturing for years at a time, but he always came back.

It was a victory that had to be followed up, and a tour through the mining camps was the obvious sequel. Traveling with his business manager, Dennis McCarthy, an old friend from *Enterprise* days, Twain traveled for a month by stagecoach over rough mountain roads, lecturing in towns with names like Red Dog and You Bet. The tour was a triumphal progress; his publicity was even more boisterous than in San Francisco. In Nevada City he advertised that after the lecture he would, if desired, perform various "wonderful feats of SLEIGHT OF HAND. . . . At a given signal, he will go out with any gentleman and take a drink" and will repeat "this unique and interesting feat" as often as requested. "At a moment's warning," he would "depart out of town and leave his hotel bill unsettled. He has performed this ludicrous feat many hundreds of times, in San Francisco and elsewhere." In Sacramento his posters notified the public that "The Wonderful COW WITH SIX LEGS! is not attached to this menagerie." Neither was "THE CELEBRATED BEARDED WOMAN" or "THE IRISH GIANT," but "THE KING OF THE ISLANDS . . . may be confidently expected."

Audiences were hungry for entertainment. "Be them your natural tones of eloquence?" inquired one listener; and Twain never forgot one introduction: "Ladies and gentlemen, this is the celebrated Mark Twain from the celebrated city of San Francisco, with his celebrated lecture about the celebrated Sandwich Islands."

His tour ended in Virginia City in November. He had left that town, had almost fled from it, under highly embarrassing circumstances, after having publicly insulted various citizens, including ladies. But all was now forgiven, Virginia was proud of his success—even the *Union* welcomed him. The flush times were over, but an audience of eight hundred, at a dollar a head, filled the Opera House. It was a homecoming; he needed no introduction. At Joe Goodman's suggestion, he arranged instead to have the curtain raised, to find him seated at the piano, playing and singing his favorite song, "I Had an Old Horse Whose Name Was Methusalem."

Twain stayed in town for several days, and one freezing

November night, as he and McCarthy were walking back
to Virginia after a lecture in nearby Gold Hill, a masked
man stepped from the shadows and pushed a revolver in
Twain's face, exclaiming "Your watch! Your money!" That
gold watch, commemorating Twain's service as governor
of the Third House, was a prized possession. More bandits
appeared, calling each other by the names of Confederate
generals, waving guns and giving Twain contradictory orders—to raise his hands, empty his pockets—and threatening to blow his head off if he didn't obey instantly. Before
fleeing, they ordered their victims to stay put for ten minutes with their hands up in the air, on pain of death. Taking
no chances, Twain forced the reluctant McCarthy, who
had been forewarned, to stand shivering with him, for
fifteen minutes.

The robbery, a hoax, was organized by Steve Gillis and
a group of Twain's old friends. Afterward, the highway-
men waited comfortably for their victim in a saloon on C
Street. There they listened sympathetically to Twain's
story, gave him some of his own money when he asked for
a loan, then followed him to the *Enterprise* office, where
Dan De Quille wrote up the story and Twain offered a
reward. They suggested that he stay on and recoup his
losses with another lecture, describing the robbery. He
agreed. Then he learned the truth and was furious—firing
McCarthy, canceling the second lecture, and returning to
San Francisco as soon as the stolen goods were returned.
"Since then," he wrote in *Roughing It*, "I play no practical
jokes on people and generally lose my temper when one is
played on me." One paper dismissed the whole episode as
a publicity stunt, another Mark Twain hoax, claiming that
he had written the story after burying his money and
watch, and that the public restoration of his belongings,
and even his anger and profanity, were all "a part of the
programme."

A second San Francisco lecture, on November 16, was
notably less successful than the first. Twain might have

been overconfident and failed to do his level best, or he might have adapted his style to the mining camps; his jokes were too coarse for the ladies, complained the *Dramatic Chronicle*. Apparently the balance between information and amusement had been upset; audiences wanted to learn as well as to laugh. The lecture had been advertised as a farewell performance, and the lecturer was scheduled to sail for the East on November 19, but his sailing was postponed for more than three weeks while he toured the surrounding towns, then spoke again in San Francisco. He must have wanted to redeem his failure; he also needed cash for the voyage. One paper coyly explained that his departure had been delayed by a "severe attack of impecuniosity"; another bluntly stated that the proceeds of the second San Francisco lecture had been seized by one of his creditors.

The smaller towns were friendly—in Oakland the city council canceled a meeting in order to hear Mark Twain—but not very profitable. Much depended on the final San Francisco appearance, and he made careful preparations. Ostensibly given in response to an invitation by twenty prominent citizens, it was advertised as a repetition of his initial lecture with the addition of "an IMPROMPTU FAREWELL ADDRESS, gotten up last week, especially for this occasion." The "farewell address" was calculated to appeal equally to the sentimental nostalgia and the civic patriotism of his hearers. After stating his intention of going home, and describing the changes that a returning exile must expect to find—"gray hairs where he expected youth, graves where he looked for firesides"—he prophesied San Francisco's future greatness, when the whole Pacific rim would "pour in upon her the princely commerce of a teeming population of 450,000,000 souls," when "the straggling town shall be a vast metropolis," when railroads would be built and factories rise, when California's "deserted hills and valleys shall yield bread and wine for unnumbered thousands." That prediction and that almost religious exaltation of the profit motive, were exactly what his audience wanted to hear. But there is no reason to doubt Mark Twain's sincerity; he shared their devotion to Progress.

The lecture was a success. With money in his pocket and favorable notices in his scrapbook, Twain could go back to the "states" and revisit his family with no danger of being taken for the prodigal returned. His four and half years in the West had been the most important of his life; he had made himself a professional writer, he had become "Mark Twain," he had begun to make himself nationally known. But publishers, magazines, audiences, critics—all were to be found in the East. If Mark Twain had stayed in San Francisco, he would never have become more than a provincial celebrity, like Ambrose Bierce. It was time to exploit the reputation the "Jumping Frog" had won for him, and to carry out some of those plans for travel that he had been making.

On December 15 the *Alta California* proudly told its readers that Mark Twain was to travel around the world as its correspondent, touring France, Italy, the Mediterranean, India, and China, free to write from whatever place, on whatever subject, he chose. Twain was not only a humorist, said the *Alta*, but "a keen observer of men and their surroundings—and unsurpassed as a descriptive writer. His letters, it predicted, would "give him a worldwide reputation."

INTERLUDE— NEW YORK

December 15, 1866, was a brilliant day, and as the *America* steamed out of San Francisco Bay, Mark Twain noted in his journal, the sun shone on the steep Marin hills, already green from the fall rains. He was on his way to a new life, but, he reflected proudly, he was "leaving more friends behind... than any other newspaperman who ever sailed out of the Golden Gate." Such a departure promised an agreeable voyage. Only one storm caught them, just out of port; a great wave smashed the starboard bulwark, and "crash went a deluge of water booming aft through steerage and forward-cabin," but Captain Ned Wakeman's seamanship brought them through without serious damage. The sunny days could be passed in reading or games, gossip about fellow passengers, and sneers at second-cabin travelers who dared invade first-cabin territory—Mark Twain traveled first-cabin.

Best of all, there were the humors of Captain Wakeman to delight in. Ned Wakeman was "fifty years old," Twain noted, "as rough as a bear . . . burly, hairy, sunburned, stormy-voiced . . . tatooed from head to foot like a Fejee Islander." He was an inveterate yarn-spinner; tall tales were his specialty, and with his "strong, cheery voice, animated countenance, quaint phraseology, defiance of grammar and extraordinary vim," he could make a story out of anything. In one of his *Alta* letters, Twain reproduced—and no doubt improved upon—a Wakeman tale about rats deserting a doomed ship: "away they galloped over that hawser, each one treadin' on t'other's tail, till they were so thick you couldn't see a thread of the cable, and there was a procession of 'em three hundred yards long . . . they'd smelt trouble!—they'd smelt it by their unearthly, supernatural instinct!" The captain was a man of action as well; discovering that a couple in their 'teens could produce no evidence of marriage, he had them summoned to his cabin at midnight, along with a parson and witnesses, ordered the ceremony performed at once, and concluded by preaching a brief sermon on the benefits of matrimony: "No more dodging—no more shirking the revenue—no more smuggling—no more sailing under false colors."

Wakeman made good copy, and the impression outlasted that short voyage.[1] He would figure in Twain's work for almost forty years: as Captain Ned Blakely in *Roughing It* (1872), capturing, trying, and hanging the murderer of his mate; as Captain Hurricane Jones, given to unorthodox biblical commentary, in "Some Rambling Notes From an Idle Excursion" (1877); as Captain Stormfield in *Captain Stormfield's Visit to Heaven*, begun in 1866 and published in part in 1907, and allegedly based on Wakeman's story of a marvelous dream; finally as Admiral Stormfield in the unfinished "Refuge of the derelicts" (1905), who makes his home a haven for failures—"Derelicts, old, battered and broken." (Stormfield was also the name of Mark Twain's final home, in Redding, Connecticut, completed less than two years before his death.)

Twain and his fellow passengers landed in Nicaragua after a two-week passage. They had to cross the isthmus by "mud-wagon" and riverboat before embarking on another ship for New York. Boarding one river steamer, Twain's bohemian dress got him in embarrassing trouble: "Man at companionway asked me—'None but 1st cabin allowed up here—you first cabin?' . . . and let a whole sluice of steerage pass unchallenged—quite a compliment to my personal appearance!" On a second boat, he alone was challenged. Trivial slights in themselves, but reminders of his still doubtful status at thirty-one.

The voyage north was a nightmare. Cholera broke out on the second day, and within five days, five men had died and been buried at sea, the last of them a clergyman who collapsed while performing a burial service and was put overboard himself a few hours later. To make matters worse, the ship's medicine locker was nearly emptied, and the engines repeatedly broke down. Luckily the passengers were not quarantined when they finally reached New York in mid-January, but the gloom of the voyage overshadowed their arrival.

The New York Mark Twain had known as a young printer in 1854, thirteen years before, had been transformed. "Instinct with a frenzied energy," he wrote, the city had become a metropolis "adorned with a hundred steeples." Its population had passed a million—half of them packed into "holes and dens and cellars of tenement houses." The scale was too large; he could not come to terms with it. It took a day to do a business errand or pay a friendly call—at least, if you walked through the rain or squeezed yourself into a crowded horsecar. In Virginia City, even in San Francisco, he had known everyone who counted; he might have been poor, but he was recognized, he was an insider. In New York he was an outsider, he

counted for nothing. People might have heard of the jumping frog, but not its creator.

He meant to change that, of course; that was why he had
come—to conquer New York. "Make your mark in New
York, and you are a made man. With a New York endorsement you may travel the country over without fear," he
told *Alta* readers. He could never build a solid reputation
on newspaper and magazine sketches; a book was essential,
offering at least a chance to earn prestige and cash. He had
brought with him his letters from the Hawaiian Islands and
a collection of his sketches. But no publisher wanted the
Hawiian letters—Twain would rework them for *Roughing
It*, but they would have to wait more than seventy years
for book publication in their original form—and even the
sketches seemed unmarketable. One publisher received
Twain in his office, learned his purpose, then "made an
imposing sweep with his right hand which comprehended
the whole room and said, 'Books—look at those shelves!
Everyone of them is loaded with books that are waiting for
publication. Do I want any more? Excuse me, I don't.
Good morning.' " Twenty-one years later, that publisher
ruefully apologized: "My chief claim to immortality is the
distinction of having declined your first book."

But that satisfaction lay far in the future. Meanwhile,
Twain did his best to cover New York for the *Alta*. He
reviewed the notorious *Black Crook* show, with its spectacular scenic effects and "dozens of clipper-built girls . . . with
only just barely clothes enough on to be tantalizing." "The
scenery and the legs are everything," he said, while the
speaking actors were "the wretchedest sticks on the
boards." Barnum's Museum he found dull; Anna Dickin-
son, feminist lecturer, impressed him with her "tremendous earnestness"; he attended a "grand Bal d'Opera,"
dressed in "flowing royal robes" and feeling "like a highly
ornamental butcher."

New York then kept the Sabbath—not a drop of liquor
could be had, all places of public amusement were closed,

and in consequence, there was a "fashionable mania" for church-going. Henry Ward Beecher, at the Plymouth Church in Brooklyn, was a star attraction, preaching to a packed house, with the aisles filled by late-comers perched on stools. The most popular preacher in America, he was a master of oratory from whom, Twain noted, a beginning lecturer might learn something about the art of blending "poetry, pathos, humor, satire and eloquent declamation." "Bishop Southgate's Matinee," on the other hand, offered pretty girls in the latest fashions, schottisches and waltzes on the organ, and a choir that sang airs from *Il Trovatore*. The bishop merely read announcements and, as Twain observed, could have been economically replaced by a bulletin board. At Saint Alban's a full "high-church" performance, with candles, a procession of surpliced clergymen, and a boy's choir chanting the litany, shocked and delighted Mark Twain nearly as much as had *The Black Crook*.

But it was a dreary season; in late February, he wrote, at the end of a "calamitous cold in the head," he "felt like the breaking up of a hard winter. I had the blues; and a ceaseless drumming and ringing in my ears; and a deadening oppression of the brain, and a horrible sense of suffocation . . . my thoughts persistently ran on funerals and suicide." He thought a visit home, his first in five and a half years, might cheer him up; at the beginning of March, Twain set out by train for Missouri, marveling at the newfangled sleeping cars and briefly noting the scenery en route—Pittsburg "a vast, impenetrable bank of black smoke, and two or three long bridges stretching across a river."

In St. Louis he saw his mother and sister and noted that steamboat traffic was flourishing again, but he showed no sign of being tempted back to the pilothouse. He was asked to conduct a Sunday school class and retold "The Jumping Frog" to rapturous applause, then tried to find a moral in the story—or so he said—and failed. He lectured in Hannibal, of course, and amused *Alta* readers with a burlesque history of the town and with the story of Jimmy Finn, the reformed drunkard. That tale would reappear in the early chapters of *Huckleberry Finn* with Huck's Pap as protagonist. He spoke also in Keokuk, Quincy, and St. Louis— still on the Sandwich Islands, for he had nothing else in his repertoire. The lectures were a success: "refined enough for the most fastidious, pointed enough for the most obtuse," said the Quincy *Herald*, while the Keokuk *Gate City* noted that Twain had outdrawn Emerson, and given better entertainment. Bad weather kept attendance down at his second performance in St. Louis, but the lecturer literally warmed up his audience by applauding himself at the first purple passage, until everyone joined in. The Midwest appreciated Mark Twain's platform humor as much as the Far West had; the East was still to be tried.

Back in New York, he at last found a publisher for his sketches: Charles Webb, an ex-Californian and old acquaintance. *The Celebrated Jumping Frog of Calaveras County and Other Sketches*, by Mark Twain, would appear in early May—an unassuming little book of not quite two hundred pages in rather large type, with a gilded frog on its cover. The author provided a burlesque dedication: "To John Smith, whom I have known in divers and sundry places about the world. . . . It is said that the man to whom a volume is dedicated, always buys a copy. If this prove true in the present instance, a princely affluence is about to burst upon The Author." The publisher, in a one-page "Advertisement," informed the public that Mark Twain, "The Wild Humorist of the Pacific Slope," had "scaled the heights of popularity at a single jump" with his "Frog." Sales were to prove moderately good for a book of its kind—about 14,000 copies over the next two years—but reviewers ignored it; except for the title piece, there was nothing to set it above the work of other humorists, or to attract an Eastern audience. Publication brought neither cash nor prestige; New York's endorsement had not been won.

Twain was determined to win it, on the platform if not on the printed page. "Frank," said Twain to Frank Fuller, another Western friend, "I want to preach right here in New York, and it must be in the biggest hall to be found." He hired the Cooper Union for the evening of May 6. The tone of his advertisements was restrained, adapted to the more sophisticated Eastern public, the posters announcing simply that "MARK TWAIN will deliver a Serio-Humorous Lecture Concerning KANAKADOM or, THE SANDWICH ISLANDS." Admission was a modest fifty cents, but Mark Twain was so nearly unknown that a theatrical magazine called him "*Seth* Twain" and went on to pronounce him "young, handsome, single, and rich." And he faced competition of a kind that hadn't existed in California. New Yorkers searching for entertainment on the night of May 6 could have chosen among such attractions as *The Black Crook*, the Imperial Troupe of Japanese Jugglers and Acrobats, the actress Adelaide Ristori (packing the theater even though she performed only in Italian and seats were priced at three and four dollars), and Schuyler Colfax, speaker of the House of Representatives, who had a much wider reputation as a lecturer than Mark Twain.

"Everything looks shady, at least, if not dark," he confessed to his mother, but "I have taken the largest house in New York and cannot back water." When advance ticket sales seemed slow, he agreed to "paper the house" and sent hundreds of complimentary tickets to school teachers. When he fearfully approached the hall that evening, Twain remembered in old age, he was amazed to find the streets jammed with people trying to get in. Probably we should discount the story of the traffic jam, but box office receipts totaled three hundred dollars, so there were at least six hundred paying customers. Ex-Governor Nye of Nevada, now Senator Nye, had promised to introduce him, but failed to appear. The lecturer seized his chance, introducing himself and delighting the audience with ridicule of the missing senator. The reviews were favorable the next morning—although Schuyler Colfax got more coverage—and the *Times* remarked kindly that "judging from the success achieved by the lecturer last evening, he should repeat his experiment at an early date." He had not set the Hudson on fire, or repeated the triumph of his first San Francisco lecture, but he had done well enough, and he twice repeated the experiment in Brooklyn and New York. There were other invitations as well, including one from the cartoonist Thomas Nast proposing a joint tour—Twain to speak and Nast to illustrate the lecture with lightning sketches.

But he had letters to write for his paper, and preparations to make—in less than a month, he would sail for Europe! He had left California with a double intention—to make himself a national figure, which was proving to be a slower and more difficult process than he had expected, and to see the world. Now those nebulous plans for travel, which had been churning in his mind for two years or more, were to be realized. In an *Alta* letter of March 2, Twain had enthusiastically reported the details of a proposed "Grand European Pleasure Trip" on board the steamer *Quaker City*, commanded by the expedition's organizer, Captain Charles Duncan. It would be the first pleasure cruise in the modern sense—or at least the first to sail from an American port. The voyage was to last nearly five months, and the itinerary was ambitious: Gibraltar, Marseille, Genoa, Naples, Athens, Constantinople, the Crimea, the ancient cities of Smyrna and Ephesus, Beirut, Joppa (modern Jaffa), Alexandria, Malta, Sardinia, Majorca, Spain, Madeira, and Bermuda. There would be time for overland travel—excursions to Paris, through Italy, across the Holy Land, to the pyramids.

The *Quaker City* was modern and comfortable, offering such luxuries as an organ and a printing press, for the ship's newspaper; there were to be theatricals and dancing on deck. It was advertised that General William Tecumseh Sherman, second-ranking hero of the Civil War in Northern eyes, would be aboard ("Your programme is all that could be desired," he had said), and it was rumored that Henry Ward Beecher himself would escort the party through the Holy Land. Many of Beecher's parishioners planned to travel with their minister. One could not simply book passage for such a cruise; all applications were to be rigorously examined by a committee. But even without that scrutiny, the company would be select. The price guaranteed that—$1,250 in gold, with another $750 at least required for excursions from the ship, at a time when first-class, round-trip passage to Europe could be had for $200.

The prospectus instantly captured Twain's imagination: "Five months of utter freedom from care and anxiety . . . and in company with a set of people who will go only to enjoy themselves." He meant to go, "provided I receive no vetoing orders from the *Alta*," and had already submitted his application, to undergo the committee's rigorous examination. "No veto. He has been telegraphed to 'go ahead,' " his editors added in parentheses. His instructions were simply "to write at such times and from such places as you deem proper, and in the same style that heretofore secured you the favor of the readers of the *Alta California*." The *Alta* was affording him even more freedom than he had enjoyed on his Sandwich Islands assignment.

Mark Twain enjoyed—perhaps needed—movement and distraction. He knew his own ignorance; a visit to Europe would be essential to his education. The assignment itself—simply to travel and to write about whatever interested him—perfectly fitted his taste and his talent; half a dozen of his later books would be constructed, in whole or in large part, around the framework of a journey. And to travel to Europe in the spring of 1867 was to be part of a great national movement. With peace and prosperity restored, and with the attraction of a world's fair in Paris, it had been estimated that at least 100,000 Americans would cross the Atlantic that year. Tourism on such a scale had never been seen before; how could Mark Twain have resisted joining this unprecedented migration?

His application passed the scrutiny of the formidable "committee"—which in fact consisted only of Captain Duncan and was accepting all comers able to pay. At Duncan's office he overheard another reporter asking what notables would be going: "A clerk, with evident pride, rattled off the names: 'Lieutenant-General Sherman, Henry Ward Beecher, and Mark Twain—also probably General Banks.' " But Sherman withdrew when Indian wars required his attention; Beecher withdrew, and forty-five members of his congregation with him; Banks had apparently never meant to go—and Mark Twain was left as the *Quaker City*'s sole celebrity.

While he planned his lectures, prepared his sketches for publication, waited for the departure date, and wondered if they would sail at all, he had to go on covering New York and writing *Alta* letters. Those letters suggest a reporter desperately hunting for copy. He visited the Blind Asylum, and on another day the Bible Institute, where a statistic caught his attention—the institute's printing house could produce "all bound and ready for shipment, TEN BIBLES A MINUTE!" The technology of printing fascinated him. He caught a glimpse of Jefferson Davis entering a hotel and was surprised that only two years after the end of the Civil War, the ex-president of the Confederacy could arrive in New York "as unheralded as any country merchant." He reported on one of Albert Bierstadt's gigantic landscapes, *The Domes of the Yosemite*, finding it "considerably more beautiful than the original." He viewed a painting by an unidentified old master and found it wanting: "six bearded faces without any body to them . . . glaring out of Egyptian darkness and glowering upon a naked infant that was not built like any infant that ever I saw, nor coloured like it either. I am glad the old masters are all dead." He preferred a pair of storytelling canvasses, one depicting a

pair of drunken squirrels sipping brandy from an over-
turned flask, and the other "two libertines of quality teasing . . . a distressed young peasant girl, while her homely
brother . . . sat by with the signs of a coming row overshadowing his face."

He tasted New York low life, too, visiting Harry Hill's
Club House, which offered "liquor, dancing, music,
'waiter girls,' low theatricals, and occasional prize fights,"
and where, he added, the most abandoned streetwalkers in
the city could be found. "Harry Hill's" he wrote, "was
where the *savants* were in the habit of meeting to commune
upon abstruse matters of science and philosophy," and he
claimed to have mistaken a tough named "Bladder-nose"
Jake for Louis Agassiz, the zoologist.

He spent one night in jail. As he explained to his readers,
he and a friend, while on their way home at midnight,
"came upon two men who were fighting. We interfered . . .
and tried to separate them, and a brace of policemen came
up and took us all off to the Station house." They were
locked up, wakened at dawn, and taken to Police Court to
wait for their hearing. Twain talked with the derelicts and
prostitutes with whom he shared the lockup, learned their
histories, noted their acceptance of their fate. In a paragraph he gives the life story of a "bloated old hag" with a
black eye and drunken leer, wearing only "a dingy calico
dress, a shocking shawl," and a pair of worn slippers. She
had been married, then abandoned by her husband; had
lived with another man and borne a child who "starved,
one winter's night—or froze, she didn't know which." She
asked him "for a chew of tobacco and a cigar," and hospita-
bly offered her flask of gin in return.

Court convened at eight, and written on a wall, he said,
was the message "THE TROUBLE WILL BEGIN AT EIGHT
O'CLOCK," the very words with which he had advertised his
first San Francisco lecture. Eventually he and his friend
were discharged. The Mark Twain of five years later, a
best-selling author and respectable householder of Hart-

ford, Connecticut, might not have confessed to such an experience, but the bohemian Twain of 1867 could describe it frankly and unapologetically, without moralizing or condescension: his jail-mates, he said, had been "a pretty good sort of people . . . though a little under the weather as to respectability . . . even the worst in the lot freely offered to divide her gin with me."

The coming voyage seemed irresistibly attractive. "We have got the pleasantest jolliest party of passengers that ever sailed out of New York," he told *Alta* readers, and he had initially been assigned "a splendid, immoral, tobacco-smoking, wine-drinking, godless room-mate"—Dan Slote, who would remain his friend for many years. But in the end they did not become roommates; as the ship's one celebrity, Mark Twain was given sole occupancy of the cabin reserved for General Sherman. With the prospect of pleasure and freedom ahead, a series of postponements of the sailing time made him frantic: "I am wild with impatience to move—move—move!" he exclaimed in a letter. "Curse the endless delays! . . . they make me neglect every duty and then I have a conscience that tears me like a wild beast." His letters the night before departure were indeed filled with gloom and self-condemnation; he blamed himself for having failed to visit Washington and find a government job for Orion. "You observe that under a cheerful exterior I have got a spirit that is angry with me and gives me freely its contempt," he confesses to his family, and writing to his old Hannibal friend, Will Bowen, he already dreads the return: "If we all go to the bottom, I think we shall be fortunate. There is no unhappiness like the misery of sighting land (and work) again after a cheerful, careless voyage."

PILGRIM

The *Quaker City* finally left her berth on the afternoon of Saturday, June 8, 1867 — only to anchor in the lower bay for two days, waiting for the sea to calm. Passengers stayed on board in a pouring rain. But Mark Twain was content — at least they were on their way, and he had escaped from the routines and responsibilities of life on land.

During those two days at anchor and the ten-day cruise that followed before they reached the Azores, he studied his fellow passengers. At breakfast the first morning, he wrote, he "was greatly surprised to see so many elderly . . . so many venerable people." He should not have been surprised; given the nature of the tour and its promotion, the travelers naturally tended to be elderly, prosperous, and pious; for many of them, the Holy Land would be the climax of the journey. The prevailing tone was set by Captain Duncan—a "psalm-singing hypocrite," according to his partner, Daniel Leary. Duncan was a phenomenon, a skipper who never swore and never drank. Once at sea, he held prayer meetings every night in the upper lounge, nicknamed the Synagogue by Twain. The program was formidable, typically beginning with a hymn, then a prayer by a passenger, another hymn, another prayer, a hymn, a reading from the Scriptures, addresses and prayers by the three ministers on board, a closing prayer by the captain— "the loudest, the longest, the most irrepressible & inextinguishable suppliant" observed Twain—the doxology, and a benediction.

If there was more than enough prayer for a pleasure cruise, there were not enough ladies. The men outnumbered them four to one, and of the seven single women on board, among seventy-six passengers, four were girls chaperoned by their parents. Male passengers included old soldiers, preachers, doctors ("I have got the bly-ake—& there's 8 doctors on board," Twain sourly noted), a newspaper publisher, and what Twain called "an ample crop of 'Professors' of various kinds," all collecting "specimens" for assorted institutions. One of these was William Gibson, collecting for the Department of Agriculture and carrying the title "Commissioner of the United States of America to Europe, Asia, and Africa." A dignitary of that tonnage, Twain commented, was surely too much for one vessel to carry; he ought to have been shipped in sections. More pompous still was Dr. Andrews, christened the Oracle by Twain, a pretentious ignoramus who regularly inflicted on his companions information he had just cribbed from guidebooks—information usually garbled in the repetition. There was Bloodgood Cutter, a Long Island farmer and compulsive poet. Mercilessly reciting his own doggerel— *"Whether we're on the sea or the land/We've all got to go at the word of command"*—or distributing his verses, printed on slips of paper engraved with his own portrait, "to any man that comes along, whether he has a grudge against him or not," Cutter established himself as the ship's bore. Although a rich man, he had hoped to earn free passage as the expedition's poet; he was to figure in *The Innocents Abroad* as the Poet Lariat, from Dr. Andrews's mispronunciation of *laureate*. Any occasion could move him to verse. Before they reached the Azores, he had composed "The Good Ship Quaker City," an "Ode to the Ocean," and "Recollections of the Pleasant Time on Deck Last Night"—"which Pleasant Time," Twain observed, "consisted of his reciting some 75 stanzas of his poetry" to a captive audience on the upper deck.

Mrs. Green, a "Frenchy-looking woman" with her dog, a "small mongrel black & tan brute with long sharp ears that stick up like a donkey's," was another oddity. She would hug her pet to her bosom, wrap her shawl around him, and "talk affectionate baby talk," or would put him down and follow him around the cabin to interrupt his "enterprises," always "of an improper and mischievous tendency," meanwhile reciting his "interminable biography" to anyone unfortunate to be nearby. And there was Judge Haldeman, who dressed like a gambler and usually appeared "very peculiar" to other passengers. No wonder—he was an alcoholic hoping to cure himself with morphine. William James, the expedition's photographer, would be remembered by all for one macabre joke. Presenting a magic-lantern show to the passengers, he announced that most of his pictures would be "of places where we expect to go." His first slide showed a Brooklyn cemetery. And there was the pious fool who inquired whether the ship "would come to a halt on Sundays." Mark Twain declared that he "basked in the happiness of . . . drifting with the tide of a great popular movement" aboard the *Quaker City*, but he already had some doubts about his company.

There were three young men on board, sent on the Grand Tour by their families. One of them, seventeen-year-old Charlie Langdon, son of a wealthy coal dealer in

upstate New York, seemed "an innocent young man . . .
well-meaning, but fearfully green, & as fearfully slow."
But green or not, Langdon and his two young contemporaries were better company than the pious elders—even the
"wide-mouthed, horse-laughing young fellow" who carried
a "monstrous compass" and kept "a wary eye on the binna-
cle compass to see that it does not vary from his & so en-
danger the ship."

He made a few friends. Dan Slote, who brought "many
shirts, and a History of the Holy Land, a cribbage-board
and three thousand cigars," was a man after his own heart;
and he enjoyed the dry wit of Dr. Jackson, the ship's sur-
geon, a specialist at guide-baiting who became his favorite
traveling companion. But although a sociable man, Mark
Twain simply could not "amalgamate" with most of the
other men on board. There was "a little difference of opinion between us," he told his *Alta* readers; "They thought
they could have saved Sodom and Gomorrah, and I
thought it would have been unwise to risk money on it."
Evangelical piety and self-righteousness called for ridicule:
one elderly passenger looked "the way God looks when He
has had a successful season," while another was "a sancti-
monious old iceberg who looked like he was waiting for a
vacancy in the Trinity." On their side, the ultrarespectable
considered Twain "a worldling and a swearer," noted that
he drank, and found that his "unfortunate habits" were not
easy to tolerate—he "knew nothing of Eastern society." He
was also the only wage earner on the excursion; simple
snobbery no doubt entered into that disapproval. It was a
clear case of incompatibility; for Twain, the male passengers would be divided into "pilgrims," the pious majority,
and "sinners," himself and a half-dozen others. When seen
at close range, that "crowd of tip-top people," as he had
called them before sailing, became "the *Quaker City*'s
strange menagerie of ignorance, imbecility, bigotry &
dotage."

Of the women on board, only two became close to

Twain—Emeline Beach, accompanying her father, and Mary Mason Fairbanks, a married woman traveling with friends. Mrs. Fairbanks's husband, apparently too busy to travel, was publisher of the Cleveland *Herald*. Twain also enjoyed the company of Julia Newell—a vigorous, self-confident, single woman, sure that she could stand all the hardships of travel as well as any man on board—but on the whole he much preferred gentler, more Victorian females. He developed a closer friendship with young Emma, as he called Emeline Beach, and was to correspond with her after their return, yet she too seems to have been a good comrade only. When a man of thirty-two opens a letter to a girl of seventeen with "AHOY SHIPMATE!" he is no danger of falling in love.

Friendship with Mrs. Fairbanks developed more slowly—she and Twain grew close only in the final weeks of the voyage—but it was to last until her death thirty years later. She was an intelligent and cultivated woman— the only person on board who spoke understandable French. Her marriage was unequal, Twain later decided; she was "a Pegasus harnessed to a dull brute of the field. Mated, but not matched." By the end of their cruise, he had decided that she was "the kindest & best lady" on the ship. "She sewed my buttons on," he confided to his family, "fed me on Egyptian jam (when I behaved), lectured me awfully on the quarter-deck on moonlit promenading evenings, & cured me of several bad habits." Plainly, their relationship was unromantic. He was thirty-one, she was thirty-nine, and that eight-year difference perhaps allowed her to play a safely maternal role. He loved being "reformed" by a sympathetic woman, and the process could be endless; "I know I shall never get reformed up to the regulation standard," he wrote later to Emeline Beach. "Every time I reform in one direction, I go overboard in another." As for Mary Fairbanks, matched with a dull husband, she could safely enjoy the attention of a brilliant, younger man. Together they would play, quite consciously, the roles of mother and son—a game that both enjoyed, and that made their intimacy possible.

Much—more than it deserves—has been made of their friendship. Paine describes Mark Twain, at the outset of the voyage, reading his letters aloud to Mrs. Fairbanks and a little circle of discerning friends, and accepting their criticism. He had in fact written no letters yet because he had seen nothing to write about, and he was an experienced, highly competent professional journalist who surely knew that none of the journal-keepers and amateur correspondents on board, who were sending letters home to newspapers ranging from country weeklies to the New York *Sun*, could teach him anything about writing. It was never his custom to ask for such criticism; in his entire career, there seem to have been at most three critics who influenced his work significantly—Bret Harte perhaps, Howells, and his wife, Livy.

Life was quiet on board, and pleasures were simple— shuffleboard, dominoes, reading in the ship's library, which seemed to consist mainly of hymnbooks and guides to the Holy Land, letter-writing, conversation, gossip, and watching for porpoises, whales, and passing ships. If Twain had seriously expected to "dance and promenade, and smoke, and sing, and make love," as he claimed, he was quickly disillusioned. Smoking was frowned on, the singing was mostly of hymns, and there was little lovemaking (there was only one shipboard romance, and it resulted in marriage three years later); during the Atlantic crossing, most passengers were too seasick for promenading. A dance was tried, but there were not enough ladies; gentlemen with handkerchiefs around their arms had to make up the sets. The *Quaker City* made a precarious platform; "When the ship rolled to starboard the whole platoon of dancers came charging down to starboard with it, and brought up in mass at the rail; and when it rolled to port, they went floundering down to port with the same unanimity of sentiment." Twain himself was a principal source of amusement; as Mrs. Fairbanks wrote for her husband's paper, "There is one table from which is sure to come a peal of laughter, and all eyes are turned toward Mark Twain, whose face is perfectly mirth-provoking." He took the lead in mock debates—"Is or is not Capt. Duncan responsible for the head winds?"—and a mock trial. One passenger, more tolerant than some, found the trial "a laughable affair" and observed that "Mr. Clemens is the ruling spirit and a capital person for ocean life."

Ten days out from New York the *Quaker City* docked at Horta in the Azores, giving the passengers their first taste of the Old World and Mark Twain the occasion to write his first letters, to both the *Alta* and the New York *Tribune*. With the Azores, the voyage ceased to be merely a pleasure excursion for him; until his return, he would be a hardworking journalist. He had contracted to write fifty letters for the *Alta*, and he provided them all, as well as others for the *Tribune*—a total of about 150,000 words. He kept a notebook as well, even during land excursions, so that most of the time when he was not actually sightseeing he must have been either writing or thinking about his writing.

Those first letters set the tone for all that followed; they are aggressively Protestant, aggressively modern, equally impatient with "jesuit humbuggery" and with the backwardness of the Portuguese islanders, who did not even want to progress. Farmers still worked their fields with wooden ploughs, "such as old Abraham used," and attempts to introduce such modern improvements as threshing machines failed because "the good Catholic Portughee crossed himself and prayed God to shield him from all blasphemous desire to know more than his father did before him." The women, Twain noted, "wear a blue cloak and a hood like a covered wagon" and seemed "the infernalest homeliest tribe on earth." It was said that they were not "virtuous," but he could not believe it—fornication with them "would come under the head of the crime without a name." (That comment stayed in his notebook.) He was curious, skeptical, irreverent—the cathedral altar was "a perfect mass of gilt jim-cracks and gingerbread" and the church was filled with "images of old rusting apostles... some on one leg and some with one eye out." But he was amused by his fellow travelers as well. How absurd they often were—astride enormous saddles on tiny donkeys, followed through narrow streets by a crowd of noisy muleteers; panicking at a restaurant bill of 21,000 reis before realizing that it translated into twenty-one dollars, covering dinner for ten.

He was duly impressed by the grandeur of Gibraltar, but Tangier, across the Strait, enthralled him: "The infernallest hive of infernally costumed barbarians I have ever come across." "We wanted something thoroughly and uncompromisingly foreign—foreign from top to bottom... nothing to remind us of any other people or any other land under the sun. And lo! in Tangier we have found it." The crowds on the streets, the "aged Moors with flowing white beards, and long white robes... Bedouins with long, cowled, stripy cloaks, and negroes and Riffians with heads clean-shaven, except a kinky scalp-lock back of the ear," and thousands of Jews in their blue gaberdines, seemed to bring the Arabian Nights to life. He made Tangier, almost unknown to Americans, the subject of two letters; it had offered one of the most exciting experiences of the voyage—all the more so because he and his companions had discovered it for themselves, because they had defied warnings of danger, because it had not been spoiled by overexpectation. No guidebooks had told them where, or to what extent, they should be thrilled.

Some passengers had left Gibraltar for Paris by train, giving themselves sixty hours for glimpsing Spain and France, but Mark Twain stayed with the ship for the more leisurely and comfortable cruise to Marseille. As they steamed through the "richly, beautifully blue" Mediterranean in fine weather, the voyage seemed a pleasure party at last. There was another dance, and the Tangier tourists

made a sensation by appearing in "Moorish" costumes—
baggy white trousers, white blouses, fezzes, and bright yellow slippers. They passed the Fourth of July at sea, celebrating with cannon (the *Quaker City* carried two, for firing
salutes), a reading of the Declaration of Independence, the
singing of "The Star-Spangled Banner," the inevitable oration ("that same old speech about our national greatness
which we so religiously believe and so fervently applaud,"
Twain called it), and a recitation by the Poet Lariat:

We have assembled on this sea
To represent our country free;
Although now in a foreign land,
By her true principles we'll stand.

The celebration concluded with champagne toasts—thirteen of them—and in that rare moment of conviviality,
even the virtuous Captain Duncan unbent: "He made a
good speech . . . the only good speech . . . he said: LADIES
AND GENTLEMEN:—May we all live to a green old age and
be prosperous and happy. Steward, bring up another basket of champagne." That evening the ship docked in
Marseille.

With Dan Slote and Dr. Jackson, Twain traveled on to
Paris by rail—through the France of the Second Empire at
the height of its power and prestige, its crushing defeat in
the Franco-Prussian War still three years in the future.
Even the countryside was orderly, Twain noted, so unlike
sprawling America; here there were no "hogwallows, broken fences, cow-lots, unpainted houses, and mud." Instead
there was "the marvel of roads in perfect repair." Sardonic
entries in his notebook—"French virtue in woman: Only
one lover & don't steal"—show that he brought along with
him the traditional Anglo-Saxon prejudices, but Paris conquered him: "music in the air, life and action all about us,
and a conflagration of gaslight every where!" Taking a
sumptuous suite at the Grand Hôtel du Louvre, the grand-

est of all grand hotels, occupying an entire block, the party proceeded to enjoy themselves. The great international Exposition, the goal of so many tourists that summer, received only a two-hour visit. Far more exciting was Paris itself, ancient yet up-to-date, with its broad avenues, newly created by order of Napoleon III, its sidewalk cafés, its glittering shop windows, and its gaslit streets, the most brilliant in the world. Paris was literally the City of Light. At Notre Dame they were shown alleged nails of the true cross and a part of the crown of thorns. They visited the Morgue, and the Jardin Mabille, for the notorious cancan: "Shouts, laughter, furious music, and bewildering chaos of darting and intermingling forms, stormy jerking and snatching of gay dresses, bobbing heads, flying arms, lightning flashes of white-stockinged calves and dainty slippers in the air, and then a grand final rush, riot, a terrific hubbub, and a wild stampede!"

They saw Paris at its most seductive, and while Twain might occasionally have been shocked, he could not resist its fascination. The evident prosperity of France, he believed, was owing entirely to Napoleon III, "the greatest man in the world today." Viewing the sultan of Turkey and the emperor together at a military review, he believed that he was witnessing a confrontation of the first century and the nineteenth—one man the embodiment of barbarism, the other, of modernity and civilization. France might be an autocracy, and every third man might wear a uniform, but it was "the freest country in the world"—for anyone who could refrain from meddling in politics. Like other Americans then and later, Mark Twain saw no inconsistency between theoretical democracy and admiration for a successful autocrat.

"I think we have lost but little time in Paris," he reported. "We have gone to bed every night tired out." In a stay of only four days he had seen the principal sights, including Napoleon III, he had shopped and dined, glimpsed the great Exposition, and even visited Ver-

sailles—"The scene thrills one like military music!" Some
of his sightseeing had been done in the company of an old
acquaintance, Lily Hitchcock of San Francisco, "a beautiful twenty-five-year-old . . . bluestocking," according to
one biographer, who happened to be staying at the same
hotel. An unsent note to her suggests intimacy but not
love; she had promised him her picture, and he addresses
her as "My dear," promising that he will return to Paris,
"& when I do the Grand Hôtel du Louvre will not be big
enough to hold both of us," but he did not mail the letter
and did not come back. Instead, he caught the train for
Marseille and his ship. "We had a gorgeous time in
Paris . . . I can't write—I am full of excitement," he
summed up for his family.

Italy came as an anticlimax, affording a steady decline in
pleasure and a crescendo of exasperation. Mark Twain and
his shipmates were traveling in midsummer heat; they were
forced to undergo periodic "fumigations" that were supposed to prevent the spread of cholera by subjecting travelers to the stench of burning lime and sulphur; guides were
ignorant and officious. Twain, like all of the *Quaker City*'s
pilgrims, rushed, rushed, rushed. He did northern Italy in
ten days, visiting Milan, Venice, Florence, Pisa, and Lake
Como, and writing several newspaper letters. It was a killing pace, yet typical. "Paris has been done in a day, the
Exposition in an hour and half!" wrote Captain Duncan in
his log. But that, he sardonically observed, was the American way. He failed to add that he himself had planned the
schedule that compelled that frantic dash through Europe.

Twain enjoyed Genoa for the beauty of its women, and
the Cathedral of Milan awed him by its sheer mass—the
cathedral held 7,148 statues, he informed his readers. Usually, his opinions were less favorable. Whatever he saw,
he judged by American standards. Lake Como might be
winding and picturesque, but its setting could not compare
with Tahoe's, while Florence's celebrated Arno, to a man

who had known the Mississippi, was simply "a great historical creek."

He was equally outraged by the omnipresent Catholic church and by the old masters. He could admire cathedrals, but the church as an institution roused centuries-old suspicions. His exasperation became too intense for humor; "relics" and "miracles" seemed the sheerest humbuggery, and he raged at both the priests—"flabby, greasy vagabonds"—who perpetrated those transparent frauds, and the servile, credulous populace that swallowed them. He could accept the human suffering involved in the building of Versailles—that was finished, it had no consequences in his own world—but here he could not forget the beggars outside the cathedrals. That impression would last; twenty years later, in *A Connecticut Yankee in King Arthur's Court*, he would present the church as exploiter of the poor and enemy of progress—the force that kept the Dark Ages dark. All of Italy seemed "one vast museum of magnificence and misery," and the splendor of the churches not only contrasted with that misery but helped produce it. "Curse your indolent worthlessness, why don't you rob your church?" he imagined himself telling the beggars of Florence. The country was, for him, "the lousiest, princeliest land on the face of the earth."

To those who revered the old masters, Italy was the Holy Land. Mark Twain, predictably, was a skeptic. For him, age added nothing to an artist's authority—America, after all, was the country of the New. And he rejected their subject matter. Madonnas and saints bored him, he knew nothing of their lives and legends; religious ecstasies were beyond his understanding; and when the painters concerned themselves with the secular world, he damned them for servility to their aristocratic patrons.

He had no training in the visual arts and almost no experience of them. He could only look, give a literal report of what he saw, and present his own reaction, often humorously heightened. Leonardo's fresco of the last Supper, for example, seemed to him to be "battered and scarred in every direction, and stained and discolored"; the legs of some Apostles were missing; the figures were "blurred and damaged." "So what is left of the once miraculous picture?" he asked; "To us, the great uncultivated, it is the last thing in the world to call a picture . . . it looked like an old fireboard." Twain would not, probably could not, make the effort necessary to imagine the painting in its pristine form, and he doubted the sincerity of those who claimed they could. Philistine, if you like—yet there seems by contrast something fraudulent in the almost contemporary remark of Théophile Gautier that while the body of the painting had disappeared, the soul survived "toute entière," or in Henry James's insisting what while *The Last Supper* is "battered, defaced, ruined," it nevertheless "remains one of the greatest works of art in the world." Twain was following in an American tradition: a few years earlier, Nathaniel Hawthorne, viewing Michelangelo's frescoes in the Sistine Chapel, had also reported precisely what he perceived and felt: "methinks I have seen hardly anything else so forlorn and depressing . . . all dusky and dim, even the very lights having passed into shadows and the shadows into utter blackness." Twain remains the plain man refusing to be humbugged, seeing just what is before him and reporting his reaction—not the guidebook's. His great strength is in his honesty; his great limitation, in his refusal to admit that others might recognize qualities that he cannot perceive, or feel emotions that he cannot share.

Rome lay ahead, the climax of an Italian tour. Twain found surprisingly little to say about it. "What is there in Rome for me to see that others have not seen before me? . . . What is there for me to feel, to learn, to hear, to know, that shall thrill me before it pass to others?" he asked, and answered "Nothing." He wrote only one newspaper letter from Rome (it was lost), and his account in *The Innocents Abroad* contains little personal experience; he offers instead a burlesque playbill for a performance at the

Colosseum—"NEW PROPERTIES! NEW LIONS! NEW GLADI-
ATORS!"—with a review by the critic of the *Roman Daily
Battle-Ax*.

With his shipboard friends Dan Slote and Dr. Jackson,
he baited the guides: when one of them had exhausted his
"enthusiasm pointing out to us and praising the beauties of
some ancient bronze image or broken-legged statue," the
travelers would look at it in stupid silence for as long as
they could hold out, and finally ask, "Is—is he dead?" reducing the guide to hopeless confusion. It was a game, but
also an assertion of their own American identity against
the overwhelming, incomprehensible past. Ancient Rome
might have been glorious, but it was also dead—they, and
their country, were alive. The nineteenth century belonged
to *them*.

Naples restored his energies, perhaps because of the contrast between his own situation and that of the luckless passengers who had stayed with the *Quaker City*; the ship was
quarantined, and all were compelled to stay on board,
sweltering in the heat, while those who had come by land,
like Twain, enjoyed complete freedom. He detested Naples, but that too gave him energy; Mark Twain was vigorous in his detestations. "See Naples and die," ran the
cliché, but Twain predictably found in the magnificent setting no compensation for filth and stinks, poverty, ignorance, and disease. Nowhere else had he seen, and been
repelled by, such masses of humanity, swarming through
narrow streets overshadowed by towering tenements, such
grotesque contrasts between riches and beggary, such credulity before a "wretched religious humbug"—the "miraculous" liquefaction of the blood of Saint Januarius. The
Neapolitan upper classes were no better than the poor; he
was shocked to see a theater audience cruelly deride "an
actress they once worshipped, but whose beauty is faded
now and whose voice has lost its former richness," hissing
and laughing while she sang, then calling her back time
after time with applause, only to hiss again when she reap-

peared. To do such a thing, he commented, a man must be "heartless, soulless, groveling, mean-spirited, cruel and cowardly. My observation teaches me (I do not like to venture beyond my personal observation), that the upper classes of Naples possess those traits of character. Otherwise, they may be very good people; I cannot say."

There was more to see than Naples; there was Vesuvius to be climbed and Pompeii to be inspected. The ascent and descent of Vesuvius filled three letters, a tour de force of comic digression and incoherence, with the writer continually trying to return to his subject—each new paragraph hopefully headed "Ascent of Vesuvius, continued"—then finding himself helplessly distracted from it. The "Descent" concludes with a passage of several hundred words on the canals of Venice, after which the writer announces "*Descent of Vesuvius—Continued.* I will speak of this in my next." There was of course no next.

Pompeii, with its pathos of the commonplace, appealed to his imagination as nothing else in Italy had. The ovens of a bake-shop or the graffiti and paintings of a bawdy house, "which no tongue could have the hardihood to describe," the ruts made by chariot wheels in stone pavements, the hollows worn in lava blocks by theatergoers, these evoked an imaginative effort that *The Last Supper* had not. Viewing them, he could almost reconstruct the past. Everything suggested receding vistas of time and the continuity of human life. His imagination stirred, he could even respond to the art of its people: "Their paintings... are often much more pleasing than the celebrated rubbish of the old masters of three centuries ago."

From Naples the *Quaker City* sailed straight for Athens, where her passengers met with a crushing disappointment. The ship was quarantined; those aboard could view the Acropolis and the Parthenon from shipboard, but they could not land. At least, not legally. The temptation was great, and in the depths of the night Twain and three companions "stole softly ashore in a small boat"—risking several months in a Greek prison if caught—and set out for the Acropolis, climbing over hills, stealing grapes to quench their thirst. At 1:00 A.M., "the citadel, in all its ruined magnificence burst upon us." It was guarded, but the guards proved accommodating; for a tip, one of them even acted as guide. There, in the moonlight, were "the noblest ruins we ever looked upon." On the marble floor of the Parthenon "in lavish profusion, were gleaming white statues of men and women, propped against blocks of marble, some of them armless, some without legs, others headless . . . They rose up and confronted the midnight intruder on every side." Athens lay below, "every house, every window, every clinging vine" distinct and clear, while the "grand white ruin of the Parthenon" rose above them. "When I forget it, I shall be dead—not before," Mark Twain would exclaim in his notebook. Then it was time to return. Escorted by a pack of noisy dogs, they reached the shore as dawn broke, Twain carrying a small marble head as a souvenir. Dodging a police boat, they reached the ship safely. Moonlight, solitude, and danger had overcome the fatigue of tourism; the Parthenon had not only been seen, it had been experienced.

Twain denounced their next stop, Constantinople, hating it as much as Naples. It was "the heart and home of human monsters," the morals of its inhabitants, whether Christian or Moslem, "consist only in attending church regularly on appointed Sabbaths, and in breaking the ten commandments all the balance of the week." Even the dogs were "mangy and bruised and mutilated . . . the sorriest beasts that live." The celebrated Turkish bath was a humbug—a favorite word in his letters—and so was the Turkish waterpipe; the women, although "rather pretty," looked like the "shrouded dead"; the dancing dervishes were only "a pack of miserable lunatics in long robes who spin round, and round, and round"; and the famed mosque of Saint Sophia, he dismissed as "the rustiest old barn in heathendom. . . . Everywhere was dirt, and dust, and dinginess, and gloom." The glamor of the East seemed a fraud, created by lying books.

Sebastopol was their next objective, and Russia came as a welcome relief after Turkey. Granted, Crimean battle-fields interested only the military men on board, and the city seemed nothing more than "a wilderness of battered-down houses" and "a forest of broken chimneys." But the new port of Odessa reminded them of home; streets were wide and straight, the town had "a stirring, business-like look," and everything seemed new. Best of all, "we con-sulted the guidebooks and were rejoiced to know that there were no sights in Odessa to see." (Howells, in reviewing *The Innocents Abroad*, would remark on the amount of "un-regenerate human nature" that it contained, and certainly in that comment Twain catches more of the human nature of the tourist than gets into most travel books.)

Russia welcomed them. The governor of Sebastopol in-quired if he could be of any assistance; all formalities were waived. To be American was passport enough. Unexpect-edly that detour into the Black Sea produced the great so-cial triumph of the voyage—a meeting with the czar and the whole imperial family, who were vacationing at Yalta in the Crimea. The travelers have been accused of "shame-lessly" running after an emperor, but an entry in Twain's notebook proves that the initiative came from the Russians; at Sebastopol, "several gentlemen insisted on our visiting the Emperor of Russia with the ship—said they would en-sure us a superb reception." The tourists declined at first, but at Odessa, by suggestion of the governor, changed their minds and telegraphed the czar to announce their coming. Twain's notebook records their excitement: "Geeminy what a stir there is! What a calling of meetings!—what an appointment of committees!—what a furbishing up of swallow-tail coats!" They were not moved by snobbery alone. Russian-American relations were at their warmest, Russia had strongly supported the Union during the Civil War, and to Americans Czar Alexander II seemed not a despot but a liberator, who had freed the serfs as Lincoln had freed the slaves.

"The passengers on board the American steam yacht *Quaker City* have been paying a pleasant, informal visit to his Majesty," Twain's next letter announced. They were received with great simplicity by the emperor and empress and their two children. The address, composed by Twain, was read to the czar; "He bore it with unflinching fortitude," Twain remarked in *The Innocents Abroad*, when the episode had become distant enough to seem comic. The czar was presented with a copy, which he handed to an official, "to be filed away among the archives of Russia— in the stove." But what an intensely satisfying moment it must have been, for a man who nine months before had been denied entrance to the first-cabin deck of a Nicaraguan riverboat, to hear the address that he had composed read aloud to the Czar of All the Russias. After some general conversation the imperial family escorted their visitors on a tour of the palace, then turned them over to the Grand Duke Michael, brother of Alexander—"a rare brick," said Twain, while his wife was "one of the pleasantest of these pleasant people"—who fed them and talked with them at his residence. Six feet tall, dressed "in the handsome and showy uniform of a Cossack officer," the grand duke charmed the travelers, but the czar impressed them more deeply. They saw absolute power over seventy million Russians embodied in this plainly dressed man who so cordially received them. There were blunders, of course: one of the passengers loudly inquired, "Say, Dook, where's your watercloset?" and Mark Twain himself, noticing that many of the Russians wore red ribbons in their buttonholes, decided to decorate himself in the same way—only to be asked, by a gorgeously uniformed grand master of ceremonies, what noble order he belonged to.

But the blunders hardly mattered; the visit had been a great success. Instead of the brief, formal reception they had expected, they had enjoyed a friendly meeting lasting several hours. Visits to the ship by Russian dignitaries followed, then a "champagne blow-out," and a ball. Twain's partner, he told *Alta* readers, was "the most beautiful girl that ever lived and we talked incessantly, and laughed exhaustingly, and neither one ever knew what the other one was driving at." He was not so decorous in his notebook, calling her "that beautiful little devil I danced with . . . in that impossible Russian dance."

Resuming their journey, the passengers were soon reminded of democratic realities. The crew amused themselves by burlesquing the imperial reception: "the cook delivered the address, and a soiled table-cloth was spread for the imperial feet." Coalheavers and foretopmen went about their work reciting Twain's opening lines: "We are a handful of private citizens of America, traveling simply for recreation—and unostentatiously, as becomes our unofficial state—and, therefore, we have no excuse to tender for presenting ourselves before your Majesty," et cetera. "I never was so tired of any one phrase as the sailors made me of the opening sentence," Twain admitted.

Returned to Constantinople, the *Quaker City* encountered exasperating delays in getting coal, and the travelers, who had already seen the sights, filled their time with souvenir-hunting—Dan Slote ordered a tombstone with his own name on it, carved and gilded in Arabic script. Delay was all the more annoying because the Holy Land, "the chief feature, the grand goal of the expedition" lay ahead of them. But they could hardly have expected the Turks to be concerned about their convenience; they had, after all, just paid a friendly visit to the Russian czar, the mortal enemy of Turkey.

When they finally sailed, the voyage became a pilgrimage. En route they stopped to visit Smyrna and the ruins of Ephesus, cities rich in New Testament associations: "Here Paul and John preached," wrote Twain in his notebook; "here the Virgin Mary lived with John & both died & were buried. . . . Here John the Baptist laboured." And here

Mark Twain's life, at least by his own account, was changed forever. Young Charlie Langdon showed him a miniature portrait of his sister, Olivia, and, writes Paine, "The delicate face seemed to him to be something more than a mere human likeness," and he resolved "that some day he would meet the owner of that lovely face."

Then, at last, the Holy Land. Saddles and bridles, revolvers and bowie knives were produced; guidebooks had warned them that Arab saddles were unsuited to Westerners, and that the country was infested with bandits. Rough traveling clothes had to be packed, along with "umbrellas, green spectacles, and thick veils" to protect them from the desert sun. Mark Twain had made other preparations as well; his notebook contains page after page of biblical citations keyed to localities he might visit. Most of the travelers seem to have accepted without question the literal accuracy of both Testaments; biblical events, locations, characters, were quite as real as those in any historical work. A group of eight, including Twain, chose the longest and most difficult route, from Beirut to Damascus, then "through all the celebrated Scriptural localities to Jerusalem," with a final visit to the Dead Sea before rejoining the ship at Joppa. They traveled in style, with nineteen servants, twenty-six pack mules, and separate tents for cooking, dining, and sleeping; there were soft beds with clean sheets, too, and carpets. They dined on "roast mutton, roast chicken, roast goose, potatoes, bread, tea, pudding, apples and delicious grapes" at a table lit by candles in silver candlesticks—all for five dollars a day, apiece. Camping out in the Holy Land surpassed all expectations. Nothing else would.

They spent twenty-four hours in Damascus—Twain lying sick with an intestinal infection—then headed south into Palestine. They had chosen the hardest route, through the most forbidding desert. As they rode south, the heat seemed intolerable to a man still weak from illness: "The sun flowed down like the shafts of fire that stream out before a blowpipe; the rays seemed to fall in a steady deluge on the head and pass downward like rain from a roof." His umbrella and dark glasses had been packed out of reach, and the glare of the sun was so intense, he observed, that "my eyes were swimming in tears all the time." The country was "a horrible, rocky desert"; he compared it to Nevada and its inhabitants to the Goshoot Indians, for him the poorest and most degraded of humanity.[1] The Palestinians aroused pity, contempt, and finally exasperation—as though they had *chosen* to be poor, hungry, and diseased. Their villages consisted of mud hovels and camel dung; Nazareth itself, the home of Jesus, could show nothing but "dirt and rags and squalor, vermin, hunger, and wretchedness; savage costumes, savage weapons and looks of hate . . . "

Travelers had lied in describing the countryside as beautiful, "a modified form of fairy-land." Even the Sea of Galilee was no more than "a solemn, sailless, tintless lake," surrounded by "a rim of yellow hills . . . and looking just as expressionless and unpoetical (when you leave its sublime history out of the question). . . as any bathtub on earth." Leaving its sublime history out of account, there was no reason to visit Palestine at all, and the sacred history could not be imagined except in terms of the present. When one of the doctors in the group washed the diseased eyes of children and was instantly surrounded by supplicants, Twain saw a reenactment of an ancient scene: "Christ knew how to preach to these simple, childish, ignorant, superstitious, disease-tortured vagabonds: *he healed the sick.*" Disillusionment with the present led to disillusionment with the past; the country and its people, he concluded, were exactly what they had always been. If its inhabitants were "savages" now, they could have been no better in biblical times—"ignorant, depraved, superstitious, dirty, lousy, thieving *vagabonds.*" Palestine could not satisfy the expectations formed by Sunday school teachings, his own childish imaginings, and the writings of devout travelers.

Their party was incompatible, divided equally between "pilgrims" and "sinners." Twain enjoyed pointing out to the pilgrims—those who had been "so wild with religious ecstasy ever since they touched holy ground that they did nothing but mutter incoherent rhapsodies about how wonderful is prophecy"—that, given time, any prophecy of destruction is sure to be fulfilled. In return, the pilgrims preached until he and his fellow sinners had been so admonished and lectured, "so put upon in a moral way . . . that their lives have become a burden to them." At Galilee the sinners had their revenge. The pilgrims' goal had been to hire a boat "and sail in very person the waters that had borne the vessels of the Apostles and upheld the sacred feet of the Saviour," Twain wrote, parodying the language of sentimental piety. "To look upon this picture, and sail upon this sea, they had forsaken home and its idols and journeyed thousands and thousands of miles, in weariness and tribulation." A boat was sighted and hailed, and the price of a cruise eagerly demanded. But when the boatman answered "Two Napoleons" (eight dollars), "faces fell, there was a pause, then 'Too much! We'll give him one!' " In an instant, "that ship was twenty paces from shore, and speeding away like a frightened thing!" The pilgrims shouted after it, offering more money, but it was useless. While they bickered and blamed each other, young Jack Moulton could not resist observing to one of the most devout, "Well, Denny, do you wonder now that Christ walked?"

Sick of heat and desert, of filthy villages and a hostile population, they made for Jerusalem, desecrating the Sabbath by riding all day. They sought Jerusalem both as a holy place and as a place to rest. It disappointed them on both scores. The city was unexpectedly small, "mournful, dreary, and lifeless," offering only more "rags, wretchedness, poverty, and dirt." In the Church of the Holy Sepulcher armed Moslem guards stood ready to keep the peace between Christians of rival sects. The sacred sites—the altar built where the soldiers divided Christ's clothing, the grotto in which Saint Helena found the True Cross, the precise spot where the risen Christ had appeared to Mary Magdalene, the alleged center of the earth—all seemed absurd frauds to Mark Twain. He could almost envy the serene credulity of the believers: "Oh for the ignorance... that could enable a man to kneel at the Sepulchre & look at the rift in the rock, & the socket of the cross & the tomb of Adam & feel & know... that they were genuine," he exclaimed in his notebook.

The travelers were sated with holy places. Bethelehem was no better than Jerusalem; in the Church of the Nativity, "beggars, cripples and greasy monks encompass you about, and make you think only of bucksheesh." Even for pious "pilgrims," a tour of the Holy Land was more likely to shake their faith than to confirm it. Mark Twain's disillusionment was complete: the country was a wasteland, its people savages, and he could not, by any effort of the imagination, relate the "holy places" to the sacred events that were associated with them. "No Second Advent—Christ been here once—will never come again," he sardonically observed in his notebook. And if, as he believed, the present Palestine was a continuation of the past, then God's Chosen People, the ancient Israelites, had been "God's chosen savages." That bitterness lasted. Nearly two months later, writing a final letter for the *Alta* in New York harbor, he sketched an ideal cruise—the ship to be commanded by Captain Wakeman, the passenger list to be made up of California friends, and the itinerary to include "forty days in London [which he had not seen] . . . five months in the Sandwich Islands, six in Egypt, forever in France, and two hours and a half in the Holy Land."

Egypt impressed him with the green fertility of the Nile and the paradoxical combination of railways and pyramids, of European Alexandria and Oriental Cairo. Entries in his notebook show the change of mood: in Alexandria, "Fine streets & dwellings. Fine shade-tree avenues. Luxurious

bowers." And in Cairo (reached by rail), "Beautiful Oriental scenery. Naked girls in the streets—finely built. Noble
shaded avenue leading to Old Cairo." (In *The Innocents
Abroad*, "naked girls in the streets" would be modified to
"a girl . . . dressed like Eve before the fall," but that conces-
sion to prudery would be balanced by the addition of
"stark naked men of superb build, bathing and making no
attempt at concealment.") The travelers were hauled up
the Great Pyramid by muscular Egyptians, and while they
admired the dramatic contrast of desert and Nile, Dr. Gibson chipped off a "specimen." They viewed the Sphinx,
providing Mark Twain with simultaneous opportunities for
a flight into the sublime and a shot at the American
souvenir-hunter: "There was dignity not of earth in its
mien," he wrote, but "while we stood looking, a wart, or
an excrescence of some kind, appeared on the jaw of the
Sphinx. We heard the familiar clink of a hammer . . . "

Dan Slote now left the party to travel through Europe
on his own, and the "sinners" gave him a farewell party in
Alexandria. On the next day, the *Quaker City* turned her
bow toward home and a succession of disappointments;
cholera prevented them from landing at Malta, Sardinia,
and Algiers. Mark Twain may have welcomed that freedom from distraction, for in Egypt he had learned that
many of his letters from France and Italy had been lost in
the mail. It was devastating news; he had no copies and his
memories had begun to fade. Instead of trying to reconstruct the missing letters, he decided to compensate for the
loss with more letters from the Holy Land—filling them
out with facts from guidebooks and with retellings of Bible
stories, since his own experiences did not provide enough
material. He was writing under pressure, with a contract
to fulfill, and if he could only meet his obligations by
stuffing his letters with borrowed history and geography,
then he would do just that—and was to do it again, under
similar circumstances, in his later career. He would be
writing almost continuously until they reached New York,

producing twenty-two letters, totaling about 44,000 words, in three or four weeks. He now asked Mary Fairbanks for help. She read his copy, corrected errors, weeded out Western slang that would have put off Eastern readers. He was grateful to her; she helped widen his audience.

That drudgery of continuous composition was relieved just once, by a week of strenuous touring in southern Spain. Twain and three companions, including Julia Newell, rode all night on horseback from Gibraltar, the only port that would admit the *Quaker City*, then traveled on by stagecoach and railroad to Seville, reaching it the following midnight. They were "somewhat tired" as a result. It was the last of Europe for them, and a satisfying conclusion. Spain seemed the country still of Don Quixote and Sancho Panza, and the Alcazar, the ancient palace of Moorish kings, struck Twain as supernaturally beautiful. The adventure must have appeared even more satisfying when they learned how thoroughly their fellow passengers had been bored at Gibraltar.

There was more boredom and bickering on the long Atlantic passage home; the captain threatened to ban smoking in private cabins; the last few days at sea were stormy. The Poet Lariat expressed himself in valedictory verse:

Long will I think of this good ship,
That conveyed me on this grand trip;
For comfort will her recommend,
To all around, both foe and friend.

Mark Twain's verdict would differ. On his first evening ashore, writing at the office of the New York *Herald*, he vented his accumulated exasperation. The nightly prayer meetings had constituted "a unique feature in pleasure excursions," shipboard life had been made up of "solemnity, decorum, dinner, dominoes, prayers, slander." The cruise had been "a funeral excursion without a corpse."[2]

AUTHOR

He had not exactly come home—he had no home, unless the United States of America could be called
one. "I have a roving commission," he had told Will Bowen
six months earlier, and that phrase described his life from
the time he left Hannibal as a boy of seventeen to make his
way to New York. He had a base, perhaps—San Francisco
and the *Alta*—and he was not yet ready to cut his California connections, but he had no intention of going back
there. He had no money and would have to begin earning
some immediately; he had no permanent employment—a
man could not make a career of writing travel letters for
the *Alta California*; he had only a gift for winning friends,
when he chose to exercise it, and a talent whose range and
value he had barely begun to understand.

But he was not overwhelmed by gloom at the end of a

pleasant voyage, as he had been on his return to San Francisco from the Sandwich Islands. Of course the voyage of the *Quaker City*, at least in its final phase, had not been very happy; no doubt that satirical blast in the *Herald*, written at the very moment of return, had provided a catharsis. With it, he had put the exasperations of the voyage behind him; now he could look ahead and confront again the familiar problem of what to do next. But this time the question had already been partly answered; before the sailing of the *Quaker City*, Senator William Stewart of Nevada had offered him a position in Washington as private secretary, and Twain had written to him in August, accepting it. There were other possibilities. Within a week of his landing, "18 invitations to lecture, at $100 each" had come in as well—he didn't accept them, preferring to widen his reputation first—and journalistic prospects were good; he expected to write from Washington for the New York *Tribune* and *Herald* while keeping up his *Alta* connection.

He left for Washington immediately. "I room with Bill Stewart and board at Willard's Hotel," he reported to his family. He had expected a sinecure, no doubt, with a modest salary, allowing plenty of time for his writing and offering an unparalleled observation post on the political scene. As for Stewart, he was enlisting the sharpest pen in the West on his side. But it was an impossible arrangement—acting as secretary with ill-defined duties to an egotistical senator and sharing his rooms as well. Whatever duties Mark Twain might have been expected to perform, however easy they might have been, they would have conflicted with other work more interesting or more important to his future. And he was a man who insisted on living in his own style; he was not likely to change his personal habits even for a senator.

The secretaryship lasted only a few weeks. Twain bore no malice for the inevitable parting, but Senator Stewart did; eventually he would offer his own, highly partisan story of their relationship in his *Memoirs*. One afternoon,

Stewart wrote, "a very disreputable-looking personage" "slouched" into his room. "A sheaf of scraggy black hair leaked out of a battered old slouch hat" (Mark Twain's bushy *red* hair was his most striking feature), and "an evil-smelling cigar butt, very much frazzled, protruded from the corner of his mouth. He had a very sinister appearance." "I have been to the Holy Land," said the visitor, "with a party of innocent and estimable people who are fairly aching to be written up," and he asked for a stake while he finished his book. The senator read a few pages of his manuscript and appointed him as clerk on the spot.

But Twain's habits were impossible. He upset the landlady, particularly by smoking in bed; she appealed to Stewart, and the senator warned his secretary more than once to behave himself, on pain of a "sound thrashing" if he did not. Twain replied, "All right, I'll give up my amusements, but I'll get even with you." And he did: "When he wrote *Roughing It* he said I had cheated him out of some mining stock or something like that, that he had given me a sound thrashing; and he printed a picture of me in the book with a patch over one eye." Nevertheless, "Clemens remained with me for some time. He wrote his book in my room, and named it 'The Innocents Abroad.' "

Mark Twain not only created legends about himself, as his biographers have had to realize, but he inspired others to create them as well. The senator's story is demonstrably false in most respects. Mark Twain did not write *The Innocents Abroad* in Stewart's rooms; he did the bulk of the work six months later in San Francisco. In *Roughing It* he did not accuse Stewart of cheating him, nor did he claim to have thrashed him. Any such claim would have been absurd; Twain was physically slight, while the senator was six feet tall and muscled in proportion. But as a description, even if exaggerated, of Twain's bohemian habits and appearance, Stewart's account has its interest.

Twain must have meant to write a book about the *Quaker City*'s voyage from the beginning. He had already tried to make a book of his Sandwich Island letters, and here was a subject with much wider interest. On November 19, the day the *Quaker City* docked in New York, the *Herald* suggested that a book about the voyage by that "most amusing American genius, Mark Twain . . . a book written from his own peculiar standpoint, giving an account of the characters and events aboard ship and of the scenes which the pilgrims witnessed, would command an almost unprecedented sale." That thought had occurred to others. Circumstances had changed for Mark Twain: a year before he had hawked his Sandwich Island letters around New York without result; now publishers were seeking him out.

The most flattering offer, and the most exciting in the prospects it opened, came from Elisha Bliss, manager of the American Publishing Company of Hartford, Connecticut. "We are desirous of obtaining from you," Bliss wrote on November 21—just two days after the *Herald*'s suggestion—"a work of some kind, perhaps compiled from your letters . . . with such interesting additions as may be proper. . . . We are perhaps the oldest subscription house in the country and have never failed to give a book an immense circulation." Subscription publishers sold books in great numbers through door-to-door canvassing. The American Publishing Company, said Bliss, had sold 100,000 copies of A. D. Richardsons's *Field, Dungeon and Escape*—an account of Civil War adventures—and "are now printing 41,000 copies of *Beyond the Mississippi*" by the same author. Those figures were enormous for an America with a total population of less than forty million and for books that sold at a minimum of $3.50 apiece—two-days' wages for a factory worker. "If you have any thought of writing a book, or could be induced to do so, we should be pleased to see you," Bliss concluded.

With its promise of fame, wealth, and vast circulation, that invitation was irresistible; it satisfied Mark Twain's most sanguine dreams. On December 2 he replied, asking for details (the delay was not owing to any lack of interest—the letter had taken that long to catch up with him in Washington) and offering to make a book out of his *Alta* letters, which had not been published in the East, after "weeding" them "of their chief faults of construction and inelegancies of expression." That was his way, it was what he had tried to do with the Sandwich Island letters. He defended his method of work to Bliss—he was not motivated simply by laziness: "When those letters were written, my impressions were fresh." He asked how big the book should be, when it would be wanted, and above all, "what amount of money I might possibly make out of it. The latter clause has a degree of importance for me which is almost beyond my own comprehension." Images of "vague, splendid, ungraspable dollars" were dancing through his mind, as they would through Tom Sawyer's when he searched for treasure—and like Tom Sawyer, Mark Twain would find a treasure.

Later that same month, on December 27, he met Olivia Langdon, Charlie's sister. The Langdons were spending the holiday season in New York City, and on one of Twain's frequent visits from Washington, he paid a call on his young friend from the *Quaker City*. He repeated the visit on New Year's Day, and two or three days later accompanied the family to hear Charles Dickens read. All Twain would remember of Dickens that evening was that he had worn "a black velvet coat with a fiery red flower in his buttonhole," and had "read the storm scene from *Copperfield*," but he never forgot that during the reading he had held hands with Olivia.

A year later he told her that their first meeting in the St. Nicholas Hotel had been decisive: "I did have such a struggle . . . to keep from loving you with all my heart! But you seemed to my bewildered vision, a visiting Spirit from the upper air—a something to worship . . . and not a creature of common human clay, to be profaned by the love of such as I." That Olivia charmed him there is no reason to doubt; that she overwhelmed him is less likely. Writing to his family on January 8, he gave no sign of such feeling, merely reporting that he had started to make New Year's calls but "anchored for the day at the first house I came to—Charlie Langdon's sister was there (beautiful girl), and Miss Alice Hooker, another beautiful girl . . . I just staid there and worried the life out of those girls. I am going to spend a few days with the Langdons in Elmira . . . as soon as I get time, and a few days at Mrs. Hooker's in Hartford, Conn., shortly."

He had met two beautiful girls and expected to visit their families—and that was all. In fact, he postponed his visit to the Langdons until the next September. But by January of the following year, his love for Olivia was so intense that it was impossible for him to believe that he could ever have seen her without instantly adoring her. By the romantic convention that he accepted, a perfect love must begin with love at first sight. But the reality was that at the time of that first meeting he did not yet think of himself as a marrying man. He was still a free-lance reporter, an unattached bohemian, quite unable to support a wife in the style he had outlined to his sister-in-law, Mollie, more than four years before, when he was expecting at any moment to strike it rich in the silver mines.

His Washington secretaryship had already ended, but newspaper engagements drew him back to the capital. He was writing now for the *Enterprise* again, for the *Alta*, the New York *Tribune*, the *Herald*, the Chicago *Tribune*, the Chicago *Republican*. It was a time of rancorous dispute between Congress and President Andrew Johnson over the issues of civil rights for blacks and the limits of presidential powers—disputes that culminated in the attempted impeachment of the President. Mark Twain's response was to burlesque the whole affair, and the legislative process in general, in a short piece called "The Facts in the Case of the Senate Doorkeeper." As doorkeeper, he charges senators admission, he continuously attempts to introduce a bill, entitled "An Act Entitled an Act supplementary to an

Act entitled an Act amendatory of an Act to Confer Universal Suffrage Upon Women," and he is finally impeached for his violations of the rules.

He had more urgent matters than politics on his mind; Bliss's offer had to be followed up, and in late January he traveled to Hartford to look into the American Publishing Company and to talk terms. Hartford impressed him with its lawns and trees, its solid prosperity and cultivated society, its two hundred years of history—all contrasting so sharply with the rawness of Virginia City and San Francisco. Writing to the *Alta*, he called Hartford "the handsomest city in the Union in the summer"; it was "the best built and the handsomest town" that he had ever seen. It was also the best behaved; there was not a drunk to be seen on the streets. He was the guest of John Hooker, Henry Ward Beecher's brother-in-law and a descendant of the Puritans. "I tell you I have to walk mighty straight," he wrote to Mrs. Fairbanks. "I desire to have the respect of this sterling old Puritan community, for their respect is well worth having—& so I don't dare to smoke after I go to bed, & in fact I don't dare to do anything that's comfortable and natural."

Despite those restrictions on his behavior, it was a thoroughly satisfactory visit. He agreed on terms with Bliss, contracting to produce a book of five or six hundred printed pages—subscription buyers liked weighty books. It would be based on his newspaper letters, and was to be completed about August 1, 1868. Making the wisest business decision of his life, he chose a 5 percent royalty instead of a $10,000 cash payment for his book. Five percent may seem unimpressive, but Twain proudly assured his family that it was "splendid" and "a fifth more than they have paid any author except Horace Greeley." (Bliss had never published Greeley, but Twain tended always to be uncertain about details.) A formal contract, "between American Publishing Company of City of Hartford and Samuel L. Clemens of New York City" would not be drawn up until eight months later, but that delay did not concern him. He trusted Bliss.

Twain came back from Connecticut in a state of euphoria; as he boasted to an old Hannibal friend, he had made a "tip-top contract . . . with the heaviest publishing house in America." But euphoria could not counter the rigors of free-lance journalism in a Washington winter, with his discontent aggravated by those glittering prospects in Hartford. It was a time of hurried writing, of discomfort and restlessness. Since leaving Stewart, he reported to his family on February 21, he had moved five times and was about to move again: "Shabby furniture and shabby food—that is Washington." He would accept no invitations to lecture; his writing made too many demands, and he was "not going to rush headlong in & make a fiasco of the thing." He broke that rule only once, when a friend, in drunken exuberance, booked a hall for a lecture by Mark Twain and notified the papers without bothering to inform the lecturer. It would have been humiliating to withdraw, explaining that he was unprepared and that his friend had been intoxicated, so he slapped a lecture together, made up of snippets from his *Alta* letters, called it "The Frozen Truth," and delivered it with surprising success.

Meanwhile, he was mastering the technique of the after-dinner speech. At a banquet of the Newspaper Correspondents' Club, he responded to the toast to "Woman." After the expected humorous disclaimer—he did not know why he had received such a distinction, "unless it be that I am a trifle less homely than the other members of the club"—he launched into a mock eulogy, enlivened by precisely calculated irreverence after his careful pauses: "she gives us good advice—and plenty of it; she gives us a piece of her mind, sometimes, and sometimes all of it; she soothes our aching brows; she bears our children—ours as a general thing." There followed a list of notable women of history, including Cleopatra, Desdemona, Florence Nightingale, and Lucretia Borgia, with a delicate reference to the nudity of "Mother Eve," and he concluded with a burst of sentiment—"Jesting aside . . . woman is lovable, gracious, kind of heart, beautiful—and a toast to the best of them all, each man's mother!" He was on his way to becoming America's favorite after-dinner speaker.

Somehow he found time to dabble in politics. He had hoped to get a government clerkship for Orion, who seemed fit for nothing else, but, as Paine remarks, "the powers were not interested in a brother." They were interested, however, in Mark Twain himself. Nineteenth-century America offered no fellowships for writers, but political patronage occasionally supplied the lack; Hawthorne, Howells, and Harte all served as consuls. To help a friend, Twain had lobbied against a candidate for the postmastership of San Francisco—a major political plum—and had been told by Stephen J. Field, associate justice of the Supreme Court, that "if I wanted the place he could pledge me the President's appointment"; a California senator guaranteed the Senate's confirmation. But on careful scrutiny the prospect seemed less alluring. The job was worth only $4,000 a year, if "honorably conducted," and it was no sinecure after all; "It is a mistaken idea that the postmaster of San Francisco, an office which wields vast political power throughout the Pacific Coast, can be an idle man." In short, he could not be postmaster and write his book too. The choice was easy; his ambitions reached higher than a postmastership.

Meanwhile, he had been gathering material for his book, collecting newspaper letters by Mrs. Fairbanks and other fellow passengers. He asked Emeline Beach for information on Murillo, then exploded, "Hang the whole gang of old masters, *I* say! The idea that I have to go drivelling about those dilapidated, antediluvian humbugs at this late day is exasperating." He thanked Mrs. Fairbanks warmly—evidently she had called his work "authentic"—there was nothing, he said, that made him prouder: "*I* don't care anything about being humorous, or poetical, or eloquent . . . the end and aim of my ambition is to be considered authentic." He reserved the right to be satirical, especially concerning Dr. Gibson, the self-styled "Commissioner of the United States of America to Europe, Asia & Africa"— "what he did in the ship is fair prey, & *don't* you plead for him."

But he had written only fragments, and he had contracted to produce a completed manuscript for a volume of five to six hundred pages by August 1. The distractions of journalism and politics left him little time or energy to construct a book. He was restless and discontented—as usual, travel seemed the answer. On impulse, he wrote to Anson Burlingame, who was soon to set out on a mission to Europe on behalf of the Chinese government, asking that he be allowed to go along as "a dignitary of some kind, and privately on my own hook as *Herald* & *Tribune* correspondent." Another old friend, Ross Browne, the new minister to China, offered him "a lucrative position on his staff," which was momentarily tempting.

Plainly, he still thought of himself as a free-lance, on a roving commission, able to escape at short notice from boredom, frustration, or unwelcome commitments by traveling—no matter where. What he really needed was time to write; he asked Bliss for an advance of $1,000, but Bliss was not in the habit of supporting his authors while they wrote their books. Suddenly he learned that the *Alta* had copyrighted his *Quaker City* letters and planned to issue them as a book. He needed them himself, and he wanted to revise them; publication of those "wretched, slangy letters" in their original form might ruin his reputation. It was the excuse that he had been looking for; within two days he had decided that he must settle the matter in California and had booked passage for the trip. "I am so glad of an escape to go to sea again," he admitted to Mrs. Fairbanks.

It had been an unsatisfying, frustrating, distracting winter, a winter of divided energies, spent in an uncongenial city. His brilliant prospects were still only prospects, and he was impatient. "We chase phantoms half the days of our lives," he grumbled to Orion; his hopes so far had turned out to be only phantoms. The inside knowledge he had gained of the political process, of lobbying, legislating, and vote-buying, the detailed portraits of senators and congressmen that went into his notebook—all this would be invaluable five years later in the writing of his first novel, *The Gilded Age*. Meanwhile, close observation of Washington, at a time of seemingly universal corruption and of bitter, partisan conflict between President and Congress, left him with a deep skepticism about the workings of American democracy.

The voyage out was eventful for one thing only, a second and final meeting with Captain Wakeman in a Panama bar. Arriving in San Francisco on April 2, he promptly settled matters with the *Alta* owners, who held copyright on his letters. They obligingly gave up their intention of publishing the letters, allowing Twain to use them instead. With that settled, he could deal with the next question, of how he could earn enough money to support himself while he wrote his book. The answer was obvious—he would lecture. California had not forgotten him, and interest in the *Quaker City*'s voyage was high; his letters were still running in the *Alta*, titillating sinners and scandalizing the pious— one minister denounced him from the pulpit as "this son of the Devil, Mark Twain."

The *Alta* had obligingly announced the arrival of "the genial and jolly humorist" Mark Twain on April 2, adding that "he proposes to lecture in a few days." Newspaper friends could be useful. The lecture was undeniably a box-office hit, with over $1,600 in gold and silver taken in, and the audience enjoyed his selection of highlights from the excursion—the visit to the czar, an account of the sultan of Turkey and his eight hundred wives, satirical comments on his fellow passengers, and irreverent descriptions of the Holy Land. He had shamelessly flattered his audience's prejudices—unconsciously in part, no doubt, for those prejudices were his own. He not only remarked that "we saw no energy in the capitals of Europe like the tremendous energy of New York, and we saw no place where intelligence and enterprise were so widely diffused," but went on to observe, in all seriousness, that "we saw nowhere any architectural achievement that was so beautiful to the eye as the national capital . . . of Washington."

But if his listeners enjoyed his performance, the newspapers were more critical, and so was Twain himself, acknowledging that it had been "a miserably poor lecture." He had tried a novelty that failed, appearing on stage in what one paper called "a singular disguise" and explaining that he was "dressed for a masquerade," turning himself into a buffoon and his performance into farce. It was an experiment he never repeated. He delivered the same lecture the next evening, without disguise, and, said the *Alta*, succeeded in breaking down "all barriers between the man on the stage and the people occupying the seats." The whole secret of Mark Twain's platform art was its appearance of complete artlessness. "Mark," wrote one reporter a few years later, "is a young man of very innocent appearance; he evidently don't mean to say anything funny if he can help it, but people will laugh at what he says in spite of his . . . embarrassed manner."

The lecture created a scandal among the orthodox, although he had promised his sister that there would "be no scoffing at sacred things in my book or lectures." It was denounced as "foul," "sacrilegious," and "sickening"; the speaker was "lost to every sense of decency and shame."[1] A month later the *Call* printed a curious story: Mark Twain had attended church, for the first time since returning from the Holy Land, and had listened to the minister denounce the ridicule of sacred things—concluding with a direct attack on Twain himself. At the conclusion of the service he had introduced himself, admitted that he deserved everything that had been said, and thanked the minister for his reproof. "In the heat of his momentary passion," the *Call* concluded, he had "written many words which his cooler judgment did not approve, and which will not appear in his forthcoming book." But that Mark Twain not only listened patiently to reproof but then did public penance for his error seems unbelievable, entirely out of character. It is likely that the story was fabricated by some reporter to edify pious readers. The *Call*'s standard of veracity was low, as Mark Twain knew from experience.

As he had done nearly two years before, he followed up his San Francisco success with a tour of the mining towns—by steamboat to Sacramento, where he found "balmy summer weather and the peaches & roses all in bloom," through the gold camps in the Sierra foothills, then over the mountains to Nevada, crossing the Sierras by rail, sleigh, and stagecoach, over thirty-foot snowdrifts. "I CANNOT GO A-MAYING TODAY, because it is snowing so hard," he reported to Mrs. Fairbanks from Virginia City on the first of May.

Snow and cold did not deter him from witnessing a hanging, for the first and only time in his life, and covering it for the Chicago *Republican*. The criminal, John Melanie, was the first man ever hanged in Virginia City, which had seen so many killings. But he had outraged public opinion by brutally murdering a woman—Julie Bulette, a popular prostitute. Twain's letter effectively combines objective description with growing revulsion, contrasted in turn with the inhuman serenity of the condemned man, who "considerately" helped to fasten the leather straps that bound his legs together. While Melanie calmly prayed, read a statement, and allowed the noose to be fastened around his neck and the black hood pulled down over his face, the suspense built steadily: "Twenty moments to live—fifteen to live— ten to live—five—three . . . then down through the hole in the scaffold the strap-bound figure shot like a dart—a dreadful shiver started at the shoulders, violently convulsed the whole body all the way down, and died away with a tense drawing of the toes downward like a doubled fist—and all was over!" And so he added one more to the store of gruesome images crowding his memory: "I can see that stiff, straight corpse hanging there yet, with its black pillow-cased head turned rigidly to one side, and the purple streaks creeping through the hands and driving the fleshy hue of life before them. Ugh!"

The return to California offered more agreeable recollections. Crossing the Sierra summit by sleigh, alternating snowstorms and moonlight, "was something magnificent—we made ten miles an hour straight along. We had no such thrilling fun in Palestine." Boarding the steamboat at Sacramento, his status as a celebrity was recognized—he was given the bridal suite; "a ghastly sarcasm on my lonely state," he called it. Then he was in San Francisco again, and it was time for serious work. There was a book to be written, and he had less than two months to do it in.

Settling into his favorite hotel, the Occidental, Mark Twain began the job of revision and addition, working through the nights. By late June he could report to Bliss that "the book is finished, & I think it will do." The *Alta* letters made up the body of his book, but he had revised and added about 35,000 words. Bret Harte had helped him; as he recalled two years later, "Harte read all the MS of the 'Innocents' & told me what passages, paragraphs & chapters to leave out—& I followed orders strictly." One example of that aid survives in an eight-page manuscript fragment concerning seasickness, apparently omitted on his friend's orders. A note in Harte's hand explains that the subject is hackneyed and "won't admit of the frozen truth without becoming rather broad." Twain deleted the slang from his writing and eliminated the character of Brown, the vulgarian. Brown's remarks were often kept, but attributed to Twain himself. The literary personality of Mark Twain was becoming more complex, able to express a wide range of style and emotion, from sublimity to burlesque. Wordiness was eliminated, comparisons intended for the Western reader were removed, possibly offensive words or passages were deleted or modified. He framed the *Alta* letters with introductory chapters on the organization of the expedition and the Atlantic crossing and with a concluding account of Egypt and the voyage home, finishing with his satirical letter to the New York *Herald*, written on the day of landing. He provided new material on France and Italy; he occasionally softened his satire; he reduced the amount of burlesque; he added contrast and variety with reminiscences from his earlier life, inserting, for example, a recollection of his journey by stagecoach from Missouri to Nevada into the description of the train ride from Marseille to Paris; paragraph by paragraph he sharpened his diction and added telling details. Those changes were important; without them the book could not have achieved the success it did. But its most controversial features, Twain's irreverence toward the old masters and the Holy Land, remained.

Those final weeks had not been all hard work; there had been time for champagne dinners at Lick House and for a reunion with Anson Burlingame, home from China after successfully negotiating a treaty with the imperial government. They talked over the possibility of Twain's accompanying Burlingame to Europe, and concluded that it "was both impracticable and inexpedient." He had invitations from "splendid friends in China & Japan," offering him "princely hospitality," he reported to Mrs. Fairbanks, but he refused them. He had promised to accept a "nice sinecure" from Ross Browne, the new minister to China, but had already booked return passage to the "states." He could not afford to travel, he explained; he had gotten himself "buried . . . under such a hill of literary obligations." It was not love that held him back; nowhere does he mention a passion for Olivia Langdon as a reason for passing up chances for travel to Europe or China. He was simply an overworked writer—not yet a lover. He found time, though, to write a lengthy article for the New York *Tribune*, extolling the treaty Burlingame had just negotiated with China and bitterly attacking the denial of legal rights to Chinese in America—the treaty allowed them to be naturalized.

With his manuscript complete, he could arrange a farewell lecture, this time more carefully prepared. His advertising was characteristic: posters carried a fictitious protest supposedly signed by a long list of Californians, ranging from Leland Stanford to "various Benevolent Societies, Citizens on Foot and Horseback, and 1,500 in the steerage," who had learned, "with the deepest concern," that he proposed to read from his forthcoming book and begged him not to—"There is a limit to human endurance." Below came Twain's reply: "I will torment the people if I want to." He announced his subject—"VENICE . . . the most venerable, most brilliant, and proudest Republic the world has ever seen"—promised "pleasant information, somewhat highly spiced, but still palatable, digestible, and eminently fitted for the intellectual stomach," added that while his last lecture had not been particularly good, "able critics" had endorsed his new one, and concluded with a promise that if allowed to talk once more he would "sail positively on the 6th of July" and stay away for two years. "Further remonstrance" followed, from the Board of Brokers, the clergy, and the police—"You had better go, yours, THE CHIEF OF POLICE"—and finally an announcement of time, place, and price of admission, with a note that the lecture would be celebrated two days after its delivery, on July 2, with fireworks, a parade, and a reading of the Declaration of Independence. It was the kind of extravaganza that California expected from Mark Twain.

He won the audience with his opening words, thanking the city for its kindness to him, particularly because there had been "such a wide-spread, such a furious, such a determined opposition to my lecturing on this occasion." ("Laughter," added a newspaper report.) "I never had such a unanimous call to—to—leave, before." ("Great laughter.") There was no doubt about his reception this time; the audience had been large and fashionable; he assured

Mrs. Fairbanks, and "I gave so much satisfaction that I feel some inches taller, now." There had been "No slang, & no inelegancies in it," he added proudly, "& I never swore once." Writing to her six months earlier, he had claimed that he had conquered the habit as thoroughly as he had conquered tobacco chewing, that at the present time "*no* man is freer from the sin of swearing" than he. Mark Twain's "reformations" were frequent and usually temporary; he was to make a similar claim to Livy during their courtship, yet throughout his life he was be notorious for his flamboyant profanity.

Was he submitting himself to Mrs. Fairbanks's influence, then, or merely making changes that he knew were necessary and allowing her, by implication, to take credit for them? Just how seriously we should take such statements is indicated by a letter he had written to her several months earlier, assuring her that in responding to the toast to Woman at a "grand banquet," he had been "frigidly proper in language & sentiment." He concluded that "with head uncovered, & in attitude suppliant but yet expressive of conscious merit, I stand before you in spirit & wait my earned 'Well done' & augmented emolument of bread & butter—to the end that I may go & slide on the cellar door & be happy." Clearly, he is playing his favorite role of mischievous, half-repentant boy—Tom Sawyer to her Aunt Polly. He enjoyed the role of prodigal almost as much; a few weeks before his final San Francisco lecture he had closed a letter to her with "The Prodigal in a far country chawing of husks," adding "P.S.—& with nobody to molest or keep him straight. (!) mild exultation." There was of course a touch of seriousness; Mrs. Fairbanks certainly believed that her advice was useful, and he might occasionally accept it. But he must always be reforming, never reformed; true "reformation" would have ended the game and left no role for her.

On July 5 he sailed through the Golden Gate for the last time. The steamer gave him free passage, another pleasure of celebrity. It was an agreeable, uneventful voyage; after three months of continuous work and travel, he could relax, organizing an evening of amateur theatricals on board, keeping a notebook once more, and writing for his own amusement. It would be years before he would enjoy that much freedom again.

On August 4 he delivered his manuscript to Elisha Bliss in Hartford. He spent two weeks in the city, giving him time enough to admire Hartford again and to report his admiration again to *Alta* readers. Homes were "massive private hotels," each one sitting "in the midst of about an acre of green grass, or flower beds . . . guarded . . . by files of huge forest trees that cast a shadow like a thunder cloud." "To live in this style," he recognizes, "one must have his bank account, of course." He still lacked that qualification. Actually, he had fallen in love not with Hartford but with Nook Farm, an affluent subdivision on the western edge of the city developed by John Hooker, who sold his land only in large parcels and only to prosperous, congenial buyers. With its trees and its little river, its wide, unfenced yards and its expensive, comfortable homes, Nook Farm was the ideal suburb. Within a few years, Mark Twain would have his wife and his bank account, and then he too would build one of those "private hotels" for himself—the most spectacular of them all.

According to Paine, an obstacle threatened publication of Twain's book at the last moment; the directors of the American Publishing Company had heard that Twain's letters were blasphemous and urged Bliss to reject the *Innocents*. A threat of resignation changed their minds: "Bliss had returned dividends—a boon altogether too rare in the company's former history." The story is dramatically appropriate—success should not be too easy, there ought to be obstacles to the publication of a major author's first successful work—but there is no supporting evidence for it. Twain stayed in Hartford for two weeks, consulting with Bliss and working on his manuscript, then returned to

New York, expecting prompt publication. He had done his part, and in late August he was free at last to visit the Langdon family in Elmira and to fall in love with Olivia Langdon.

LOVER

The Langdons were the first family of Elmira. Jervis Langdon was a self-made man who had slowly accumulated a fortune in the coal business. He was not quite a millionaire, but there was a solidity to his wealth lacking in the mushroom fortunes of California, a solidity equal to that of his great, gloomy mansion. Jervis Langdon was a solid man, and an honorable one. He had labored diligently in his calling and been rewarded. He was a man of conscience; he had been an active abolitionist, a member of the Underground Railroad, at a time when most respectable people considered abolitionists to be fanatical agitators. His religious faith was unquestioning, his behavior upright whatever the consequences. The charter of the Langdons' church stated that "no intoxicating liquors shall be used by the members," but his piety did not show itself only in a

narrow puritanism. His honesty could be quixotic; engaged
in a lawsuit, he sent all the evidence he had collected to his
adversary so that they could stand on an equal footing and
the case could be decided on its merits. He was nevertheless—consequently, he might have said—consistently
successful in business. A formidable man, perhaps an ad-
mirable one.

His daughter, Olivia, then twenty-three, seemed a
model of Victorian womanhood. Delicately beautiful, shy,
"refined," conventional in her manners, her piety, and her
tastes, she appeared to embody that purity and spirituality
which the Victorian male regarded as the peculiar property
of the female. Woman, at least the upper-class woman, was
the civilizer, the guardian of manners, culture, morals, and
religion. Physical delicacy seemed the outward sign of in-
ward purity; robust health could appear almost vulgar in
comparison. Olivia's frailty would have had another charm:
it implied her need for masculine protection, perhaps especially flattering to a man himself physically slight, as Mark
Twain was.

At sixteen Olivia had suffered a mysterious affliction.
After a fall on the ice she had remained bedridden and paralyzed for two years; she could be painfully hoisted to a
sitting position only with a pulley fastened to the ceiling.
Then Dr. Newton, a faith healer, visited Elmira. The
Langdons called him in, he threw open the curtains, raised
the window of the sickroom, and by prayer and laying on
of hands persuaded Olivia to walk. She would never be
strong—she could not walk more than a quarter of a mile
without exhausting herself—but in spite of constantly recurring illnesses and prostrations, she managed to live for
almost another forty years, to bear four children, and to
lead a surprisingly full and active life. As yet, though, she
knew little of the world and was unsure of her own powers.
She had been sheltered and petted by her family, particularly by her adoring father: "He was her idol and she his,"
her own daughter would write.

At a distance of well over a century, one can only guess at the nature of that "illness." The manner of her cure suggests that it had no organic basis, or that such basis had vanished. But it did serve to delay her entrance into the world, her marriage, and her departure from the beloved home. Such cases were then so frequent that a Dr. George Beard, who made a specialty of the subject, called it "the American disease." Men could be affected, though less often; at nearly the same age, young Henry James suffered a similar injury, "a horrid and obscure hurt," which prevented him from fighting in the Civil War and seems to have crippled him sexually for life. These conditions were, said Dr. Beard, "diseases of civilization . . . of the nineteenth century";[1] they were frequently "the result in whole or in part of disorder of the reproductive system." Hopelessness was a common symptom: a deep-rooted sense of inadequacy for the tasks of life. Such cases were especially common at the ages of fifteen or sixteen. He cured his patients, by his own report, with massage and electric shock—treatment that would also have depended on suggestion for success. Olivia must have been ready to return to the world; Dr. Newton allowed her an honorable escape from her sickbed.

Into this decorous and prosperous household came an extraordinary intruder—Mark Twain, with his drawl and his jokes, his disreputable clothes and frontier manners, his stories of a world nearly incomprehensible to Elmira. His highly unsuitable traveling accessories—"a yellow duster and a very dirty old straw hat"—must have startled the Langdons. He, in turn, was struck by the closeness of the family, by their fondness for Olivia and their demonstration of it: "Her father and mother and brother embrace and pet her constantly, precisely as if she were a *sweetheart* instead of a blood relation." That open show of affection had not been the custom in the Clemens family, or in Hannibal; "Our village was not a kissing community."

A cousin of Olivia's, Hattie Lewis, was also visiting; she

recalled that "we rode, walked, & sang together, for Mr. C. had a very sweet tenor voice." Quickly enough, his choice between the two women was clear. Hattie possessed a sense of humor and Olivia did not, but Mark Twain preferred Olivia's seriousness to Hattie's nonsense. To make things easier, Hattie departed, after giving her cousin "a hint of what I thought Mr. C. had in his mind & heart," and hinting also that she hoped Olivia's answer would be favorable. Before his two-week visit was over, Mark Twain did ask his question, and Olivia, predictably, refused. But her rejection was not total; he might write to her as to a sister, she told him, and in that permission her final acceptance could be foreseen.

He had never seriously considered marriage before. When Mrs. Fairbanks, six months earlier, had advised him to find a wife, he had laughingly agreed—"I want a good wife—I want a couple of them if they are particularly good." She "would be a perpetual incentive to progress . . . progress from house to house because I couldn't pay the rent." He had a "roving commission" and no fixed income—sometimes no income at all. Now, with his book awaiting publication, with his success as a lecturer, with his steadily growing reputation, he could consider marrying. He had been a bohemian long enough; he was thirty-two and ready to settle. "Livy," as he instantly called her, satisfied his conscious or unconscious requirements; she was beautiful and entirely feminine. Her frailty brought out his protective instincts. She was to be the angel in his house—charming, sympathetic, self-denying—and angels must be ethereal. Twain was unworthy of Livy—he took that for granted. Men always were unworthy of the women they loved. Eight months earlier he had jokingly told Mrs. Fairbanks that if he were settled, he would "swindle some girl" into marrying him, "but I wouldn't expect to be 'worthy' of her. I wouldn't have a girl that I was worthy of.

He wrote his first letter to Livy on September 7, the day before his departure, addressing it to "My Honored

Sister." The fortnight he had spent in her house, he said, had been "the sole period of my life unmarred by a regret." If he had failed in his suit, still "It is better to have loved & lost you than that my life should have remained the blank it was before." He was strong, he could bear suffering: "Of old I am acquainted with grief, disaster & disappointment." It is the language of his day—artificial, yet wholly sincere, his natural language in moments of profound emotion. Deeply in love for the first time in his life, he truly saw his past as "idle," "blank," and "dark," truly saw himself as hopelessly unworthy yet in part redeemed by love. The sincerity of his promise never again to speak "of this dead love whose requiem I have been chanting" is more doubtful. She had pledged herself to pray for him daily— a promising sign—and he in turn pledged that he would at least "grow *worthier* of your prayers, & your good will & sisterly solicitude." The letter is signed, cautiously, "Your affectionate Brother, Saml. L. Clemens."

After traveling with Charlie to Cleveland for a visit to Mrs. Fairbanks, and on to St. Louis to see his family, Twain commenced his courtship by letter. There had been encouragement. "Write me something from time to time— texts from the New Testament, if nothing else occurs to you," he had begged in his first letter, and Livy had written. She sent something better than texts—her picture— and she promised to pray for him. She could not love him, she said, but she would try to make a Christian of him and in the process, as he later claimed to have foretold, "she would unwittingly dig a matrimonial pit & end by tumbling into it." In fact, that prophecy would be only half fulfilled; Livy would marry him, but he would never become a Christian. Meanwhile, tact was essential. His reply spoke of "the high honor & respect I hold you in, my sister," with no mention of love, although love is implied in every sentence. Instead he promised to pray with her, as she had asked. Returning from St. Louis, he found time for a brief visit to Elmira, which was extended by a lucky accident. As he and Charlie were starting off in a buggy to catch a train, the horse started violently. The buggy's seat was loose and flew out onto the driveway—"I lighting exactly on my head in the gutter & breaking my neck in eleven different places," as he explained to Mrs. Fairbanks. But after a day or two of sympathetic nursing, he had recovered enough to go on to Hartford, where he learned that his book was expected to appear in March.

The trip was memorable for other reasons: "Set a white stone—for I have made a friend," he wrote Livy. That friend was the Reverend J. H. Twichell, pastor of the Asylum Hill Congregational Church in Hartford. A devout but broadly tolerant Christian who had experienced the bloodiest campaigns of the Civil War as an army chaplain, often sharing his blanket in the field with a Catholic priest, Twichell knew the world and did not take his ministerial role with undue solemnity. Knowing that people were constrained by the presence of a minister, he often traveled incognito. He had a gift for friendship; in a formal age, he was universally known as "Joe" to his parishioners. "You are acquainted with him as soon as you take him by the hand," Mark Twain observed. He possessed a sense of humor as well; he was not offended at hearing his church called the Church of the Holy Speculators, in view of its wealthy congregation. Having met him at a church sociable, on Sunday Twain "went with him to the alms house & helped him preach & sing to the inmates (I helped in the singing, anyhow.)" They found time to hike together into the countryside; having "seen a New England forest in October," Twain wrote to the *Alta*, he had "looked upon almost the fairest vision the earth affords." Their instant liking for each other was to ripen into one of the three intimate friendships of Twain's adult life.

The fall lecture season would begin in a few weeks. Success mattered more than ever before; a growing reputation might impress the Langdons, and Jervis Langdon must be convinced that Mark Twain could support a wife. Twain himself may have needed convincing. He prepared himself carefully. His subject would be the voyage of the *Quaker City*, using material drawn from his forthcoming book; his title was "The American Vandal Abroad," with *Vandal* signifying a well-meaning, naïve barbarian."

His effects were carefully calculated: "We close with a starchy & a high-toned glimpse at each of the most imposing pictures we saw—Gibraltar, St Peters, Venice, the Pyramids, Damascus, &c—fireworks, you know, then, finis," he told Mrs. Fairbanks. There was a moral—The Vandal should travel to broaden his mind—but it was "an entirely gratuitous contribution & will be a clear gain to the societies employing me," he observed, "for it isn't deduced from anything . . . in the lecture." "Scattered throughout," he added, "would be the most preposterous yarns," which was what the societies paid him for, "to relieve the heaviness of their didactic courses." He would express that self-concept often; his audience was the mass audience, not the cultured elite: "I must not preach to a select few . . . lest I have only a select few to listen, next time, & so be required to preach no more." What was true of lecturing was true of literature; he set himself to become, quite literally, the People's Author, as Bliss would christen him in his advertising, and with rare exceptions he would continue to be satisfied with his chosen role.

The season opened for him in Cleveland, on November 18. That choice was no accident; the support of the Cleveland *Herald*, the paper published by Abel Fairbanks, Mrs. Fairbanks's husband, could be invaluable. More than a week in advance, the *Herald* began printing notices and reminders of the lecture and reprinting Twain sketches. Mrs. Fairbanks reviewed the lecture, characteristically praising its "beauty and poetry" and congratulating "Mr. Twain" for "having conclusively proved that a man may be a humorist without being a clown" and for "recognizing in his audience something more than merely a desire to laugh," and the *Herald* offered its readers a sample guaranteed not to raise a grin—Twain's apostrophe to the Sphinx: "There was dignity not of earth in its mien," et cetera. It was a prose lyric, which would become the most admired purple patch of *Innocents Abroad*. The audience had come prepared to be pleased, defying rain and snow, and Twain had quickly established his uniquely intimate relation with them—so intimate that when he lost his place, he asked his listeners to help him find it. He triumphed again in Pittsburgh, competing with the popular actress Fanny Kemble, who was booked on the same evening. She drew an audience of two hundred, against his fifteen hundred. On the twenty-third, he was to appear in Elmira.

His postal courtship, meanwhile, had continued, suffering and surviving setbacks. He had sometimes forgotten the need for tact, had expressed his love too directly, and had been rebuffed; he contritely admitted the justice of Livy's rebuke for a letter of "hotblooded heedlessness." Now he could try the power of personal persuasion, for in Elmira he would of course be staying with the Langdons. While the family was at breakfast, so Paine reports, "a bushy auburn head poked fearfully in at the door, and a low humble voice said: 'The calf has returned; may the prodigal have some breakfast?' "

Before that visit ended, Olivia had accepted him. The Elmira lecture did not meet his own standards; his delivery was "lame," the whole performance seemed to him a "botch"—not surprisingly, with the Langdons in the audience. But the most important hearer was satisfied. Twain reported the chronology of love to Mrs. Fairbanks: Livy had "felt the first symptom" before he commenced, and the lecture itself "brought the disease to the surface." On Tuesday she avoided him "because her parents said NO absolutely (almost). Wednesday they capitulated & marched out with their side-arms—Wednesday night she said over & over & over again that she loved me but was sorry she did & hoped it would yet pass away—Thursday . . . said she was *glad* and *proud* she loved me!" He heads his letter to Mrs. Fairbanks "Paradise, November" and signs it "Yrs in ecstasy." In his exaltation, he vowed a new life—he would "touch no more spirituous liquors," he would "seek the society of the good," he would "be a Christian." Then he left, for propriety's sake, but now he could write not to an "Honored Sister" but to "My Dear, Dear Livy." Within six weeks of her first refusal, he had won her consent. Even as impatient a man as Mark Twain could hardly have expected better. Leaving home would be hard for Livy; to think of having her parents grow used to her absence "so that at last they would cease to miss me, made me feel as if I wanted father to put his arms about me & keep me near him always—always." But she had made her choice, her lover over her father, and it was irrevocable.

The victory was not quite complete; the engagement was conditional. Livy "must have time to prove her heart & make sure that her love is permanent," and Twain must prove—to her, to her parents, to himself—that he could "settle . . . & create a new and better character." If only he were not a humorist! "She thinks a humorist is something perfectly awful. I never put a joke in a letter without a pang," he explained to Mrs. Fairbanks. He must become a Christian, as the Langdons understood that term. Only then could he "take the sun out of their domestic firmament, the angel out of their fireside heaven." He had no real doubt of Livy's feelings, but she would never marry without her parents' full approval, and that might be harder to win. To the Langdons he must have been an extraordinary phenomenon, quite unclassifiable. Was he a Christian, by the standards of the Congregational church? Was he even a gentleman? They knew nothing of his antecedents. Would he be a faithful and loving husband? Could he support their daughter as she deserved? His only visible asset was his talent—that was undeniable, to be sure, but undeniably it had not yet produced any spectacular results.

On December 1 Mrs. Langdon wrote to Mrs. Fairbanks,

asking for information. At first, she said, she and her husband had instinctively resisted his proposal: "Our parental hearts said no—to the bare thought of such a stranger, mining in our hearts for the possession of one of the few jewels we have." She did not need, she said, "to be assured that he is a man of genius"; she was concerned with his moral nature. Granting that "he seemed to have entered upon a new manner of life, with higher and better purposes actuating his conduct," her question was "from what standard of conduct...did this change...commence?" She makes a quintessentially Victorian distinction: "Does this change... make of an immoral man a moral one, as the world looks at men? or—does this change make of one, who has been entirely a man of the world, different in ... that he resolutely aims to enter upon a new, because a Christian life?" She was inquiring about both his past and his future—had he been "immoral," that is, sexually free? If so, the Langdons could never have given him their daughter. Or had he been merely a "man of the world," who might drink, swear, smoke, and travel on the Sabbath? Had he simply begun to behave in a "moral" manner by conventional standards, or was he seeking spiritual regeneration?

Jervis Langdon's approach was similar, but more businesslike. If Mark Twain applied for the position of son-in-law, he must expect to supply character references. Accepting that logic, and admitting that much of his conduct in the West had not been likely to recommend him "to the respectful regard of a high eastern civilization" (although, he added, "it had not been considered blameworthy there, perhaps"), Twain offered an impressive list of names, including the governor and chief justice of Nevada and the superintendent of the U.S. Mint in San Francisco, and various clergymen, as well as Joe Goodman and other newspaper friends. He realized too late that those friends could know nothing of his transformation; "they knew me as a profane swearer," he explained to Mrs. Langdon, "as a man . . . not averse to social drinking; as a man without religion; in a word, as a 'wild' young man—though never a dishonorable one, in the trite acceptation of that term."

While he waited for the replies, there were other activities and interests in plenty. He had lectures to deliver, as he ranged from New Jersey to Iowa City during December and January; he had plans to make—he must settle somewhere and secure a steady income; he had almost daily love-letters to write, in envelopes addressed to Charlie Langdon, for the engagement was still tentative and private. He could be as hot-blooded as he liked now—"I press this loving kiss upon your lips, my darling Livy & waft you a fond Good-night." His letters are voluminous, rhetorical, emotional. He is filled with self-condemnation and regret for his past life, seeing in it only "*thirty-three years* of ill-doing and wrongful speech"; he analyzes his spiritual condition, confessing that "I am 'dark' yet—I see I am still depending on my own strength to lift myself up, & upon my own sense of what is right to guide me in the Way"; he is overcome by unreasoning fears, he dreams that he has lost her to a rival—"You sprang up & said 'No!—it is over for all time!' And you fled away and left me prostrate upon the floor." Measuring his spiritual progress, he finds himself still "in the infancy of Christianity," but asserts his determination: "I *can* be a Christian—I *shall* be a Christian."

In his desperation he cries out: "Men as lost as I have found a Savior, & why not I?" But desperation and determination were finally not enough. "Why not I?" Because in the end he could never surrender his reliance on his own strength and his own sense of right, he could not experience conversion. His new faith was an idolatry, a worship of Livy, not of Christ: "I believe in you, even as I believe in the Savior . . . I have faith in you—a faith which is as simple & unquestioning as the faith of a devotee in the idol he worships." She continued to be angelic for him; receiving her picture, he wrote ecstatically to Twichell, "When

I opened the little velvet case . . . lo! a messenger-angel out of upper Heaven was roosting there . . . a marvel of beauty." Her image alone compelled respect: "*Any* man's unconscious impulse would be to take his hat off in its presence."

In return, said Mark Twain, she expressed her love, "with Miltonic ponderosity of diction," signing her letters, "with stately and exasperating decorum. 'Lovingly, Livy L. Langdon.' " She sent him printed sermons by Henry Ward Beecher, and her own as well, so "full of a simple trust and confidence," said her lover, that they "would win the heart of a savage." But her letters do not survive; we know them only from Mark Twain's comments. She was uneasy about his reputation as a humorist; as she explained to her mother, she wanted the public, "who know him now only as the 'wild humorist of the Pacific Slope,' to know something of his deeper, larger nature." He seemed to share her feeling, advising her not to read a word of the *Jumping Frog* book: "I hate to hear that infamous volume mentioned . . . I'll never write another like it."

Fixed in Elmira, Livy worried about her lover's apparently incurable tendency to wander, and he defended himself: his roving had resulted from necessity, and "it is my strong conviction that, married to you, I would never desire to roam again while I lived." No doubt he believed what he said—that he had been "a wanderer from necessity" three-fourths of the time and "a wanderer from choice only one fourth," but his past did not support the claim. In 1869, as in 1864, he could truthfully have said that he had never stayed in one place for six months since he was seventeen. And he would wander again, both with and without Olivia, after his marriage.[2]

But Livy had confidence in him and so, in the end, did her father. As Twain remembered, when he reached Elmira in late January, Jervis Langdon held a private interview with him, telling him that his references unanimously agreed that he was "a brilliant, able man, a man with a future" and that he "would make about the worst husband on record."[3] Did Twain have any other friend to suggest? He did not. "Jervis Langdon held out his hand. 'You have at least one,' he said. 'I believe in you. I know you better than they do.' " Unreliable as Mark Twain's memory could be, something like this must have happened. On January 28 he confided to Joe Twichell that he had won a "*conditional* surrender" from the Langdons—provided that he could show that he had "done nothing criminal or particularly shameful in the past" and that he will proceed to "establish a good character. . . and *settle down*." The Langdons overcame their doubts, and on February 4, 1869, he was "duly & solemnly & irrevocably engaged" to "the best girl in the world, & the most sensible." As Twain described it to Twichell, the scene between the lovers was intensely emotional and religious: "On bended knees, in the presence of God only, we devoted our lives to each other & to the service of God." The Langdons had surrendered.

A few days in Elmira, triumphant announcements to family and a few friends, and it was time to return to the lecture circuit, to receive again those precious, voluminous letters. But his own letters had begun to change; they were no longer all passion and piety. While Livy attempted to save his soul, he improved her mind, with due respect for female purity, of course. He sent her books with passages underlined for her attention, and commented on his own reading—incidentally training her to become a writer's wife; he reread *Gulliver's Travels*, saw it as "a scathing satire . . . upon the English government," wondered at "the turbid sea of Swift's matchless hate." He felt that he understood it for the first time and offered to "mark it and tear it until it is fit for your eyes." He warned her, regretfully, against reading *Don Quixote*—"one of the most exquisite books that was ever written," but "neither it nor Shakespeare are proper books for virgins to read until some hand has culled them of their grossness." As a married woman, presumably, she would be free to read Cervantes and Shakespeare; the Victorian age had more than one double standard. Clearly, his rigid sense of propriety was not taught to him by Livy Langdon; it must have been ingrained from his childhood. Livy, for her part, taught him to "unravel the marvelous ravings" of Elizabeth Barrett Browning, to decipher her "impenetrable sentences" and bring the sense to light.

Together they enjoyed the puns, the gentle humor, and placid moralizing of Oliver Wendell Holmes's *Autocrat of the Breakfast Table*, making it a "courting book," reading and marking a few pages, then exchanging it between themselves. Nothing there could sully a virgin's purity. Already he foresaw the pattern of their life together; his visions, he wrote to her, "always take one favorite shape—peace, & quiet—rest, & seclusion from the rush & roar of the world. You and I . . . reading & studying together when the day's duties are done—in our own castle, by our own fireside." It was a prediction that rarely came to pass, at least not for long at a time. He needed the rush and roar of the world; he cherished the thought of retreat more than the reality. When they were married, Livy was to mend his manners, to "civilize" him and make him "a model husband & an ornament to society." Over a year later he summed up her accomplishments to Mrs. Fairbanks: "She has attacked my tenderest peculiarities and routed them. She has stopped my drinking, entirely. She has cut down my smoking, considerably. She has reduced my slang & boisterousness a good deal. She has exterminated my habit of carrying my hands in my pantaloons pocket & has otherwise well nigh taught me how to behave in company." Evidently his earlier reformations under Mrs. Fairbanks's tutelage had left much to be desired, or he had backslid sadly. Livy did not ask for this role, he cast her in it. He would enjoy describing her to close friends as a kind of domestic tyrant, a dragon of propriety—taking it for granted that anyone who knew the frail and gentle Livy, and possessed a sense of humor, would see the joke. Contemporaries did; modern scholars have sometimes failed to, finding Livy guilty not only of mending her husband's manners but of steadily undermining, finally destroying, his genius.

Livy continued to fill his mind; a letter to his mother is dated and addressed to "Livy, Feb. 23, 1946 [*sic*]" and opens "Dear Liv Mother—You are mistaken. I hardly ever think of Livy." But he could tease Livy now in his letters, even about her father's business: "The subject of coal is very thrilling. I listened to it for an hour—till my blood curdled in my veins, I may say." He described the case of an employee who had asked for a raise because his salary was too small to support his family. The logical conclusion, from a business point of view, was simply to cut down the family to fit the salary. "Business is business, you know."

His lecturing ended in early March. It had been a strenuous season; he had spoken fifty or so times, zigzagging across the whole northern tier of states, except New England, and paying frequent visits to Elmira. He had endured the discomforts of winter travel—slow, unheated trains, nights without sleep, meals snatched when the chance offered; he had been exasperated by dull audiences and reviewers—one small-town paper observed that people "would have enjoyed his lecture much more if he had told them when to laugh"—and he had less to show for the season than he might have expected. Lecturing at a hundred dollars an appearance, "a pop," sometimes less, and paying his own expenses was no way to grow rich; he had spent half his takings. But he had profited in other ways: he had survived his first regular season and had established himself as a performer, he had learned that he could please Eastern audiences, he had added to his reputation and advertised his forthcoming book. He considered a spring tour of California but decided against it; Livy had "half a mind to forbid the California journey," he told Mrs. Fairbanks; "She is a small tyrant physically, but a powerful one when she chooses to let herself out." But that was part of his joke; in fact, he did not want to separate himself from her for three months.

For eight months Twain's manuscript had been resting in the files of the American Book Company while Bliss promoted his current best-seller, a life of General Grant. Now the printing began. By the end of March Twain was in Elmira, reading proof with Livy, and so part of his prophecy had already been fulfilled. A pleasant, carefree time it must have been—he could even make jokes now. Several acquaintances had died, and the Langdon greenhouse had been emptied to provide flowers for funerals. When Twain came in, "with an air of dejection, & heaved a vast sigh," Livy inquired anxiously what was the matter. He answered, "I have been in the conservatory, & there is a perfect *world* of flowers in bloom—& we haven't a confounded corpse!" We can imagine Livy's cry, mingling consternation and delight—"O Youth!" He was ten years older than she, and looked his age, but she had already given him that inspired nickname and would use it through all their life together. With his varying moods, his impulsive, often irrational, likings and dislikings, his sudden, overwhelming enthusiasms—whether for a new friend, a new book, or a new invention—with his continuously sanguine temperament, he would always be the youth in their marriage.

The galleys came in slowly; by the middle of April he was only half through, and not until June, after more travel to Hartford and more proofreading sessions with Livy, was the work finished. There was a title to be chosen also; in retrospect, *The Innocents Abroad* appears inevitable, entirely right—but it did not seem so at first to author or publisher. Twain had originally intended *The New Pilgrim's Progress*, but that might seem excessively irreverent—to many readers, John Bunyan's *Pilgrim's Progress* ranked next to the Bible in sanctity. He offered alternatives, *The Innocents Abroad* or *The Exodus of the Innocents*. He preferred the first, but Bliss was unenthusiastic; it would do only if Twain could think of nothing better. He could not. His proposals—*The*

Crusade of the Innocents, The Irruption of the Jonathans—show him groping frantically. Mrs. Fairbanks, appealed to, could propose only grotesqueries—*Alonzo and Melissa*, or *The Loves of the Angels*. "Rubbish," Twain frankly called her suggestions. The choice was finally made on April 30: "'The Innocents Abroad,' or 'The New Pilgrim's Progress' seems to be the neatest and the easiest understood—by farmers and everybody—suppose we adopt it."

With his work done, he waited impatiently through June and July for his book to appear. To his family, he accused himself of idleness; in the past fourteen months, he said, he had "earned just *eighty dollars*" by his pen—"altogether the idlest, laziest 14 months" he had ever spent. As usual, he exaggerated his self-accusation, forgetting that he had also completed a lecture season, written a book, and carried on a courtship. Naturally, he had found time for only a few short pieces. It has been noticed, though, that the words "nigger" and "darky" disappeared from his printed writing, although not entirely from his journals and letters, during the year 1867, and that in the proofreading of *Innocents* every "nigger" had been changed to "negro." Mark Twain was "de-Southernizing" himself, consciously overcoming old habits and prejudices—partly due, no doubt, to the influence of the Langdons. But he was also making himself an *American* writer, rather than a Southern or a Western one.

By far the most interesting piece of journalism he had done recently was an "Open Letter to Commodore Vanderbilt," printed in *Packard's Monthly*. The letter must have seemed a piece of impertinence, from an almost unknown young journalist to the richest man in the United States; Cornelius Vanderbilt's fortune was estimated at more than one hundred million dollars. There is no subtlety, no satire, in the piece—it is a blast of invective. Vanderbilt, said Twain, was "the idol of a crawling swarm of small souls," infatuated dollar-worshipers who "swing their hats and shout hallelujah" for every action of their hero. The mayor of New York, for example, had compared him to Franklin, Andrew Jackson, and Lincoln as an example of the American self-made man. Vanderbilt was not only corrupt, mean, vindictive—that was to be expected—but a bore "whose flattest sayings are spread across the country" by an adulatory press. "Do something useful in the few years you have left," Twain urged him, but realized that it would be more in character for him to buy his eternal salvation at bargain price, with a deathbed repentance. Twain's indignation is powerfully expressed but purely personal. The system that created Vanderbilts, or made such careers possible, is left unmentioned; the letter deals with its subject purely as an individual sinner, not as representative of a class or as a product of the American economic and political system.

Meanwhile, no book appeared. At the end of July Twain exploded in a bitterly sarcastic letter to Bliss, pointing out that *Innocents* had originally been scheduled as a "fall book"—for the fall of 1868, that is—and asking, "After it is done being a fall book [for the fall of 1869] upon what argument shall you perceive that it will be best to make another spring book of it again? And—When it is done being another spring book again, upon what argument shall you perceive that it will be best to-to-to—" In a lengthy reply, Bliss soothed and explained and pointed out discrepancies in Twain's accusations, humorously advising him in the future to "just come out and call me a d———d cheat & scoundrel—which will really . . . cover the whole ground & be a great deal more brief," and sent his angry author three presentation copies. One of them, gilt-edged, went to Olivia. It was a masterly performance but was hardly needed. Twain might seem the most irascible of authors, but to send an exasperated letter was for him a satisfying action in itself. He was quite ready to be pacified; a week later, although the situation had not changed, he acknowledged that he had written "a wicked letter," and when he saw the finished book, it seemed "the handsomest book of the season." When a month had passed, and the success of *Innocents* was already beyond doubt, he admitted that he had been wrong. "But I am only impatient about things once or twice a day—and then I sit down and write letters. The rest of the time I am serene." Recognizing his own inflammatory temper, he would sometimes deliberately work off his anger in a furious letter, never meant to be mailed.

In fact, Bliss had been hard at work. The printing of *Innocents* had begun in February; canvassers had been recruited and the sales campaign had commenced months before Twain's letter. The success or failure of a subscription book was decided by the preliminary canvassing. Long before the books began to issue from the bindery, the agents—disabled war veterans, school teachers, clergymen—would receive their prospectuses, including table of contents, fifty or so selected pages—with enticing illustrations, their sample bindings, and their order forms. Elaborate instructions from the publisher emphasized the importance of hard work and positive thinking, provided ready answers to all possible objections from the prospect. Practical advice on sales technique was offered—when a prospect asked for the price, the canvasser should always quote the most expensive binding first, then work down. There were even instructions for making a quick and graceful exit after the sale was closed. Then the canvass would commence. In the glow of Mark Twain's imagination it became more than simply a sales campaign; it was a continent-wide military operation, with its "foragers" and "skirmishers" besieging the villages and penetrating every corner of the country.

Canvassers practiced the hard sell, and it would be naive to see them as missionaries of culture. Profit came first. Yet while the book agent might seem a bore and a nuisance to sophisticated city-dwellers, he or she was often a welcome visitor in the countryside, breaking the isolation of hamlets and farms. And, undeniably, the canvasser carried books where otherwise books would never have gone. When a book of his sold 60,000 copies, Twain once remarked, he knew that 50,000 of them "went to people who don't visit bookstores." The books were expensive by the standards of the time; at $3.50 in the cheapest binding, *Innocents* was double the price of the average book in a bookstore. Designed for an unsophisticated public, subscription books were likely to be gaudily bound and abundantly illustrated. Readers liked pictures but were not particular about quality or authenticity—Bliss sometimes transferred cuts from one book to another.

Solid, factual works were in demand: such titles as P. T. Barnum's *Struggles and Triumphs*; Horace Greeley's *American Conflict*, a history of the Civil War; or Matthew Smith's *Twenty Years Among the Bulls and Bears of Wall Street* lured the buyer. "Mighty few books that come strictly under the head of *literature* will sell by subscription," Twain once observed, and his friend Howells suggested that if Twain's own books sold, they did so only because "the subscription public never knew what good literature they were." But Howells, as editor of the highbrow *Atlantic Monthly* and a novelist who published only through regular channels, naturally despised the subscription public, and perhaps envied his friend's success.

The books were for display as much as for use—center table books, they were called. One reader who first encountered *Innocents* in his childhood recalled the typical setting: the marble-topped table with its "heavy mahogany legs chiselled into writhing curves." On it rested the family Bible, flanked by subscription books, usually added to at the rate of one a year, each one "thick and heavy and emblazoned with gold," with texts featuring "platitudes, patriotism, poetry"—bearing such titles as *Mother, Home, & Heaven, Poetic Gems, Lives of the Presidents*, or *Manual of Deportment and Social Usage*. It was a surprise—and a blessed relief—to find the *Innocents* in that tiresome company.

Subscription publishing offered a writer access to a great

audience, unreachable through conventional publishers; it offered sales and profits on a scale unapproached by "trade" firms and their authors. Of the classic nineteenth-century American writers, no other approached Twain's sales—his least successful book sold better than Henry James's most popular novel, *Daisy Miller*—or Twain's earnings—$105,000 from his subscription books between 1869 and 1881. By contrast, Harte's *Luck of Roaring Camp*, published at the height of his popularity, sold 26,000 copies in two years, bringing him royalties of slightly more than $3,000; Howells's *Foregone Conclusion*, his best-selling novel, earned him about as much. Authors could not have survived on such earnings alone; the novels of Howells and James, for example, were commonly serialized, and the serial rights brought more than the books. But while subscription publication might bring riches, comparatively speaking, to a lucky author, it had its drawbacks: subscription books were not considered "literature," they were not often reviewed by the major journals, and subscription authors might not be taken seriously by polite, or intellectual, readers. The long delay in Mark Twain's recognition by "serious" readers and critics was due not only to his classification as a "humorist"—lowest species of the literary world—but to the way his books were sold.

Twain's decision to publish with Bliss helped determine his career as a writer—determined it for the worse, some critics believe. "The standards by which he gauged his success—40,000 advance orders and impressive royalty checks . . . often served as substitutes for literary or aesthetic value," one scholar has written. Subscription publishing taught him to consider his books as merchandise; to satisfy the need for sheer bulk, he might extend them far beyond their proper length, stuffing them with irrelevant or inferior material, as he did with *Roughing It* and *Life on the Mississippi*. Certainly Twain could be crass enough at times, gleefully calculating his sales and royalties, gloating to a friend that thirty tons of paper had gone into the printing of *Innocents Abroad*. But would his books have been written at all without the prospect of those sales and royalties? Probably he desired an audience at least as much as money, but the audience could be measured only through sales figures. And it was not the American Book Company, but his training as a newspaperman, beginning in the office of the Hannibal *Journal*, that taught him to aim for the widest readership and to consider his own writings as salable merchandise. Subscription publishing made him literally the people's author; his career and his work are unimaginable without it.

The success of *Innocents* was all that Mark Twain could have expected, probably even more than he had hoped for. Within a year the book had sold almost 70,000 copies, about equally divided between the basic $3.50 cloth binding and the $5.00 leather-bound version. During that first year, Twain received an average of from twelve to fifteen hundred dollars a month. For the only time in his life, he was thoroughly satisfied with a publisher and told him so: Bliss was "running" the book "in staving, tip-top, first-class style"; he was a general who had planned and executed a brilliant campaign, successfully maneuvering his army of canvassers across the continent. Sales slowed after the first year, but in three years *Innocents* reached the 100,000 mark, and to the end of Twain's life it remained his most popular work. The Innocents traveled farther in book form than they ever had on the *Quaker City*: "I have seen the book in logging camps in Wisconsin & mining camps in Colorado, in the farm houses of the North-West," his shipmate Jack Van Nostrand noted in 1875, and a year earlier Charles Warren Stoddard, a California friend, reported seeing in the Vatican picture gallery "a lovely girl, dreaming over the pictures" and holding in her hand not a Baedeker but *The Innocents Abroad*.

What did the subscribers get for their $3.50 or $5.00? Physically, a thick book in a thick binding, with abundant, generally bad, illustrations—visible value for money. They also received a rich entertainment, a book that was, and remains, unique. Books of travel were commonplace, to be sure; Irving, Cooper, Longfellow, Emerson, Hawthorne, Howells, James, all produced one or more. But this book was different. Bliss's advertising had been precisely accurate in promising "a description of the Countries, Nations, Incidents and Adventures, seen and passed through by the party, as they appeared to the eyes of the AUTHOR, *Differing materially in several points* from descriptions usually given." And perhaps different most of all in that, as the author explained in his preface, he made "small pretense of showing anyone how he *ought* to look" at the sights of Europe— instead suggesting to the reader "how he would be likely to see Europe and the East if he looked at them with his own eyes instead of the eyes of those who traveled in those countries before him." Readers enjoyed the author's iconoclasm, whether at the expense of the old masters or the Holy Land, and his habit of evaluating everything in American terms. Clearly his irreverence was a "tip-top feature," Twain wrote to Bliss, adding with tongue in cheek that he wished of course that there were not an irreverent word in the book. *The Innocents Abroad* expressed a brash self-confidence growing out of Union victory in the Civil War, a conviction that the future belonged to America— Europe could have the past. And finally, its pleasures could be shared; it was ideal for reading aloud in the family circle.

Innocents differed in another important respect from its predecessors—it was better written. As one of Twain's most perceptive critics has observed, its style is characterized by a remarkable "purity of diction and total clarity." Twain had shown his mastery of the vernacular in "The Jumping Frog"; with *Innocents* "he proved himself a master of the English language." The subscription public responded to those qualities. The general verdict was summed up by Josh Billings, a fellow humorist: "It [*Innocents*] has all the integrity of the multiplication table, and at

the same time, is as full of deviltry as 'Gulliver's Travels.' "
It's a proof of continuing life in the book that after more
than a hundred years, *Innocents* retains its power to scandal-
ize; "an anomaly of embarrassing chauvinism and the pur-
plest prose," one recent scholar has called it, somehow
forgetting that it is funny.

For a subscription book, *Innocents* received a considerable
amount of attention from reviewers. It was pirated in Canada and published in England, and the British reviewers
admitted that this unknown American could be amusing,
even though "in the presence of the ancients he generally
indulges in facetiousness of a low order," and there was
some uneasiness as to just when he was joking. Still, "his
fun, if not very refined, is often tolerable in its way."
American reviewers produced the standard adjectives for
American humor—"audacious," "exaggerated," "extravagant." In the *Overland Monthly* Bret Harte wrote that
Twain's rank as the "foremost among Western humorists"
was now confirmed. The *Nation* found him guilty of the
usual faults of American humorists but placed him at the
head of the class. References to Twain as a "Western" humorist would soon disappear. With *Innocents* he had expressed the attitude of a new generation toward Europe,
and had permanently established himself as a national
writer. He had found his audience.

Best of all, and most unexpected, the book was approved
by the austerely intellectual *Atlantic*, which was accepted
without question as the highest critical authority in the
land. But the *Atlantic* had heard of him; a year before, one
regular contributor, James Parton, had suggested that the
magazine could be made much more popular by printing
"more articles connected with life than literature" and by
engaging "a writer named Mark Twain." The *Atlantic*'s reviewer praised Mark Twain's humor, based on "excellent
sense and good feeling," his realism, and his satire, concluding that while "it is no business of ours to fix his rank
among the humorists California has given us . . . we think

he is, in an entirely different way from all the others, quite
worthy of the company of the best." That reviewer was the
magazine's young associate editor, William Dean Howells;
reviewer and author would shortly commence a lifelong
friendship. Perhaps the most penetrating comment came
more than twenty years later from Thomas Sergeant Perry,
who drew an unexpected parallel between Whitman and
Twain, finding them "fellow-workers—one with a mysti-
cal seriousness, the other with a chilling contempt—in the
task of exploding conventions." Twain's contempt for the
past, Perry believed, expressed the true feelings of America, outside of the "thin varnish of European cultivation on
the seashore." That may well have been the final effect of
Innocents, although Twain lacked Whitman's consistency of
attitude and purpose; he was not consciously urging the
Muse to "cross out those immensely overpaid accounts,
that matter of Troy and Achilles's wrath, and Aeneas's,
Odysseus's wanderings," and emigrate to America.

Whatever his hopes might have been for *Innocents*, in
planning his future as a married man, Mark Twain had
placed no reliance whatever on the book. He knew the
financial inequality of his marriage—Livy would be a
wealthy woman; when her father died a year later, she inherited a quarter of a million dollars—and he was sensitive
to it. "Her father's family expenses," he reported to his
own family with a touch of awe, "are forty thousand dollars a year." He could easily have been accused of marrying
for money, and one cynic did exactly that; Ambrose Bierce,
in San Francisco, observed that marriage was usually committed by a person laboring under temporary insanity, but
in Twain's case "it was the cool, methodical, cumulative
culmination of human nature, working in the breast of an
orphan hankering for some one with a fortune to love, some
one with a bank account to caress."

He had to establish himself, and at first, at least, he
meant to do it without his father-in-law's help—"I have
paddled my own canoe so long that I could not be satisfied

now to let anybody help me." For a moment the Tennessee Land offered hope, but as usual it disappointed. Jervis Langdon offered $30,000 in cash and stocks for it, but Orion insisted that Langdon should go into partnership with the Clemenses instead, and no more was heard of that offer. Twain needed permanence and security; his solution was natural for a writer who still thought of himself as a newspaperman. The success of *Innocents* had surprised him too; he did not know if it could be repeated, he had no clear plans for a second book. Journalism offered a career; authorship, apparently, did not. He intended, as he explained to Mrs. Langdon, to "buy a remunerative share in a newspaper of high standing, & then instruct & elevate & civilize the public." He wanted to buy into the Hartford *Courant*; Abel Fairbanks's Cleveland *Herald* was a possibility also, but Mark and Livy preferred "the quiet moral atmosphere of Hartford to the driving, ambitious ways of Cleveland . . . what we want is a home." He would hardly say that to Mrs. Fairbanks, but he did tell her that "this thing of settling down for life" was "the solemnest matter" that had ever come into his calculations. Consequently, "I must not make a mistake."

But the *Courant* editors were reluctant. They hardly knew what to make of Mark Twain and must have wondered what sort of colleague he would prove on a family newspaper in the quiet, moral atmosphere of Hartford; they delayed, they asked for advice, and in the end they rejected him. Throughout that spring and early summer he inquired and negotiated. He considered the New York *Tribune*, but shares were unavailable, and New York would have seemed an odd location for a couple seeking a "moral and religious atmosphere." For months the Cleveland *Herald* appeared the likeliest choice; there, he told Mrs. Fairbanks, he and Livy could "nestle under your wing . . . & have you teach us to scratch for worms." Finally, however, the price was too high ($50,000 for a one-fourth interest), and he would be expected to serve as political editor—he, a man who hated politics and was sick of making new beginnings. To become political editor of the *Herald* would be to commence "*another* apprenticeship, tacked on to the end of a foolish life *made up* of apprenticeships."

Suddenly a new possibility offered itself, and Twain impulsively seized it. In early August he learned of an opening at the Buffalo *Express*, and on August 12 wrote to Bliss that he had bought a one-third interest in that "exceedingly thriving paper." Jervis Langdon, who had business interests in Buffalo, had learned of the possibility and advanced the purchase price of $25,000. The *Express* already had a business manager and a political editor; Mark Twain was to be a sort of general and contributing editor; his hours and duties were not very clearly defined. The position seemed ideal and he began his duties enthusiastically, announcing himself on August 14 to "the unoffending patrons of the paper, who are about to be exposed to constant attacks of my wisdom and learning," promising not to use slang or vulgarity or profanity and not to write poetry "unless I conceive a spite against the subscribers." Some of his contributions were hardly genteel; an early piece offered subscribers appropriate last words of famous persons: Joan of Arc—"Tramp, tramp, tramp, the boys are marching." Mrs. Fairbanks, of course, rebuked him for irreverence.

But he had hardly settled into his new role of editor and proprietor when he began to prepare for the coming lecture season. In mid-August he had told Bliss that he would not be lecturing: "When I got to counting up the irons I had in the fire (marriage, editing a newspaper, and lecturing) I said it was most too many, for the subscriber." Yet by September, he had committed himself to a tour. He was deeply in debt for his share in the *Express*, he would be married in February, and he needed ready money. As for having many irons in the fire, that was not a problem but a necessary condition of life for Mark Twain. He was restless besides. Charlie Langdon was setting off around the world: overland to California, by the route that Twain had taken

eight years before, with time there for the "Big Trees &
Yosemite," then across the Pacific to Japan and China, on
to Egypt, with a journey up the Nile, to the Holy Land,
to Russia, and finally to Paris, where he would meet the
Langdon family, including Mark and Livy, in the summer
of 1870 for a tour of England and Germany. "I feel a sort
of itching in my feet," Twain admitted to Mrs. Fairbanks,
"and if my life were as aimless as of old, my trunk would
be packed, now."

With his second regular season scheduled, he had become a confirmed lecturer, taking part in a uniquely American institution—characteristic of a nation devoted to
self-improvement but preferring to gain it by listening
rather than by laborious reading. Throughout the North-
east and the Middle West—the custom had never taken
root in the South, and the far West was too sparsely popu-
lated—every town had its "lyceum society" or lecture committee, organizing an annual "course" of lectures. It
seemed as though everyone lectured: feminists, explorers,
reformers, generals; Barnum, the showman and humbug;
Frederick Douglass; Robert Ingersoll, the freethinker;
Horace Greeley. Humorists lectured, and so did serious
writers: Poe, Whitman, Melville, and Harte tried the platform, while Emerson supported himself by it through
much of his life. Standards were relaxing in the post–Civil
War years; audiences were expecting to be entertained as
well as to be inspired or instructed. In conservative eyes,
"triflers and buffoons" were taking over the field; from
Mark Twain's point of view, he was simply making up for
the losses incurred by the "house emptiers," the dull, serious speakers. Offering both humor and enlightenment,
Twain was emphatically a house filler, and in steady demand.

The business had been organized under the auspices of
James Redpath's Boston Lyceum Bureau. For a 10 percent
commission Redpath would advertise lecturers, set their
fees, negotiate with committees, make engagements, and

schedule their seasons. His publication, *The Lyceum*, offers a fascinating insight into the culture and taste of Victorian America. There was Josh Billings on "Milk"—"A Plaintive Discourse on Nat'ral History"; a Professor Atkinson on "English Poetry and How to Study It," Charles Barnard on "My Jack-Knife and How to Use It"—on the "theory and practice of pruning"; the Reverend James Clarke—clerics made up a good part of Redpath's list—on "Why Should Not Women Vote." All these speakers and topics were available at only $50 each. Higher-priced attractions included Wirt Sikes on "After Dark in New York," at $75 to $100; the Turkish consul-general in New York on "Social Life in Turkey," "illustrated with appropriate costumes; the speaker chants the cry of the Muezzin and performs the genuflexions of Musulman worship," at $100 to $150 plus expenses; Olive Logan on "Paris, the City of Luxury," at $200. And Mark Twain—"This celebrated humorist . . . his first season in New England. Lyceums must apply for him at an early date"—at $100, "with modifications," a euphemism indicating discounts for small towns. Twain's fee of $100, "with modifications," was respectable, although well below Olive Logan's and not to be compared with the $500 a night that Henry Ward Beecher could command. He was not yet a star of the first magnitude. He had announced a new topic, "Curiosities of California," but had not been able to prepare it and fell back on that well-tried favorite, "Our Fellow Savages of the Sandwich Islands." He opened his season with tryouts in Pittsburgh, then faced his major test in Boston. The Boston audience—"4,000 critics," said Mark Twain—was considered the most demanding in the country, and the Boston papers could make or break his New England tour. He succeeded, the audience laughed like other audiences, and the papers were favorable; he must have felt that if he could please the Bostonians, he could please anyone.

For a while, Boston became the headquarters from which he journeyed to outlying towns, returning to enjoy the company of fellow lecturers, exchanging stories and platform tips, sometimes watching their performances and learning from their failures. Almost forty years later Twain still remembered the miserable fate of the lecturer who saw half his audience rise en masse and walk out of the hall, and who "stood choking and gasping for a few minutes, gazing in a white horror at that retreat, then . . . turned drearily away and wandered from the stage." They had been obliged to leave in order to catch the last suburban train, but nobody had thought to warn the speaker.

Probably it was at this time that he met the associate editor of the *Atlantic*, William Dean Howells, who had reviewed *Innocents* so favorably. Intellectual, reserved, prudish, Howells was fascinated by the spectacle Twain presented in the *Atlantic* office, with "his crest of dense red hair, and the wide sweep of his flaming moustache, wrapped in a great sealskin coat"—a most un-Bostonian costume that embarrassed Howells when they took to the street together. It was an acquaintance of opposites that a few years later would turn into a lifelong friendship, with Howells criticizing, even proofreading, Twain's works, and with the two men gleefully planning joint literary projects that were meant to earn fortunes for them both, but somehow never did. Their relationship found expression in the most entertaining correspondence in American literature and was movingly recorded in Howells's memoir, *My Mark Twain*.

Through December and January Twain explored Connecticut and Vermont, with excursions to New York City, Philadelphia, and upstate New York. He lectured almost nightly, although in his new-found religiosity he had stipulated that he would not speak on the Sabbath. He experienced the usual trials, from officious committees that allowed him no peace or privacy, and from incompetent chairmen who embarrassed him with fulsome flattery and bored the audience with dreary attempts at humor. By mid-December he had begun introducing himself: "Ladies and gentlemen: the next lecture in this course will be delivered this evening by Samuel L. Clemens, a gentleman whose high character and unimpeachable integrity are only equalled by his comeliness of person and grace of manner. And I am the man!"

Offstage, he generally wanted to be left alone, but he was likely to be dragged out for an obligatory tour of the town sights, usually in freezing weather, in an open carriage or sleigh: "the mayor's house; the ex-mayor's house; the house of a State Senator; house of an ex-Governor . . . the plaza, the place where the park is going to be—& I must sit & shiver & stare . . . while my friend gushes enthusiastic statistics and dimensions." A hotel might offer "shabby bed, shabby room, shabby furniture, dim lights," but at least, unlike the private homes where he was sometimes lodged, it gave him privacy, did not require him to sit up late making conversation, and allowed him to smoke cigars, put his feet on the furniture, scatter newspapers about the room, and drop his dirty linen on the floor. He could fill his free time instead with reading, or with writing to Livy. But the worst possible disaster was for his lecture to be printed, in whole or in part, in the local paper—for the jokes to be extracted like raisins from a fruitcake, for surprise to be lost, for the whole performance to seem flat and stale to the audience in the next town.

Lecturing had its trials—hardship, boredom, loneliness, fatigue—and as often as any actor making positively his last appearance on any stage, Twain would announce his determination never to be dragged onto the platform again, then would change his mind. He made another American tour in 1871–72, he lectured in England in the late fall of 1873, he would make a reading tour of eastern America and Canada with the novelist George Washington Cable in 1884–85, and he toured the world—Canada, the Pacific Northwest, New Zealand, Australia, India, South Africa—in 1895–96. And there were special engagements, benefit performances, innumerable after-dinner speeches;

till the end of his life, Mark Twain could not stop talking. He did not do it only for money; he could generally have earned more, with considerably less effort and discomfort, by writing. The reward remained the platform itself, the irreplaceable satisfaction—so rare for an author—of seeing an immediate, visible response from his audience, the opportunity of exercising a unique skill, the delight of holding an audience in his hand and *tickling* it—as Howells, an indifferent speaker himself, once described his friend's easy mastery over his listeners. And after Artemus Ward died of tuberculosis in England in 1867, Twain had no real rival.

That his audiences were pleased there can be no doubt, but what they actually heard can only be guessed at. Mark Twain's voice was later to be recorded by Edison, but those records were destroyed in 1914 by a fire in the Edison laboratory. His texts can be reconstructed, but the printed words are nearly as incomplete as an unperformed score. By all accounts he was a master of the pregnant pause, with the courage to wait and the sensitivity to time his delays exactly. Twain's comment on Ward applies perfectly to himself: "There was more in his pauses than in his words . . . no reporter's pen could do him justice." His voice was low—there were complaints about that, but it meant that his audiences had to pay attention; everyone mentioned his "drawl"—he exaggerated it until it was perhaps a third slower than average spoken English. He memorized his lectures, using only brief, pictorial notes. Reading from a prepared text instantly destroyed the illusion of spontaneity that he aimed at creating, and prevented him from gauging the response of his audience. Listeners sometimes believed that he was improvising; the jokes were "uttered as if he had just thought of them a minute before, and didn't perceive the point of them quite as soon as the audience." As Twain described his method to his manager, Redpath, "I rely chiefly for my effects on a simulated unconsciousness and intense absurdity." Like his own Simon Wheeler, narrator of the "Jumping Frog,"

he could "string incongruities and absurdities together...
and seem innocently unaware that they are absurdities."
Calculated repetition of an obviously dull, banal story was
a risky variation on the basic technique; as the apparently
witless lecturer repeated the same boring anecdote for the
third or fourth time, waiting hopefully for the laugh that
did not come, tension would build and build until finally
it exploded in laughter.

His letters to Livy continued, but they became more
concrete, more earthy; there was less mention of spiritual
aspirations, more comment on books. He was reading *Gil
Blas*, a picaresque novel of the early eighteenth century that
was to have its influence on *Huckleberry Finn*, but he was
not marking it for her. It would offend her delicacy, "& I
prefer not to have that dulled in you"—as though "delicacy" were a valuable property that must not be allowed
to depreciate. Charles Reade's *The Cloister and the Hearth*, a
historical novel of the early Renaissance, enthralled him,
everything in it was good. Instead of marking passages, he
wanted simply to write "I love you Livy" in the margin.
He gave her detailed, often satirical accounts of life on the
lecture circuit. He vigorously defended his habit of smoking, denying that it injured his health in any degree, offering to stop if Livy herself desired it, but implying that the
opposition came from her family instead. He had given up
profanity, he had stopped drinking—first "strong liquors,"
then "all other liquors"—because she wished it, he had
tried to keep his hands out of his pockets and to stop
sprawling in easy chairs, and that was enough. As a conces-
sion to her prejudice, however, he limited his smoking to
Sunday afternoons; he explained to Twichell that he was
humoring Livy, just as he would stop using sugar in his
coffee if she wished it. He was to take up smoking again
under the stress of writing his next book, *Roughing It*, in
the following year; none of those reforms were to last long.

Meanwhile, the process of conversion had come to a halt;
Mark Twain was no longer denouncing his unregenerate

condition or struggling to become a Christian. Learning
that the Hartford *Courant* owners, who had been so contemptuously indifferent a few months before, were now
eager to have him sell out of the *Express* and buy into their
paper, he could express a thoroughly unchristian sentiment: "Revenge is wicked, & in every way unbecoming, &
I am not the man to countenance it or show it any favor.
(But it is powerful sweet, anyway.)" He rejoiced in the sale
of *Innocents*; 12,000 copies in December—"Nothing like it
since *Uncle Tom's Cabin*." With his royalties he bought a
$10,000 life insurance policy for himself and settled it on
his mother; he hoped to have paid off $15,000 of debt by
February. On her side, in her first surviving letter, Livy
offered what Twain called "solid chunks of wisdom" to her
"good youth." They should be patient with Orion, recognizing that God had not given him "money making wisdom" but had endowed him with a "beautiful spirit"
instead; their own happiness in each other should make
them better able to help others "whose backs seem almost
broken" with care.

Suddenly time was running out. The wedding was
scheduled for February 2, and in mid-January Livy had
gone to New York with her father to buy her trousseau.
Mark delivered his final lecture on January 19, then hurried
to Elmira. On the envelope of his last letter before their
marriage, methodical Livy wrote, "184th—last letter of a
17-months correspondence." Mark Twain's wedding day
began auspiciously with the postman bringing him a royalty check of $4,000, representing three-months' sales of
The Innocents Abroad. Its arrival was no lucky coincidence;
the author had arranged for it with his publisher. It served
to remind everyone, including himself, that at thirty-four
he was as successful in his own trade as his father-in-law
to be, Jervis Langdon, had been in the coal business.

The wedding of Olivia Langdon and Samuel Clemens,
commonly known as Mark Twain, was celebrated that
evening in the Langdon home, solemnized by the presence

of two ministers—Thomas K. Beecher of Elmira, family pastor of the Langdons, and the groom's Hartford friend Joe Twichell. Both Langdons and Clemenses were in attendance; Twain's sister Pamela and her daughter, Annie, came all the way from St. Louis at his expense. Jane Clemens, then in her late sixties, did not make the long journey, but the groom was supported by the presence of his close friend and surrogate mother, Mrs. Fairbanks of Cleveland.

Accompanied by Langdons, Beechers, Clemenses, and Mrs. Fairbanks, Mark and Livy set out the next day for Buffalo in a private railway car, a "palace car"—the epitome of luxurious travel. They reached Buffalo at nine that evening, and there Jervis Langdon, that solid man, played a magnificent practical joke, the great extravagance of his life. Since the groom did not feel that he could afford to give his bride a home of her own immediately, the Langdon agent in Buffalo, a Mr. Slee, had been instructed to look up a suitably refined boarding house. In nineteenth-century America, as foreign visitors regularly noted with surprise, newlyweds often lived in boarding houses until they could afford to set up housekeeping.

Slee had found the ideal place, Twain was told, and he was waiting at the station with a cavalcade of sleighs. Everyone bundled in and drove off. Somehow Mark and Livy's sleigh became separated—he worried because their guests might arrive at the boarding house first—but at last it turned onto what appeared to be a fashionable street and stopped in front of a new and obviously expensive house. The door opened, showing the rest of the wedding party already arrived. The new couple were led on a tour of the house, showing off the blue satin drawing room and a "sanctum" in scarlet for Twain himself. Slowly he realized that it was theirs. House, lot, furniture, carriage, and servants were all a splendid gift from his father-in-law. Supper was served, then the guests departed, leaving "Youth" and Livy to begin their life together.

EPILOGUE

The Buffalo home was actually to play a minor role in their lives. Jervis Langdon died of cancer the next summer. Returning to Buffalo after nursing him, Livy collapsed from exhaustion. A succession of illnesses followed: a guest's lingering death from typhoid fever, Livy's own miscarriage and bare survival — the child, prematurely born, surprisingly lived for a year and a half, causing continuous anxiety. The house became filled with hateful associations; they learned to detest Buffalo as well, and Twain sold his interest in the *Express* at a loss. He was to be an author now, not a newspaperman, and they could move to Hartford at last. There he would build the unique mansion still preserved as the "Mark Twain home," there his three daughters would be born, there he and Livy would live the most active and satisfying years of their lives, there he would write *Tom Sawyer* and *Old Times on the Mississippi* and much of *Huckleberry Finn*. Mark Twain's apprenticeships had ended; the time of accomplishment was at hand.

Acknowledgments

This book could hardly have been written without my use of the letters, manuscripts, and documents preserved at the Mark Twain Papers, at the University of California at Berkeley. Particularly valuable was the opportunity of using the texts and the annotations that the staff of the Mark Twain Papers have prepared for the first volume in a forthcoming edition of Twain's collected letters. The University of Alberta not only provided money for travel and research but also, through study leaves and release from teaching duties, gave me what every scholar most needs—time.

For Further Reading

Much of Mark Twain's early writing—personal letters as well as journalism—has never been collected. The standard edition of his letters, *Mark Twain's Letters* (New York: Harper & Bros., 1917), edited by his first biographer, Albert Bigelow Paine, is highly selective and sometimes omits portions of letters, without indication to the reader. The recent book of Twain's letters, edited by Charles Neider, is simply a selection from Paine's selection. The first volume of a complete edition of Mark Twain's letters, covering the period of this biography, is scheduled for publication by the University of California Press in 1986.

His earliest journalism is most conveniently available in *Early Tales and Sketches*, volume 1, 1851–64, edited by Edgar Branch and Robert Hirst for the University of California Press (1979) as volume 15 of its ongoing *Works of Mark Twain* series. It includes much previously unpublished or uncollected material, a lengthy study of Twain's development as a writer, as well as historical and biographical information about each of the items printed. It omits the Snodgrass letters, which are reserved for a future edition of Twain's travel writings, but these are available in *The Adventures of Thomas Jefferson Snodgrass*, edited by Charles Honce (Chicago: Pascal Covici, 1928). Finally, volume 1 of *Mark Twain's Notebooks and Journals* (Berkeley: University of California Press, 1975), edited by Frederick Anderson, Michael B. Frank, and Kenneth M. Sanderson, contains the full text of Twain's eleven surviving notebooks from the period 1855–70, with extensive annotations. It supersedes Paine's selective and sometimes expurgated edition of *Mark*

Twain's Notebook (New York: Harper & Bros., 1935). Two editions of Twain's *Autobiography* are available, both incomplete: *Mark Twain's Autobiography*, edited by Paine in two volumes, and *The Autobiography of Mark Twain, Including Chapters Now Published for the First Time*, edited by Charles Neider (New York: Harper & Row, 1959). Most of the *Autobiography* was written—or more accurately, dictated—in the author's old age and does not follow chronological order; instead, Twain simply chose to talk about whatever happened to interest him at the moment. Paine respects this "organization"; Neider rearranges the material, presenting it in chronological order. His version is more inclusive than Paine's, and certainly more convenient. More excerpts from the *Autobiography*, including some dealing with Twain's Hannibal and San Francisco years, are available in Bernard De Voto's *Mark Twain in Eruption* (New York: Grosset & Dunlap, 1940). But the complete *Autobiographical Dictations*, as they should be called, can be seen only among the Mark Twain Papers at the University of California at Berkeley.

No "definitive" biography of Mark Twain exists. Paine's *Mark Twain: A Biography*, in three volumes (New York: Harper & Bros., 1912), is a richly detailed portrait—long, leisurely, sympathetic, even worshipful at times. As Twain's private secretary during his last years, Paine had the enormous advantage of intimate acquaintance with his subject and provides material available nowhere else, but the greatest value of his work is that it presents Mark Twain's life as Mark Twain himself would probably have seen it. (Indeed, Twain's conversations with Paine made him a collaborator in his own biography.) Paine's weaknesses are his occasional sentimentality and prudery, his acceptance of some of Mark Twain's legends about his own life as fact, and the imbalance of his work—fully one-third of it is given to the last decade of Twain's life. DeLancey Ferguson, in his brief *Mark Twain: Man and Legend* (Indianapolis: Bobbs-Merrill, 1943), offers a reliable and sympathetic study, often replacing fable with fact. Justin Kaplan's *Mr. Clemens and Mark Twain* (New York: Simon & Schuster, 1966) is thoroughly researched and modern in its approach. But it omits the first thirty years of its subject's life and is written to a thesis suggesting a fundamental duality in Twain's nature between the artist "Mark Twain" and "Mr. Clemens"—husband, father, businessman, respectable citizen, and celebrity. For an especially vivid sense of Mark Twain's personality, rather than for the facts of his life, one should turn to *My Mark Twain* by William Dean Howells (New York: Harper & Bros., 1910). A major American writer himself, Howells knew Twain longer and more intimately than anyone else who has written about him. Howells's little book, written with deep feeling, not only is the record of a forty-year friendship but offers the best portrayal of Mark Twain that we have.

A book that is not a biography itself but that has probably had more influence than any biography on the modern view of Mark Twain is Van Wyck Brooks's *The Ordeal of Mark Twain* (New York: E. P. Dutton, 1920). Brooks's presentation of Twain as an artist frustrated by a hostile, anti-intellectual environment and by his own concessions to American materialism and conventional morality has influenced nearly all subsequent scholarship, most notably Kaplan's *Mr. Clemens and Mark Twain*. Brooks was answered in *Mark Twain's America* (Boston: Little, Brown, 1932) by Bernard De Voto, who estimated Twain's accomplishment more highly than Brooks and saw it as inseparable from the environment in which he came to maturity.

For the Hannibal years, *Tom Sawyer* and *Huckleberry Finn* provide less fact than atmosphere. The first seventeen chapters in Neider's edition of the *Autobiography* deal with the same period; they are colorful and often unreliable. A less affectionate view, also by Twain himself, can be found in "Villagers, 1840–43," a piece clearly not written for publication. It is available in *Mark Twain's Hannibal, Huck and Tom*, edited by Walter Blair (Berkeley: University of

California Press, 1969). Dixon Wecter's *Sam Clemens of Hannibal* (Boston: Houghton Mifflin, 1952), which ends with Sam's leaving home in 1853, is solidly factual, a storehouse of information about Hannibal and the Clemenses rather than a coherent narrative.

Some of Sam Clemens's letters from the East—those written for publication—have been collected by Edgar Branch in *Mark Twain's Letters in the Muscatine Journal* (Chicago: The Mark Twain Association of America, 1942). *Mark Twain: Businessman*, edited by Samuel Charles Webster, the grandson of Twain's sister Pamela, contains interesting letters and family reminiscences, largely gathered from Webster's mother, Annie, who was Mark Twain's niece. For Twain's career as a pilot, the first source, inevitably, is *Life on the Mississippi* (1883, often reprinted), which incorporates and expands on the articles that Twain had contributed to the *Atlantic Monthly* in 1874–75 under the title "Old Times on the Mississippi." Twain filled out the book with an account of river life as he saw it on a return visit in 1882, and with a good deal of miscellaneous material. Chapter 38, "The House Beautiful," supplements the description of the Grangerford home in chapter 17 of *Huckleberry Finn* as a satirical dissection of upper-middle-class culture in the Old South.

Neither "Old Times" nor *Life on the Mississippi* deals with Sam Clemens's career on the river in the two years after he earned his pilot's license, but much information can be found in the annotated piloting notebooks published in the first volume of *Notebooks and Journals*, in Sam's letters, and in the first volume of *Early Tales and Sketches*, which prints his four known sketches from the period. And *Before Mark Twain: A Sampler of Old, Old Times on the Mississippi*, edited by John F. McDermott (Carbondale: Southern Illinois University Press, 1968) entertainingly supplements "Old Times" with accounts of river life by a variety of early travelers—describing the discomforts and hazards of steamboat life as well as the bullies and gamblers who infested the boats but are overlooked by Mark Twain.

For Mark Twain's Western career, the first source is *Roughing It*—with reservations. Twain makes himself a representative character, exaggerating his own youth and ignorance, ascribing experiences to himself because they seemed typical of the time and place. *Roughing It* has surprising gaps as well; it says nothing at all about the imbroglio that led to Twain's departure from Virginia City, and it gives only three chapters, out of seventy-nine, to his life in San Francisco. Letters, mostly to Orion Clemens and to his mother and his sister, Pamela, are available in *Mark Twain's Letters* and *Mark Twain: Businessman*.

The reader who wishes to study Twain's writing for the period must go to a variety of incomplete and sometimes overlapping sources. No complete file of the *Enterprise* survives. Luckily, other papers regularly reprinted Twain pieces of general interest; much of his Nevada work has thus been recovered and is collected in *Mark Twain of the Enterprise: Newspaper Articles and Other Documents: 1862–1864*, edited by Henry Nash Smith (Berkeley: University of California Press, 1957). Twain's contributions to the *Golden Era* are gathered in *The Washoe Giant in San Francisco*, edited by Franklin Walker (San Francisco: George Fields, 1938). His *Californian* pieces—later and generally more interesting—are found in *Sketches of the Sixties by Mark Twain and Bret Harte* (San Francisco: John Howell, 1927). *Mark Twain's San Francisco*, edited by Bernard Taper (New York: McGraw-Hill, 1963), prints work from a variety of journals, but all dealing with San Francisco. Taper offers the most entertaining selection available, and adds interest by including contemporary cartoons of San Francisco life by Edward Jump, a talented artist and friend of Mark Twain's. *Early Tales and Sketches* remains incomplete, excluding "social and political commentary; literary, theatrical, and art criticism; travel writings." General background on the San Francisco literary scene of the 1860s can be found in Franklin Walker's *San Francisco's Literary Frontier*

(Seattle: University of Washington Press, 1969).

Mark Twain revised and condensed his Hawaiian letters for *Roughing It*, eliminating his imaginary companion, the vulgarian Brown. *Mark Twain's Letters from Hawaii*, edited by A. Grove Day (New York: Appleton-Century, 1966), prints the originals. His career as a lecturer begins with his return from Hawaii and can be followed in detail in both Paul Fatout's *Mark Twain on the Lecture Circuit* (Bloomington: Indiana University Press, 1964) and Fred Lorch's longer and more exhaustive *The Trouble Begins at Eight: Mark Twain's Lecture Tours* (Ames: Iowa State University Press, 1968). The texts of his "Sandwich Islands" and "American Vandal" lectures, along with the address to the czar and his first recorded after-dinner speech, to the Washington Press Club on "Woman—the Pride of Any Profession and the Jewel of Ours," are given in Fatout's *Mark Twain Speaking* (Ames: University of Iowa Press, 1976).

Twain's letters to the *Alta California*—collected in *Mark Twain's Travels with Mr. Brown*, edited by G. Ezra Dane and Franklin Walker (New York: Knopf, 1940), are the main source of information for his New York interlude; added details about the journey across Nicaragua and the plague-stricken voyage to New York are contained in notebook 7. The newspaper letters have considerable historical interest, documenting New York life at many levels. More can be learned about the picturesque Captain Wakeman in his *Log of an Ancient Mariner* (San Francisco: A. B. Bancroft, 1878), ghost-written by his daughter after Mark Twain had declined Wakeman's invitation to write the book. The "Colloquy Between a Slum Child and a Moral Mentor," a vitriolic satire on Victorian complacency, can be found in *Mark Twain's Satires and Burlesques*, edited by Franklin Rogers (Berkeley: University of California Press, 1967).

The cruise of the *Quaker City* is documented first in the three notebooks that Twain kept on the voyage, then in *Traveling with the Innocents Abroad: Mark Twain's Original Re-*

ports from Europe and the Holy Land, edited by Daniel Morley McKeithan (Norman: University of Oklahoma Press, 1958), which reprints his letters for the *Alta California* and New York *Tribune*, and finally in *The Innocents Abroad*, each successive version more carefully written, and more discreet, than the one before it. *Innocents* can be found in any collected edition of Twain's works, but for full period flavor it should be read in the American Publishing Company edition of 1869, with its hundreds of woodcuts. James M. Cox offers a perceptive critical study in "Professional Traveler," the second chapter of his *Mark Twain: The Fate of Humor* (Princeton: Princeton University Press, 1966). And finally, Dewey Ganzel's *Mark Twain Abroad: The Cruise of the Quaker City* (Chicago: University of Chicago Press, 1868) offers a factual account and incidentally demonstrates the slightness of Mrs. Fairbanks's influence on Twain's writing.

For the period between Mark Twain's return from Europe and his marriage to Olivia Langdon, the two most important sources, intensely personal and deeply revealing, are two editions of his letters, both prepared by Dixon Wecter: *Mark Twain to Mrs. Fairbanks* (San Marino, Calif.: Huntington Library, 1949) and *The Love Letters of Mark Twain* (New York: Harper & Bros., 1949). Twain's notebook 11, kept during his return voyage from California in July of 1868, contains one of the best of his early burlesques, "The Story of Mamie Grant, the Child-Missionary," and a fragment of science fiction, dealing with a transatlantic balloon voyage. Hamlin Hill's *Mark Twain and Elisha Bliss* (Columbia: University of Missouri Press, 1964) gives information about the publication of *The Innocents Abroad* and a highly unfavorable view of subscription publishing and its effects on Mark Twain. Hill's edition of *Mark Twain's Letters to His Publishers: 1867–1894* (Berkeley: University of California Press, 1967) includes Twain's letters to Bliss concerning *Innocents*. Critics of Mark Twain have concerned themselves principally with his later work, but valuable discussions of the early journalism, and of *The Innocents Abroad*, can be found in the opening chapters of Henry Nash Smith's *Mark Twain: The Development of a Writer* (Cambridge: Harvard University Press, 1962) and James M. Cox's *Mark Twain: The Fate of Humor* (Princeton: Princeton University Press, 1966), the only book-length study of Twain's humor. Finally, any topic concerning Mark Twain can be followed up in Thomas Tenney's monumental bibliography, *Mark Twain: A Reference Guide* (Boston: G. K. Hall, 1977), and its annual supplements in the journal *American Literary Realism*.

Author's Notes

LITTLE SAM. Albert Bigelow Paine, *Mark Twain: A Biography* (New York: Harper & Bros., 1912). Dixon Wecter, *Sam Clemens of Hannibal* (Boston: Houghton Mifflin, 1952). "Jane Lampton Clemens," in *Mark Twain's Hannibal, Huck and Tom*, edited by Walter Blair (Berkeley: University of California Press, 1969).

1. The Clemens family already included Orion, born in 1825; Pamela, born 1827; Pleasants Hannibal, who died at the age of three months; Margaret, born 1830; and Benjamin, born 1832. There would be one child after Sam—Henry, born in 1838. Margaret and Benjamin would both die in their childhood.

TOM SAWYER DAYS. Mark Twain: *The Adventures of Tom Sawyer* (1876), *The Adventures of Huckleberry Finn* (1884). "Villagers," in *Mark Twain's Hannibal, Huck and Tom*, edited by Walter Blair (Berkeley: University of California Press, 1969). Albert Bigelow Paine, *Mark Twain: A Biography* (New York: Harper & Bros., 1912). Dixon Wecter, *Sam Clemens of Hannibal* (Boston: Houghton Mifflin, 1952). *The Autobiography of Mark Twain*, edited by Charles Neider (New York: Harper & Row, 1959). *Mark Twain's Autobiography*, edited by Albert Bigelow Paine (New York: Harper & Bros., 1924). William Dean Howells, *My Mark Twain* (New York: Harper & Bros., 1910). *Mark Twain's Letters to Will Bowen: "My First & Oldest & Dearest Friend,"* edited by Theodore Hornberger (Austin: University of Texas Press, 1941). Van Wyck Brooks, *The Ordeal of Mark Twain* (New York: E. P. Dutton, 1920). Bernard De Voto, *Mark Twain's America* (Boston: Little, Brown, 1932).

1. Sam could have gained the basis of a literary education from his school readers. The literary content of their prose selections was high, and surprisingly contemporary, with selections from such writers as Irving, Carlyle, Lamb, Longfellow, and Dickens. ("The Death of Little Nell," from *The Old Curiosity Shop*, was already a favorite.) But they were also relentlessly theistic and moralistic. McGuffey's *Eclectic First Reader*, for example, includes this catechism:

"Do you know who made the sun?"

"God made it."

"God made the moon and all the stars. How good God is to us; he gives us all we have and keeps us alive." Poems were likely to be didactic, sentimental, funerary—with such titles as "The Early Doomed," "To Wee Willie," "The Mourner" (*Low she lies, who blest our eyes/Through many a sunny day.*), "Temperance Ode" (*Dash to the earth that bowl!/Dare not its sweets to sip,/There's peril to the soul/If once it touch the lip*), or "The Dying Spaniel" (*Old Oscar, how feebly thou crawls't to the door/Thou who wert all beauty and vigor of yore*). Mark Twain's lifelong delight in collecting and ridiculing specimens of this sort, as in his account of the drawings and verses of Emmeline Grangerford, in chapter 17 of *Huckleberry Finn*, surely dates back to his schooldays.

APPRENTICE. Mark Twain, *The Adventures of Tom Sawyer* (1876). *The Autobiography of Mark Twain* edited by Charles Neider (New York: Harper & Row, 1959). *Mark Twain's Autobiography*, edited by Albert Bigelow Paine (New York: Harper & Bros., 1924). *Early Tales and Sketches*, vol. 1, 1851–64, edited by Edgar M. Branch and Robert H. Hirst (Berkeley: University of California Press, 1979). "My First Literary Venture," *The Works of Mark Twain*, vol. 7. *Mark Twain's Letters to Will Bowen: "My First & Oldest & Dearest Friend,"* edited by Theodore Hornberger (Austin: University of Texas Press, 1941). "Villagers," in *Mark Twain's Hannibal, Huck and Tom*, edited by Walter Blair (Berkeley: University of California Press, 1969). Albert Bigelow Paine, *Mark Twain: A Biography* (New York: Harper & Bros., 1912). Dixon Wecter, *Sam Clemens of Hannibal* (Boston: Houghton Mifflin, 1952). William Dean Howells, *My Mark Twain* (New York: Harper & Bros., 1910).

1. In September of 1850, Orion commenced publication of a weekly paper, the Hannibal *Western Union*, and Sam apparently came to work for him the following January. Six or seven months later, Orion bought the Hannibal *Journal* and began publishing under the consolidated title of *Journal and Western Union*, soon shortened to the simple *Journal*. He did his best to keep those glowing promises to his subscribers, not only printing Dickens but writing to Emerson and Oliver Wendell Holmes, offering them five dollars each for contributions. They did not reply.

2. Reading E. W. Howe's *Story of a Country Town* in 1885 (a book credited with beginning a literary "revolt against the village" that lasted into the twentieth century), Twain praised the accuracy of Howe's "pictures of that arid village life." "I know, for I have seen it all, lived it all." But, generally, he did not choose to write it.

JOURNEYMAN. *Mark Twain's Letters*, edited by Albert Bigelow Paine

(New York: Harper & Bros., 1917). *Mark Twain's Notebooks and Journals*, vol. 1, 1855–73, edited by Frederick Anderson, Michael B. Frank, and Kenneth M. Sanderson (Berkeley: University of California Press, 1975). Typescripts and proofsheets of *Collected Letters of Mark Twain*, now under preparation at the Mark Twain Papers, University of California, Berkeley, first volume scheduled for publication in 1986. *Mark Twain's Letters in the Muscatine Journal*, edited by Edgar M. Branch (Chicago: Mark Twain Association of America, 1942). *The Adventures of Thomas Jefferson Snodgrass*, edited by Charles Honce (Chicago: Pascal Covici, 1928). Newspaper clippings at the Mark Twain Papers.

1. The impersonality of the letters may seem disappointing. Van Wyck Brooks complains that the young Clemens "seems to have experienced few of the characteristic thoughts or feelings of youth. Never a hint of melancholy, of aspiration, of hope, depression, joy, even ambition!" But the letters were meant for the public, and Sam would not have confessed his innermost feelings in them. Neither would he have uselessly distressed his family by reporting his fears and anxieties. And like most Americans of his day, Sam Clemens could not afford the luxury of a prolonged adolescence; as an identifiable stage of life, with its unique psychological characteristics and problems, adolescence could hardly exist at a time when boys of fourteen were expected to have finished school and to be self-supporting.

2. Abolitionist agitation was increasing in the North, and Sam Clemens's Southern prejudices intensified in response. Seeing the courthouse in Syracuse, he wrote to his mother, "called to mind the time when it was surrounded with chains and companies of soldiers to prevent the rescue of McReynolds' nigger by the infernal abolitionists. I reckon I had better black my face, for in these Eastern States niggers are considered better than white people." That outburst seems to anticipate the fury of Huck's Pap at seeing a free Negro, in chapter 6 of *Huckleberry Finn*.

3. Sam copied from the Reverend George S. Weaver's *Lectures on Mental Science According to the Philosophy of Phrenology* (1852). His interest in phrenology was shared by one other major American writer of his time, Walt Whitman, who used such phrenological terms as "adhesiveness" and "amativeness" in early editions of *Leaves of Grass*. Although Twain did not use the jargon of phrenology, he made literary use of the "science" in chapter 20 of *Huckleberry Finn*; the Duke is ready to "take a turn at mesmerism and phrenology when there's a chance," and carries printed placards announcing that "the celebrated Dr. Armand de Montalban of Paris" would "lecture on the Science of Phrenology" and "furnish charts of character at twenty-five cents apiece." But while he would feel only

an amused skepticism toward phrenology itself, the theory of the temperaments permanently influenced his thought. Writing to his mother and sister in 1862, he would describe himself as a person "endowed with an uncongealable sanguine temperament... who cannot by any possibility, discover any but the bright side of a picture." And a theory of inborn temperaments, perhaps modifiable by "training," would be central to the determinism of his later years.

4. Cincinnati offered other cultural opportunities besides the conversation of Macfarlane. Sam could have heard Emerson speak on "The Conduct of Life," or Senator Thomas Hart Benton of Missouri on "The State of the Union," in a lecture series sponsored by the Young Men's Mercantile Library. Admission was twenty-five cents per lecture.

5. In January the printing house for which Sam worked printed an edition of 2,000 copies of *James's River Guide*. Setting that book in type might have helped to revive his interest in piloting and might have influenced that sudden decision.

PILOT. Mark Twain, *Life on the Mississippi* (Boston: James R. Osgood and Co., 1883). *Early Tales and Sketches*, vol. 1, 1851–64, edited by Edgar M. Branch and Robert H. Hirst (Berkeley: University of California Press, 1979). *Mark Twain's Notebooks and Journals*, edited by Frederick Anderson, Michael B. Frank, and Kenneth M. Sanderson (Berkeley: University of California Press, 1975). *Mark Twain's Letters*, edited by Albert Bigelow Paine (New York: Harper & Bros., 1917). *Collected Letters of Mark Twain*, scheduled for publication by the University of California Press, Berkeley, 1986. *Mark Twain's Letters to Will Bowen: "My First & Oldest & Dearest Friend,"* edited by Theodore Hornberger (Austin: University of Texas Press, 1941). Albert Bigelow Paine, *Mark Twain: A Biography* (New York: Harper & Bros., 1912). Newspaper clippings at the Mark Twain Papers, University of California, Berkeley. Bernard De Voto, *Mark Twain's America* (Boston: Little, Brown, 1932). *Mark Twain: Businessman*, edited by Samuel Charles Webster (Boston: Little, Brown, 1946). Allan Charles Bates, "Mark Twain and the Mississippi River" (unpublished doctoral dissertation, University of Chicago, 1968). William Lewis Herndon and Gibbon Lardner, *Exploration of the Amazon*, 2 vols. (Washington: Robert Armstrong: Public Printer, 1853–54).

1. Mark Twain first recounted his apprenticeship, under the general title "Old Times on the Mississippi," as a series of articles on the *Atlantic Monthly* between January and August of 1875. In his book *Life on the Mississippi* (1883) he introduced the "Old Times" series with three chapters of history, including a long passage describing Mississippi raftsmen from the still unpublished manuscript of *Huckleberry Finn*, then

printed the complete "OldTimes," added five more chapters to the story of his apprenticeship, including the quarrel with Brown, the loss of the *Pennsylvania*, and the death of Henry, and filled out the book with a lengthy account of his voyage up the river, as a passenger, in 1882.

2. A letter from Sam to Orion and Mollie, dated March 9, 1858, shows that Sam was directly responsible for Henry's going on the river: "Henry was doing little or nothing here, and I sent him to our clerk to work his way for a trip, by measuring woodpiles, counting coal boxes, and other clerkly duties.... He may go down again."

REBEL. Mark Twain, "The Campaign That Failed" (1885). Albert Bigelow Paine, *Mark Twain: A Biography* (New York: Harper & Bros., 1912). *Mark Twain: Businessman*, edited by Samuel Charles Webster (Boston: Little, Brown, 1946). *Mark Twain's Letters*, edited by Albert Bigelow Paine (New York: Harper & Bros., 1917). Allan Bates, "Mark Twain and the Mississippi River" (unpublished doctoral dissertation, University of Chicago, 1968). Notebook 38.

1. Besides Mark Twain himself, the major writers of the post–Civil War period were to be William Dean Howells, Henry James, and Henry Adams. James was incapacitated by a mysterious injury, apparently to his back; Howells and Adams both spent the war years abroad—Howells as American consul in Venice (reward for a campaign biography of Lincoln), and Adams as secretary to his father, the American ambassador to England.

MINER. Mark Twain, *Roughing It* (1872). *Collected Letters of Mark Twain*, scheduled for publication by the University of California Press, Berkeley, 1986. *Mark Twain's Letters*, edited by Albert Bigelow Paine (New York: Harper & Bros., 1917). *Mark Twain's Notebooks and Journals*, vol. 1, 1855–73, edited by Frederick Anderson, Michael B. Frank, and Kenneth M. Sanderson (Berkeley: University of California Press, 1975). Albert Bigelow Paine, *Mark Twain: A Biography* (New York: Harper & Bros., 1912). *Mark Twain: Businessman*, edited by Samuel Charles Webster (Boston: Little, Brown, 1946). J. Ross Browne, "A Peep at Washoe," *Harper's New Monthly*, December 1860 and February 1861.

1. According to Sam's account in his letter to Orion, two or three men armed with revolvers entered the hole: "We went up and demanded possession, and they refused," saying "they were in the hole, armed, and meant to die in it, if necessary." Sam jumped in, and again demanded possession. "They said I might stay in it as long as I pleased, and work—but they would do the same. Our boys will try to get there first in the morning."

2. That outing seems to have been principally a much-needed vacation. Sam had planned it several weeks in advance: "I shall go on a walking tour of 40 or 50 miles shortly, to get rid of this infernal place for a while," he had written to Orion on July 9. He and Higbie made a visit to Mono Lake in the Sierras (described in chapters 38 and 39 of *Roughing It*) and "had rare good times out there fishing for trout & hunting," as Sam wrote to a friend, William Claggett, on September 9.

REPORTER. Mark Twain, *Roughing It* (1872). *Collected Letters of Mark Twain*, scheduled for publication by the University of California Press, Berkeley, 1986. *Mark Twain's Letters*, edited by Albert Bigelow Paine (New York: Harper & Bros., 1917). *Early Tales and Sketches*, vol. 1, 1851–64, edited by Edgar M. Branch and Robert H. Hirst (Berkeley: University of California Press, 1979). *Mark Twain of the Enterprise: Newspaper Articles and Other Documents: 1862–1864*, edited by Henry Nash Smith (Berkeley: University of California Press, 1957). *The Washoe Giant in San Francisco, Being Heretofore Uncollected Sketches by Mark Twain Published in the Golden Era in the Sixties*, edited by Franklin Walker (San Francisco: George Fields, 1938). *Mark Twain's San Francisco*, edited by Bernard Taper (New York: McGraw-Hill, 1963). Albert Bigelow Paine, *Mark Twain: A Biography* (New York: Harper & Bros., 1912). *Mark Twain: Businessman*, edited by Samuel Charles Webster (Boston: Little, Brown, 1946). Paul Fatout, *Mark Twain in Virginia City* (Bloomington: Indiana University Press, 1964). George D. Lyman, *The Saga of the Comstock Lode: Boom Days in Virginia City* (New York: Scribners', 1934). J. Ross Browne, "Washoe Revisited" in *Adventures in the Apache Country* (New York: Harper & Bros., 1869).

1. While Sam Clemens was a miner, he played the part to the limit. But the beard would quickly be shaved, the rough clothes replaced by a broadcloth suit. Reporters were gentlemen and dressed accordingly.

2. The Virginia City that Mark Twain knew is gone. The mines were exhausted almost a century ago, and the miles of tunnels are sealed. Most of the town has simply disintegrated; only the ore dumps and the cemeteries, a mansion or two and a few churches, the opera house and the solid brick buildings along C Street are left. But the *Enterprise* building is among them, and the basement where Mark Twain wrote his stories can be inspected. And as one climbs back into the daylight, looking up at the bare flank of Mount Davidson, or at endless vistas of mountain and desert, a timeless and powerful sense of place can be felt.

3. The murderous violence of Virginia City had little in common with the stereotypes fostered by Western novels and films. The badmen, or "chiefs," were as likely to use Bowie knives as pistols, and seem often

to have been sadistic cowards, carefully choosing their victims in order to build up their scores—friendless drifters were favorite targets.

4. Fourteen years later, at a dinner honoring the poet Whittier, Mark Twain was to repeat the pattern of the "Bloody Massacre" hoax, again taking a risk, miscalculating his audience's response, and enormously exaggerating the consequences. Instead of presenting the expected tribute to Whittier, Twain apparently decided to startle his hearers with a humorous fantasy in which three ruffians impersonated three distinguished men of letters, Emerson, Longfellow, and Holmes—all of whom were present. The audience was not amused, a few newspapers criticized the speech, and Twain believed that he had committed an unforgivable, unforgettable gaffe, and had probably ruined his career.

5. The *Enterprise* accused the *Union* of "treason" (that is, of Confederate sympathies) and called it the "Virginia Daily Stultifier . . . bartered, abandoned, unprincipled and daily stultifying itself." The *Union*, in return, labeled the *Enterprise* "Our Treasonable Contemporary" and denounced the Virginia City *Bulletin* as "that venal, purchasable smut machine." For the Gold Hill *Daily News*, the *Union* was "a contemptible, word-eating, blackmail sheet." But no one had been personally insulted, and no duels followed.

BOHEMIAN. Mark Twain, *Roughing It* (1872). *Collected Letters*, scheduled for publication by the University of California Press, Berkeley, 1986. *Mark Twain's Letters*, edited by Albert Bigelow Paine (New York: Harper & Bros., 1917). *Early Tales and Sketches*, vols. 1 and 2, edited by Edgar M. Branch and Robert H. Hirst (Berkeley: University of California Press, 1979). *Mark Twain's Notebooks and Journals*, vol. 1, edited by Frederick Anderson, Michael B. Frank, and Kenneth M. Sanderson (Berkeley: University of California Press, 1975). *The Washoe Giant in San Francisco*, edited by Franklin Walker (San Francisco: George Fields, 1938). *Mark Twain's San Francisco*, edited by Bernard Taper (New York: McGraw-Hill, 1963). *Sketches of the Sixties by Mark Twain and Bret Harte* (San Francisco: John Howell, 1927). *Mark Twain in Eruption*, edited by Bernard De Voto (New York: Grosset & Dunlap, 1940). *Clemens of the Call: Mark Twain in San Francisco*, edited by Edgar M. Branch (Berkeley: University of California Press, 1969). Albert Bigelow Paine, *Mark Twain: A Biography* (New York: Harper & Bros., 1912).

1. If Orion agreed to this bargain, he did not keep it; he never became a preacher—perhaps because he could never hold to any religious conviction long enough. Somehow he would raise money to return to the East, where, among other activities, he pursued his trade as a printer for a time, tried to invent a flying machine, set himself up on a chicken

farm (subsidized by Mark Twain), dabbled in politics—unsuccessfully, of course, attempted to write science fiction in the style of Jules Verne, and finally "practiced" law with one or two clients a year, supported by a pension from his brother.

CORRESPONDENT. Mark Twain, *Roughing It* (1872). *Collected Letters of Mark Twain*, scheduled for publication by the University of California Press, Berkeley, 1986. *Mark Twain's Letters*, edited by Albert Bigelow Paine (New York: Harper & Bros., 1917). *Early Tales and Sketches*, vols. 1 and 2, edited by Edgar M. Branch and Robert H. Hirst (Berkeley: University of California Press, 1979). *Mark Twain's Notebooks and Journals*, vol. 1, edited by Frederick Anderson, Michael B. Frank, and Kenneth M. Sanderson (Berkeley: University of California Press, 1975). *Mark Twain's Letters from Hawaii*, edited by A. Grove Day (New York: Appleton-Century, 1966). Albert Bigelow Paine, *Mark Twain: A Biography* (New York: Harper & Bros., 1917). Paul Fatout, *Mark Twain on the Lecture Circuit* (Bloomington: Indiana University Press, 1964). Fred W. Lorch, *The Trouble Begins at Eight: Mark Twain's Lecture Tours* (Ames: Iowa State University Press, 1968).

1. On January 7, 1884, he wrote to his friend Howells that "I have saturated myself with knowledge of that unimaginably beautiful land & that most strange & Fascinating people," in order to write a novel based on fact—the life of a man of mixed blood (part white and part Hawaiian) born under the old religion but Christianized and "civilized" by the missionaries, who (just before his wedding) discovers that he has leprosy and exiles himself to the leper colony on Molokai. The "hidden motive" of the book, said Twain, "will illustrate... that the religious folly you are born in you *die* in, no matter what apparently reasonabler religious folly may seem to have taken its place meanwhile."

2. According to a clipping from the San Francisco *Examiner* in a scrapbook belonging to Mark Twain (now preserved at the Mark Twain Papers), not only was he funnier than Artemus Ward, in both his written and his oral humor, but "He can talk seriously as well as humorously." His only fault was occasional "coarseness," but even "his roughness is the roughness of the crude diamond." Twain felt a rivalry with Ward, and the similarities between them seem obvious: Twain's own description of Ward's technique, in a lecture given during the 1871–72 season, applies equally to himself: "His inimitable way of pausing and hesitating, of gliding in a moment from seriousness to humor without appearing to be conscious of so doing, cannot be reproduced.... There was more in his pauses than in his words." Content, however, was widely different: Ward offered nonsense, while Twain offered sense.

INTERLUDE—NEW YORK. *Collected Letters of Mark Twain*, scheduled for publication by the University of California Press, Berkeley, 1986. *Mark Twain's Letters*, edited by Albert Bigelow Paine (New York: Harper & Bros., 1917). *Mark Twain's Notebooks and Journals*, vol. 1, edited by Frederick Anderson, Michael B. Frank, and Kenneth M. Sanderson (Berkeley: University of California Press, 1975). *Mark Twain's Travels with Mr. Brown*, edited by Franklin Walker and G. Ezra Dane (New York: Knopf, 1940). Albert Bigelow Paine, *Mark Twain: A Biography* (New York: Harper & Bros., 1912).

1. Wakeman's vigor, his jollity, his vehemence, fascinated Twain; but most of all, the attraction may have been that he so perfectly filled his clear and limited role, that he so obviously and completely was exactly what he seemed to be, that he could act instantly, appropriately, without anxiety or regret.

PILGRIM. *Collected Letters of Mark Twain*, scheduled for publication by the University of California Press, Berkeley, 1986. *Mark Twain's Letters*, edited by Albert Bigelow Paine (New York: Harper & Bros., 1917). *Mark Twain's Notebooks and Journals*, vol. 3, edited by Frederick Anderson, Michael B. Frank, and Kenneth M. Sanderson (Berkeley: University of California Press, 1975). *Traveling with the Innocents Abroad: Mark Twain's Original Reports from Europe and the Holy Land*, edited by Daniel Morley McKeithan (Norman: University of Oklahoma Press, 1958). Mark Twain, *The Innocents Abroad* (Hartford: American Publishing Co., 1869). Dewey Ganzel, *Mark Twain Abroad: The Cruise of the Quaker City* (Chicago: University of Chicago Press, 1968). Albert Bigelow Paine, *Mark Twain: A Biography* (New York: Harper & Bros., 1912). Justin Kaplan, *Mr. Clemens and Mark Twain* (New York: Simon & Schuster, 1966).

1. Herman Melville had toured the Holy Land ten years earlier and in his journal had summed up his impressions of the landscape in even harsher words: "bleached—leprosy—encrustation of curses... bones of rock... *the unleavened nakedness of desolation*," and concluded that "I have little doubt the diabolical landscape of Judea must have suggested to the Jewish prophets, their ghostly theology." Melville of course was not writing for publication.

2. Twain's intention in writing that letter for the *Herald*, he told his family, had been to "make the Quakers get up & howl," and he succeeded. When not writing for print, he was even harsher: "psalm-singing cattle" he had called his fellow passengers in a letter to Joe Goodman a month earlier, and writing to J. R. Young, on November

22, he referred contemptuously to "the Quaker City's strange menagerie of ignorance, imbecility, bigotry & dotage."

AUTHOR. *Collected Letters of Mark Twain*, scheduled for publication by the University of California Press, Berkeley, 1986. *Mark Twain's Letters*, edited by Albert Bigelow Paine (New York: Harper & Bros., 1917). *Mark Twain's Notebooks and Journals*, edited by Frederick Anderson, Michael B. Frank, and Kenneth M. Sanderson (Berkeley: University of California Press, 1975). *Mark Twain to Mrs. Fairbanks*, edited by Dixon Wecter (San Marino, Calif.: Huntington Library, 1949). *Mark Twain: Businessman*, edited by Samuel Charles Webster (Boston: Little, Brown, 1946). Albert Bigelow Paine, *Mark Twain: A Biography*, (New York: Harper & Bros., 1912). *Mark Twain's Letters to His Publishers, 1867–1894*, edited by Hamlin Hill (Berkeley: University of California Press, 1967). Hamlin Hill, *Mark Twain and Elisha Bliss* (Columbia: University of Missouri Press, 1964).

1. "What did I ever write about the Holy Land that was so peculiarly lacerating?" Mark Twain complained to Mrs. Fairbanks on June 17. "The most strait-laced of the preachers here cannot well get through a sermon without turning aside to give me a blast. The last remark reported to me from the pulpit is 'this son of the Devil,' Mark Twain."

LOVER. *Collected Letters of Mark Twain*, scheduled for publication by the University of California Press, Berkeley, 1986. *Mark Twain's Letters*, edited by Albert Bigelow Paine (New York: Harper & Bros., 1917). *The Love Letters of Mark Twain*, edited by Dixon Wecter (New York: Harper & Bros., 1949). *Mark Twain to Mrs. Fairbanks*, edited by Dixon Wecter (San Marino, Calif.: Huntington Library, 1949). *Mark Twain's Letters to His Publishers, 1867–1894*, edited by Hamlin Hill (Berkeley: University of California Press, 1967). Albert Bigelow Paine, *Mark Twain: A Biography* (New York: Harper & Bros., 1912). Paul Fatout, *Mark Twain on the Lecture Circuit* (Bloomington: Indiana University Press, 1964). Fred W. Lorch, *The Trouble Begins at Eight: Mark Twain's Lecture Tours* (Ames: Iowa State University Press, 1968). James M. Cox, *Mark Twain: The Fate of Humor* (Princeton: Princeton University Press, 1966). George M. Beard, *A Practical Treatise on Nervous Exhaustion, Its Symptoms, Nature, Sequence, Treatment* (New York: E. B. Treat, 1894).

1. Dr. Beard provided an impressive list of phobias likely to result from "nervous exhaustion," including not only the familiar claustrophobia and agoraphobia, but astrophobia (fear of stars), topophobia (fear of places), mysophobia (fear of contamination), anthropophobia (fear of society)—culminating in phobophobia (fear of fears) and pantophobia (fear

of everything). Other symptoms included both impotence and temporary paralysis, as in Livy's case, from which sufferers "sometimes recover very suddenly and unexpectedly," as Livy had done.

2. He had known himself better when he wrote to Will Bowen, on the day before the *Quaker City* sailed, that cheerful voyages always bring one back to land, and to work, but "I have a roving commission, anyhow, and if I don't like to land when we get back, I will just shift on to some other ship."

3. The replies to Jervis Langdon's inquiries do not survive, but in writing to C. W. Stoddard (August 25, 1869), Mark Twain confided that one of them, from a clergyman, "came within an ace of breaking off my marriage by saying 'Clemens is a humbug ... a man who has talent, no doubt, but will make a trivial use of it,' " while another predicted that Twain "would fill a drunkard's grave." As he summed up, no doubt with some exaggeration: "The friends that I had referred to in California said with one accord that I got drunk oftener than was necessary and that I was wild and Godless, idle, lecherous, and a discontented rover & they could not recommend any girl of high character and social position to marry me."

4. Mark Twain was experiencing what he himself would call, when writing to Mrs. Fairbanks a few weeks before his wedding, "the frenzy, the lunacy of love." Naturally reserved, for all his apparent sociability, for once in his life he allowed himself to be swept away by an irresistible flood of emotion. And he could hardly help seeing the woman who inspired that emotion as something more than human, or seeing all of his past life as worthless in comparison to it. As on the occasion of Henry's death, his expression of feeling seems exaggerated, even hysterical—but he had no other vocabulary for deep personal feeling.

His newfound piety was a part of that frenzy, and would subside with it. For a time he believed that he believed, even claiming, to Mrs. Fairbanks, that he was a Christian at last. But his religious enthusiasm had begun to moderate before his wedding, and within a few years he had substituted for the personal God of traditional Christianity, who confined His interest to humanity and to earth, a God of the gigantic universe revealed by modern astronomy, who did not concern himself with trifles. In 1878 he would tell Joe Twichell, "I don't believe in your religion at all.... I don't believe one word of your Bible was inspired by God.... I believe it is entirely the work of man from beginning to end—atonement and all." Instead of converting her lover, Livy in time would lose her own faith.

INDEX